THE EUROPEAN HISTORY SERIES

SERIES EDITOR

KEITH EUBANK

ARTHUR S. LINK
GENERAL EDITOR FOR HISTORY

THE RUSSIAN REVOLUTIONARY INTELLIGENTSIA

SECOND EDITION

PHILIP POMPER

WESLEYAN UNIVERSITY

HARLAN DAVIDSON, INC.

WHEELING, ILLINOIS 60090-6000

Library of Congress Cataloging-in-Publication Data

Pomper, Philip.

The Russian revolutionary intelligentsia / Philip Pomper. — 2nd ed.

p. cm. — (The European history series)

Includes bibliographical references and index.

ISBN 0-88295-895-X

1. Soviet Union—Social conditions—1801–1917 2. Revolutionaries—Soviet Union. 3. Intellectuals—Soviet Union. 4. Socialism—Soviet Union. I. Title. II. Series: European history series (Wheeling, Ill.)

HN523.P674 1993

305.5'52'0947—dc20 92-5628

CIP

Cover illustration: Conspiracy in Russia—a Nihilist meeting surprised.
North Wind Picture Archives.

Manufactured in the United States of America

97 96 95 94 2 3 4 5 MG

FOREWORD

Now more than ever there is a need for books dealing with significant themes in European history, books offering fresh interpretations of events which continue to affect Europe and the world. The end of the Cold War has changed Europe, and to understand the changes, a knowledge of European history is vital. Although there is no shortage of newspaper stories and television reports about politics and life in Europe today, there is a need for interpretation of these developments as well as background information that neither television nor newspapers can provide. At the same time, scholarly interpretations of European history itself are changing.

A guide to understanding Europe begins with knowledge of its history. To understand European history is also to better understand much of the American past because many of America's deepest roots are in Europe. And in these days of increasingly global economic activity, more American men and women journey to Europe for business as well as personal travel. In both respects, knowledge of European history can deepen one's understanding, experience, and effectiveness.

The European History Series introduces readers to the excitement of European history through concise books about the great events, issues, and personalities of Europe's past. Here are accounts of the powerful political and religious movements which shaped European life in the past and which have influenced events in Europe today. Colorful stories of rogues and heroines, tyrants, rebels, fanatics, generals, statesmen, kings, queens, emperors, and ordinary people are contained in these concise studies of major themes and problems in European history.

Each volume in the series examines an issue, event, or era which posed a problem of interpretation for historians. The chosen topics are neither obscure nor narrow. These books are neither historiographical essays, nor substitutes for textbooks, nor monographs with endless numbers of footnotes. Much thought and care have been given to their writing style to avoid academic jargon and overspecialized focus. Authors of the European History Series have been selected not only for their recognized scholarship but also for their ability to write for the general reader. Using primary and secondary sources in their writing, these authors bring alive the great moments in European history rather than simply cram factual material into the pages of their books. The authors combine more in-depth interpretation than is found in the usual survey accounts with synthesis of the finest scholarly works, but, above all, they seek to write absorbing historical narrative.

Each volume contains a bibliographical essay which introduces readers to the most significant works dealing with their subject. These are works that are generally available in American public and college libraries. It is hoped that the bibliographical essays will enable readers to follow their interests in further reading about particular pieces of the fascinating European past described in this series.

Keith Eubank
Series Editor

CONTENTS

PREFACE
TO THE SECOND EDITION

The first edition of this book was written in the late 1960s, a period of neo-Stalinism. Times have changed. Stalinism in Russia is dead; now the Soviet period of Russian history itself is over. What role did the revolutionary intelligentsia play in this extended tragedy? Do they bear any responsibility for Russia's failure to achieve either liberal or social democracy in 1917? Was there something pathological about the entire intelligentsia tradition, or did a recessive trend within an otherwise healthy, progressive movement triumph? Such questions about the fate of the revolutionary movement cannot be answered without examining the Russian Empire's unique character. We must ask: Did Russia's authoritarian culture and a police mentality infect the revolutionary subculture and poison the postrevolutionary politics of the victorious Bolsheviks, or did the Soviet regime grow out of the intelligentsia movement's inherent defects? Was Russia in 1917 in the midst of a promising modernizing trend that was interrupted and then destroyed by world war, revolution, and civil war, or was it still a thoroughly backward land ruled by a reactionary regime whose policies prepared the ground for totalitarianism?

The preceding questions were very probably inspired by another one: To what source do we trace the monstrous human costs of the Soviet period? And an even more basic question underlies it: Why can't the Russians be more like us? The Western democracies modernized at considerable social cost and pain—pain, in fact, that inspired the Marxian and other revolutionary visions. But from the perspective of the late twentieth century, the old democracies can comfort themselves with the thought that they modernized without the additional agony of totalitarianism. This sense of relative success, not to speak of historical grace, in the global trend toward modernization encourages scholars in the Western democracies to assume a 'clinical' posture in talking about Russia's past. Of course, we judge when we 'diagnose' and affirm our own values when we judge.

Any useful study of the Russian revolutionary movement must address these questions and problems of perspective. In undertaking this revision more than twenty years after the publication of the first edition, I am even more fully aware than I was earlier of the difficulty of doing justice to the history of a movement whose ideas remain alive and still affect millions. I ended the first edition by describing the history of the Russian revolutionary intelligentsia as tragic. The ensuing years have not yet changed that judgment, although tragedy, like all things in history, is not endless.

Ph. P.
Middletown, Conn.

1 / THE RUSSIAN REVOLUTIONARY INTELLIGENTSIA AS A HISTORICAL MOVEMENT

There have been several studies of the origin, evolution, and meaning of the word *"intelligentsiia,"* as well as a great number of attempts by members of the Russian revolutionary intelligentsia to define their own historical movement. Such studies make clear that the collective noun *intelligentsiia* is not simply a Russian variation of "intellectuals," granting that there is sufficient confusion over the latter word too. The definition that I present below is, I believe, fairly close to the spirit of *intelligentsiia.**

The intelligentsia are distinguishable from both intellectual workers and pure intellectuals, from the former by their concern with ultimate questions, and from the latter by their active commitment to human self-fulfillment. They tend to reject the idea of engaging in any cultural activity for its own sake, viewing the arts and sciences as activities which may help them in their larger quest. Having internalized the idealizations of art and science and the images of good and evil, order and chaos, fulfillment and unfulfillment contained therein, the intelligentsia in a changed historical environment either revivify these images or expose their inadequacy. Critics in the intelligentsia do not merely establish a new canon or set new criteria for the arts and sciences. The most important thinkers revitalize and transform religious worldviews, or even create new secular ones more suit-

* Throughout this book I shall use the more familiar English spelling of this word, as both noun and adjective.

able to the historical moment. The intelligentsia tend to be mobilizers who assail the tolerance of the banal evils that follow from the domestication of once militant and uncompromising religious visions. Sometimes such thinkers experience crises of faith. They abandon theological categories of good and evil and seek answers in the secular world of science. The power of the old faith and the passionate quest of the believer, however, carry over into the secular realm.

Neat boundaries cannot always be drawn between the world of faith and of putative scientific truth. The revitalizers of religion and the creators of secular ideologies labor in the same vineyard. Given the existential stakes—salvation, human dignity, the meaning of history, in short, the greater scheme of things and the human place in it—the intelligentsia's passionate longings deeply affect their creativity. The great ideologues who address the most painful questions of the human condition are prone to wishful thinking. Their "solutions" sustain them through their own crises and serve larger communities in crisis as well. At their very best, intelligentsia thinkers fashion remarkable systems of thought offering hope for affirmative, purposeful action in the service of humanity.

The word "ideology" first appeared in 1796 in the work of the French *philosophe* Destutt de Tracy, who influenced Thomas Jefferson as well as the Russian Decembrists. At first "ideology" carried positive connotations as an all-embracing science of ideas with progressive aims. This word, however, became tarnished when Napoleon blamed ideology for undermining his power, but especially when Marx designated it an instrument of the ruling class. The word is currently used neutrally to describe developed doctrines containing ideas of evils to be combatted and goods to be pursued in a secular context. Most scholars of such doctrines recognize that ideologies confer meaning—they help make sense of an ever-changing world. But people create ideologies, and when we study ideologies we also study people.

Historians must trace the formation of ideology in several contexts: in the cultural milieu of the major ideologues, in the subculture that these individuals inspired and sometimes led, in the followers who took their work in sometimes surprising directions, and in the larger community which shaped the movement by either thwarting or trying to realize the goals of the intelligentsia. For instance, we might imagine the discomfort that Nicholas Chernyshevskii or Karl Marx, the two most powerful influences on the Russian revolutionary subculture, might have felt in seeing the rise and triumph of Bolshevism. Certainly Lenin and his followers had altered their original revolutionary doctrines in fundamental ways. Fyodor Dostoevsky, who repented of his youthful revolutionism, vividly portrayed in his novels the troubled evolution of intelligentsia doctrine and the tortured career of the idea of freedom in the Russian revolutionary movement. Others who remained committed to revolutionism nonetheless showed prophetic insight in recognizing the dangers of leading doctrines or tactics. The revision, abandonment, replacement, or 'betrayal' of ideologies by followers all are recurring themes in the history of the intelligentsia, as are the noble aspirations and sometimes saintly self-sacrifice of generations of revolutionaries.

The Russian revolutionary movement passed through so extended a development that it remains an especially interesting historical laboratory for studying revolutionism. Aside from studying "isms," we should also examine the anatomy of the movement. Here methodological questions arise: How should we study the transformation of ideologies in a movement? How does practice affect theory? How do styles of leadership affect ideology? Can we discern patterns or "laws" in the movement? Marx and Friedrich Engels attempted to answer these questions when they pioneered the "sociology of knowledge," a discipline that seeks to ground ideologies in the concrete circumstances and interests of social groups. They wanted to dispel any illusion that ideologies spring from individual creativity or change simply by circulating through the minds of individuals. In the view of Marxians, social classes either extend their power and control or struggle against the power and control of other classes. They do so partly by means of ideologies. An intelligentsia movement, in this view, is really an instrument in a larger struggle of social classes. Later theorists in the Marxian tradition viewed the intelligentsia as independent actors serving their own cause but retained the notion that ideologies are connected with socioeconomic or sociocultural conditions. For example, some scholars find it significant that so many leading figures in the revolutionary intelligentsia came from "marginal" social and cultural backgrounds. In any case, social classes no longer seem as monolithic and their historical roles as unambiguous as they did to Marx and Engels.

Beginning in the late nineteenth century, Marxians had to face hard facts that seemed to defy their expectations: the adaptability of capitalism; the persistent "problem" of the historically "doomed" but still numerous peasantry; the autonomous role of power structures (elite groups, bureaucracies, security forces, the military); the increasing social weight of the professional stratum in modern society; the failure of the factory proletariat to play its predicted historical role; the continuing power of nationalism, religious movements, and ethnicity; and, perhaps most important of all in the long run, the growth of the women's movement. All of these and other factors forced many Marxians to revise Marx and Engels's thought or to abandon the system entirely.

The relative importance of individual leaders also remains a vexing issue for practitioners of the sociology of knowledge. Most contemporary historians would agree that even the greatest historical actors need a supporting cast. They would not all agree, however, that the role of individuals is merely instrumental to social forces. Lenin and Stalin particularly loom as figures who need to be examined and explained, so vast do their roles in history seem. How do Marxians place Lenin's unique role in perspective? Whether Marxist or non-Marxist, few students of the October Revolution of 1917 and its aftermath believe that history would have been the same if Lenin had died before 1917. Trotsky, who had to reconcile the role of individuals with the dialectic of class struggle in his historical works as well as in his political career, devised a Marxian solution: Individuals can hasten or retard historical development; they can affect the timetable but not the fundamental dialectic of historical change. Thus without Lenin, the October Revolution might not have happened, and the 'victory' of the proletariat might have been delayed. Trotsky, moreover, believed that Lenin's leadership derived its inspiration and strength from its proletarian support. In his analysis of

Stalinism, however, Trotsky saw Stalin as the instrument of the *apparat* (party bureaucracy).

Trotsky's approach still satisfies many, but other scholars point out that both Lenin and Stalin often acted against the wishes of the majority and still had their way. Lenin, in this less charitable view, virtually kidnapped the revolution and with it Russia's chances for achieving a less painful, nontotalitarian, Western-style form of development. He distanced himself from other Marxists by insisting on a direct path to socialism under the domination of a single party. Lenin, in effect, changed the rules of the game, purged the revolutionary ranks of all except those who accepted his form of party discipline, and established a dictatorship in the name of the proletariat. Stalin, in his turn, demolished the very *apparat* that had served Lenin and him so well in struggles against earlier opponents. Once he suspected a group of disloyalty, Stalin disposed of that instrument of power and forged new ones. His position was so unassailable and role so crucial that when he faced the greatest threat to his survival in the opening days of World War II, no one dared remove him. It is therefore important to study Stalin as an individual, not merely as the instrument of a social group, and to investigate how his individual pathology affected his most destructive policies.

The application of normative psychological terms to individuals does not raise any great problems, so long as care is taken with diagnoses. The use of such psychological descriptions does, however, raise problems when applied to groups. Nevertheless, the following proposition will be offered here: Groups, however admirable their purpose and overall composition, can and sometimes do select pathological leaders. The history of the modern era provides striking illustrations of this proposition, and the Russian revolutionary subculture yields some excellent specimens. Dostoevsky especially offers valuable insight into the "demons" in the movement, although it should be kept in mind that his characters are exaggerated versions of historical personalities.

The great Russian literature of the nineteenth and early twentieth centuries both enriches and complicates the search for the sources of ideologies and styles of leadership, not to speak of pathologies, in historical sociocultural groups. In the absence of adequate data and methods for sampling the attitudes of such groups, historians have recourse to literature. We must not, however, delude ourselves into believing that the interpretation of literature yields a necessarily accurate method for studying the social psychologies of historical groups. When, for example, we try to establish the mentality of the Russian *dvorianstvo* (gentry) and succeed in finding connections between the ideas of this class and that of the intelligentsia, we often do not stop to think that our "success" is based on the use of typologies. We attribute to the gentry ideas that we believe they ought to have possessed, given their position and interests, and then find those echoes in literature. Although the typological approach has no rock-bottom empirical foundation and is more impressionistic than scientific, it is nonetheless a fruitful one. We shall use typologies in this study.

The Russian *dvorianstvo* were undergoing a series of transformations in the nineteenth century, having undergone a number of previous historical changes. The search for common denominators in the *dvorianstvo* psychology becomes increasingly difficult as the nineteenth century progresses. Russian literature of this period abounds with a variety of *dvorianstvo* types. The major reason for the increasing heterogeneity of the gentry was the demand of the Russian imperial governments that they acquire new skills and assume leadership in all areas of modernization, while at the same time guarding and perpetuating Russia's traditional institutions and culture. This self-contradictory demand generated considerable confusion within the ranks of the *dvorianstvo* and gave rise to a variety of responses. We can identify several basic responses and establish subgroups corresponding to them. Needless to say, the groups described in the following paragraphs are abstract and idealized categories.

One such group that felt threatened by modernization was the traditionalists, who believed that Russia's strength lay in the ways of the past and who wanted to preserve the old military and administrative structure that they had staffed and run with the help of subordinates from other estates. Their ideological attitudes are perhaps best exhibited in Nicholas Karamzin's *Mem-*

oir on Ancient and Modern Russia (1811). Traditionalists feared the encroachments of parvenu bureaucrats from other estates and loss of their special relationship to the throne. One might characterize this anxiety as that of a decadent *noblesse d'épée* which could no longer fulfill the needs of a modernizing state and society. In general, they were represented by conservative Romantic ideologies.

Another group, the rational bureaucrats, accepted the responsibilities of modernization and were content to serve the dynasty in spite of its sometimes capricious and self-contradictory demands. The rational bureaucrats embraced a great number of philosophies, but were fundamentally legalistic and gradualistic in their approach. Their idea of service was somewhat more abstract than that of the traditionalists in that they were more concerned about their relationship to state and society than to the throne. In this respect, the rational bureaucrats were acting in accordance with the express wishes of Peter I (1689–1725), whose reforms were the major impetus that pushed the *dvorianstvo* estate into two centuries of disequilibrium. The rational bureaucrats' position was often threatened by the rulers, who encouraged them to produce modernizing reforms and then, feeling threatened, formed alliances with the traditionalists against them. This was one of the great ironies of the modern period of Russian history. Having forced the Russian gentry to become the major agency of modernization in the empire, the rulers discovered that they themselves were not able to accept the reforms proposed by elements of the gentry. By the end of the eighteenth century, it was clear that a small minority within the gentry were sufficiently taken by the ideas of the Enlightenment to sacrifice both their own privileged position and the throne's absolutism.

The career of Michael Speransky during the reigns of Alexander I (1801–1825) and Nicholas I (1825–1855) strikingly illustrates the problems of the rational bureaucrat in the context of Russia's dynastic politics. Speransky's unsuccessful constitutional project is in retrospect one of the clear signs that Russia's perpetually insecure rulers could not be relied upon to support the reformers in any project that would threaten the conservative majority of the *dvorianstvo* or the throne's own authority. The coups, attempted coups, and assassinations of the period 1730–1801 had made it abundantly clear that no ruler could flout the wishes of the *dvorianstvo*. Thus, rational bureaucrats like Speransky were a resource that the rulers sometimes used to modernize the bureaucracy, improve the economy without abolishing serfdom, uphold legality and justice without creating a constitution, and expand education without undermining the privileged position of the *dvorianstvo*. These proved to be herculean tasks, and the rational bureaucrats were mistrusted by the right and despised by the left for their efforts.

The intelligentsia, a third group that emerged during the transformation of the *dvorianstvo*, were an unforeseen and unintended consequence of cultural change. They, more than any other group within the *dvorianstvo*, developed a sense of mission that was unconstricted by estate, dynastic, or even national loyalties. To assume that the intelligentsia's sense of mission was somehow associated with the outlook of the *dvorianstvo* is to deny the intelligentsia's self-image as a group outside the estates, bound together by experiences that transcended their upbringing. It is methodologically impossible to determine precisely the origins and boundaries of the intelligentsia. On the one hand, one may assume, as do some investigators, that the kinds of "alienation" that arose from the ambiguities of the *dvorianstvo's* position (or even from gentry techniques of child rearing) in the eighteenth and nineteenth centuries were coextensive with the kind of alienation characteristic of members of the intelligentsia. An excellent example of this approach is Martin Malia's thesis that ". . . the democratic ideal arose in Russia, not by direct reflection on the plight of the masses, but through the introspection of relatively privileged individuals who, out of frustration, generalized from a sense of their own dignity to the ideal of the dignity of all men."[1] Marc Raeff, in a more recent work, develops at greater length a methodologically similar though substantively different thesis:

1 Martin Malia, *Alexander Herzen and the Birth of Russian Socialism* (New York, 1965), p. 421.

> On the contrary, conscious of their basic rootlessness and alienation from the people, the élite of the nobility hoped to give a new meaning to their function in the state without abandoning the tradition of service, which was *the* stable element of their existence. The men who reached adulthood in the first fifteen years of the nineteenth century shared the characteristic intellectual and psychological traits of the eighteenth century nobility. But they were the first to give those traits full scope in their public and private lives. In this respect they were but following in the footsteps of A. Radishchev, who had first drawn the practical conclusions of the elite's relationship to the state that had nurtured it and their cultural responsibility to the people.[2]

On the other hand, one has the testimony of the group itself, increasingly self-conscious and self-examining, desperately trying to explain and validate its own alienated mentality:

> Our literature has created the morals of our society, has already educated several generations of widely divergent character, has paved the way for the inner *rapprochement* of the estates, has formed a species of public opinion and produced a sort of special class in society that differs from the *middle estate* in that it consists not of the merchantry and commoners alone but of people of all estates who have been drawn together through education, which, with us, centered exclusively in the love of literature.[3]

These are the words of Vissarion Belinsky, one of the most influential members of the intelligentsia, written at a time (1847) when the term "intelligentsia" was still not used to denote the "special class" whose existence and origin is discussed in the above quotation.

In Russia during the first half of the nineteenth century the gentry were the major source of social thought—whether elitist or democratic—simply because they had the easiest access to higher education. But not all literate members of the gentry became members of the intelligentsia. The Russian imperial governments were able to recruit a sufficient number of able men

2 Marc Raeff, *Origins of the Russian Intelligentsia* (New York, 1966), p. 168.
3 Ralph E. Matlaw, ed., *Belinsky, Chernyshevskii, and Dobroliubov: Selected Criticism* (New York, 1962), p. 6.

from the higher and middle strata of society—both gentry and nongentry—to enter the twentieth century as a major, though relatively declining, world power. When we compare the dimensions of the intelligentsia at any given moment in the nineteenth century with the dimensions of the larger educated community working at bureaucratic or professional employments, we discover that they were a rather small proportion of that community. And the *revolutionary* intelligentsia was relatively minuscule. Privilege was a necessary condition of the emergence of the intelligentsia, but neither a sense of privilege nor any other attitude peculiar to the *dvorianstvo* is a sufficient explanation for the formation of the radical mentality of the revolutionary intelligentsia or its democratic outlook. The privileged and cultured, therefore, at first provided recruits for the intelligentsia, but social and cultural background alone did not determine its membership. In fact, the increasing heterogeneity of the *dvorianstvo* and the infusion of recruits from other estates after the 1840s obscures to a greater extent the precise sources of intelligentsia radicalism. To be sure, it is still possible to match different styles of thought and leadership to distinct social and cultural groups. Nevertheless, commitments to the revolutionary movement were basically individual responses to culture and to new ideas taught in universities, institutes, and especially study circles. Such ideas, however appealing to an alienated group, did not inspire all to action. Education, even education biased toward liberal and radical ideas, cannot by itself create a radical. Only a handful of those exposed to complex theoretical formulations of human progress and self-fulfillment will dedicate their lives to them; even fewer will creatively amend or extend them. We must conclude that the creative radicalism of the revolutionary intelligentsia sprung from varying individual responses to social and cultural milieus.

The interaction of the intelligentsia subculture with the regime, the larger society, and mainly European cultural and political developments produced a discernible pattern of change in the revolutionary intelligentsia. A roughly cyclical pattern emerged: First a major figure or figures in the literary world (the world of ideas and intellectual styles) took an imported liberal or socialist doctrine and placed a distinctly Russian stamp on it; the ideas spread to younger, mainly student radicals in the university cities and from there to the provinces; after a *kruzhok* (study circle) period of self-education in radicalism, the students quickly organized themselves into conspiratorial groups for purposes of educating (some would say propagandizing) the *narod* (the people, mainly peasants); the failure of propaganda campaigns to open the eyes of the peasants gave way to short-term efforts to radicalize them through agitational methods that were not always scrupulous; after the failure of both propaganda and agitational methods for a variety of reasons, the revolutionaries then turned their attention to struggling with the regime itself through terrorism; the failure of terrorist methods led to a crisis of faith and ushered in the dominance of a new "ism"; a new cycle began.

Two complete cycles of roughly this sort dominated the history of the Russian revolutionary movement: the first, nihilism (1855–1869); the second, populism (1870–1883). "Populism" and "nihilism" connote rich varieties of revolutionary expression (but both terms, "nihilism" in particular, fail to convey very precisely the meaning of the doctrine). Both ideologies demarcate distinct periods of development that were punctuated by a sense of defeat. To be sure, neither the period of nihilism nor populism ended in a sense of total defeat—historical movements never end so neatly and abruptly—but the revolutionaries knew that they had to rethink their position and regroup. So, too, the phases of each cycle were never distinct: there was considerable overlap; different tactics coexisted; even different theories coexisted. A given tactic or theory was only relatively dominant.

The final acts of the revolutionary drama presented an even more complex picture: during the period between the late 1890s and 1917 several revolutionary doctrines and parties contended; mass movements responded to propaganda and agitation; other groups joined frustrated students and their followers to engage in terror, which assumed major proportions after the revolution of 1905 as Nicholas II's regime reasserted its control. Yet we find the broad features of earlier cycles repeated: Marxism became a relatively dominant doctrine in the intelligentsia after the mid-1890s; over the next two decades the Russian Marxists followed the typical phases of the movement. Despite a doctrinal aversion to terror, they engaged in terrorist acts (principally in combat groups and bands involved in "expropriations") in the period 1905–1908. In the earlier cycles, terrorist methods seemed to be the last flare-up of a failing movement, but in the final struggle against the Tsarist regime in 1917, those who were willing to use extreme tactics, who showed the most combativeness, and who organized themselves along paramilitary lines were also the ones most suited to take power in a chaotic situation. The mere willingness to use terror, however, did not assure success for any group in the struggle for power in 1917.

Paradoxically, and tragically, the quest of the nineteenth-century intelligentsia for meaning in history, for scientific truth, for the freest and the most just social order contributed to a penchant for doctrinal orthodoxy and eventually to the rise of one of the most brutal, repressive, and, in its own way, conservative of all modern regimes. To deride the intelligentsia and its doctrines in general is fashionable today, but clearly, given the wide spectrum of positions and leaders, not all deserve to be blamed equally for the disasters of the Soviet period. The story that follows will show that a sort of political ecology determined the tragic outcome of the revolutionary process and the ascendancy of the most ruthless leadership. The dynamics of revolutionary subcultures and the crucial role of leadership and organization in a chaotic contest for power played a greater role in the tragedy than did the intelligentsia's agonizing pursuit of truth, freedom, and social justice.

2 / LOST GENERATIONS

THE DECEMBRISTS

The appearance of the Russian intelligentsia was a symptom of broad historical changes in eighteenth- and nineteenth-century Russia. One is tempted to say flatly that the intelligentsia was an unintended consequence of actions taken by Russia's rulers to establish the country on an equal footing with other European powers. But we must consider also the complicated matter of cultural imitation, in which a nation finds that it must create a nonclerical, highly educated class out of necessity, but at the same time is sufficiently attracted to new cultural forms to pursue them for their own sake. Of course, a nation has no intentions; the rulers, the court, indeed all of those groups who either were forcibly exposed to Western culture or pursued it voluntarily, were living points of contact between Russian and European culture. The motives of these points of contact, or agencies for cultural importation, varied. For example, while Peter the Great was fundamentally interested in European technology and became a great admirer and importer of the culture of maritime nations like England, Holland, and Sweden, his daughter Elizabeth, a frivolous soul, was more interested in *bals masqués*. A Russian court gentleman of Elizabeth's reign, no longer forced to study technical subjects as under her father's rule, learned rather to speak French and to be charming in the French manner.

Inevitably, imitators of the cultural life of the capital appeared in the provinces, and, just as inevitably, xenophobic reactions to the new forms occurred in every layer of Russian society. These reactions were particularly strong during periods of domestic strain, when all evils were attributed to the influence of foreigners. The great victory over Napoleon in 1812 was accompanied by a reaffirmation of traditional values and a revival of the belief that Russia's strength lay in its ancient customs and institutions. However, by the beginning of the nineteenth century an irreversible trend had been established. Elements of the nobility, emancipated in 1762 from compulsory military service to the state, had outstripped the throne in the pursuit of European culture. The first clear manifestation appeared during the reign of Catherine the Great. Catherine, who fancied herself an agency of the Enlightenment, actively sought the approval of the French *philosophes* and tried to rule as an enlightened despot. However, toward the end of her reign she persecuted Enlightenment-influenced critics such as Nicholas Novikov and Alexander Radishchev, whom, in view of internal unrest and the external threat of the French Revolution, she saw as subversives. Alexander I in many ways repeated Catherine's career.

Unquestionably, an extraordinary transformation had taken place in Russia during the one hundred years that followed the death of Peter the Great. At the beginning of the eighteenth century, Peter had dragged an unwilling, tradition-ridden Muscovite nobility into the modernizing European world. By the end of the eighteenth century, some of the newly educated, newly leisured nobility were bringing pressure to bear upon fearful and reluctant rulers. When the principle of autocracy was threatened, the throne became a conservative force, thrown back upon sometimes uncomfortable alliances with the conservative elements in the nobility, who formed an overwhelming majority. Thus began the painful process of reform and reaction that continued until 1917.

The failures of Peter the Great, Catherine II, Alexander I, and later, Alexander II can be explained at least to some extent by the disparity between their goals and the desires and capacities of the population at large. There simply was no solid constituency for modernization in Russia. Neither the court, the extended nobility, the clergy, nor the numerically insignificant urban middle class could effectively lead the vast and backward empire into the modern world. Russia's enlightened despots, while trying to demonstrate their capacity to create the future, revealed instead their inability to deal with the present. The Decembrist movement was a symptom of this failure.

There is hardly a major episode in the Russian revolutionary movement that was not associated, directly or indirectly, with foreign events. The history of the Decembrist movement is bound up with the Napoleonic Wars, especially the period 1812–1815 when Russian armies moved into central and western Europe in the aftermath of Napoleon's disastrous Russian campaign. Evidently, men of all ranks experienced a great psychological letdown after the dramatic campaigns and peace conferences. Some of the letdown could be attributed to propaganda that inevitably accompanies a patriotic war effort. Numerous documents attest to this. In a letter written a year after the Decembrist uprising, one of the major participants, Peter Kakhovskii, wrote:

> Napoleon's dominion, the war of 1813 and 1814, in which all of the peoples of Europe were united, summoned by monarchs, fired up by the appeal to liberty and to a new civic order—by what other means could countless sums be collected from citizens, how else could the armies be led? They preached liberty to us in manifestoes, in appeals, and even in orders. They lured us on, and with our whole hearts we believed them, sparing neither our blood nor our possessions.[1]

Alexander Bestuzhev made the same point in a letter to Tsar Nicholas I:

> The government itself pronounced the words "liberty, liberation!" itself disseminated writings on Napoleon's misuse of unlimited power, and the Russian Monarch's appeal resounded on the banks of the Rhine and the Seine. The war was still going on when returning troops first began to spread grumbling in the masses. "We shed blood. . . and are still forced to perform *barshchina* [labor rent owed by Russian serfs to their landlords]. We saved our homeland from the tyrant, but the lords still tyrannize us." The army, from generals to soldiers in the ranks, upon returning could talk about nothing but how good

1 A. Borozdin, ed., *Iz pisem i pokazanii Dekabristov* (St. Petersburg, 1906), p. 12.

> life was in foreign lands. A comparison with their own naturally led to the question, Why isn't it like that at home?[2]

The war effort tended to magnify the expectations that had been growing in the liberal segment of Russian society since the reign of Catherine II. Alexander was still expected to carry through the projects begun before the wars. Now that he had vanquished "tyranny" in Europe, it was believed that he would have to grant freedoms in Russia at least equivalent to those that he had restored elsewhere. Within a very short period of time, these expectations were totally frustrated, and young liberals began to discover that the patriotism and struggles of the war years were not necessarily leading to liberation at home. The real struggle lay ahead. In the postwar period a new generation came of age abruptly and bitterly.

> In 1814 life for youth in Petersburg was tiresome. In the course of two years, events had passed before our eyes which had determined the fate of nations and to some degree we had been participants in them. Now it was unbearable to look at the empty life in Petersburg and listen to the babbling of the old men who praised the past and reproached every progressive move. We were a hundred years ahead of them.[3]

Ivan Iakushkin's memoirs reveal consciousness of the growing distance between generations. His feelings of suppressed vitality and of thwarted energies were commonly experienced by the young officers who later joined secret societies, contemplated the assassination of Alexander I, and engaged in the armed rebellion of 1825 against Nicholas I.

The experiences of the war had also created an unusual emotional bond between Alexander I and the liberal young officers in his army. Many of them had seen him in reviews, and some had served him in an immediate capacity. Close contact made the emperor more human, more accessible, and also more easily despised when they concluded that he was a tyrant. The gentry

---

2 Ibid, pp. 35–36. Also, see the appendix in Anatole Mazour, *The First Russian Revolution* (Berkeley, Calif., 1937), pp. 275, 278. I have attempted to improve upon Mazour's translations of the documents in Borozdin's collection.

3 Quoted in Mazour, p. 56. I have slightly altered the translation.

had learned during the era of palace revolutions that the throne was both accessible and vulnerable. Alexander I's father, Paul I, had been assassinated because he had tried to rescind some of the advantages and freedoms won by the nobility in previous reigns. The belief that a tyrannical emperor could be disposed of by a strategically placed group of officers still seemed reasonable during the reign of Alexander I. When the love of the young officers for Alexander turned to hate, the vague dreams of the secret societies began to take the form of a plot to assassinate the emperor.

The idea that Alexander was a tyrant and that he had betrayed Russia was inspired by both his foreign and his domestic policies. In foreign policy, Alexander had committed Russia to a defense of legitimacy in Europe, especially after the Congress of Troppau (1820). Alexander, whose grand schemes for international peace and constitutional reform had been rejected at the Congress of Aix-la-Chapelle (1818), came to see things Metternich's way. Alexander's acquiescence at Troppau repeated in the realm of foreign policy his earlier abandonment of projects for reform within Russia. Fear of revolution in Russia and Europe took precedence over all else in Alexander's political actions at home and abroad between Troppau and his death in 1825.

The major faults of Alexander's domestic policy after 1815 issued from his immoderate love of order and discipline. This peculiar trait was largely a consequence of the fascination with Prussian models that had been perpetuated in the tsars from Peter III (1761–1762) on. In Alexander, Prussianism was combined with an intellectualized passion for law and order. However, especially in the postwar period, the concrete results were shaped by the advice of Count Alexis Arakcheev, virtual prime minister. At Alexander's command, Arakcheev attempted to carry over military modes of organization and discipline into domestic institutions. The military-agricultural settlements that he created in the postwar period were supposed to yield great military, economic, and social benefits, but they became instead a symbol of inhuman oppression and vast bungling. Finally, attempts in the postwar period to maintain a high degree of army discipline produced a revolt in October 1820 of the Semenovskii regiment, an elite regiment of guards which the emperor often commanded himself. The mutiny reinforced Alexander's fears and probably influenced significantly his foreign policy decisions at Troppau.

Another side to Alexander's complex personality, his religious fervor, expressed itself in both foreign and domestic politics, especially after 1815. There is no need to investigate the emperor's wanderings through a variety of religious experiments. They all reinforced his belief in his own moral superiority and mission. In foreign policy, Alexander's religiosity led chiefly to the Holy Alliance, which was insignificant in comparison with the treaty arrangements that he entered into with Austria and Prussia. Domestically, however, his religious leanings strongly influenced secular education. Thus, it is not difficult to understand why the young liberals who had fought in the Napoleonic campaigns felt that their sacrifice had been squandered, their patriotism misused, and their trust in Alexander betrayed. In this atmosphere, associations that might have had primarily cultural significance underwent a metamorphosis and became centers of conspiracy.

Some of the roots of the Decembrist movement can be traced to the attempts of the idealists within Europe's aristocracies to replenish their spiritual zeal and to resume leadership of European society. Large numbers of the European aristocracy were unwilling to surrender their medieval heritage of ritual and hierarchy to the abstract and generalized natural order of Enlightenment philosophers. However, they were unable to preserve medievalism intact, and a variety of syncretic doctrines, combining this-worldly and other-worldly concerns and both modern rationalistic and Romantic elements, appeared during the eighteenth century. The Masonic lodges fulfilled the desire of idealistic aristocrats to band together as a moral and intellectual elite, while at the same time providing them with the elaborate rites that they evidently still needed in order to feel consecrated to a higher cause. Masonry eventually served a wide variety of both aristocratic and nonaristocratic groups with conflicting aspirations, both in Europe and Russia; it permitted them, whatever their cause, to move through life with a sense of righteousness and benevolence.

The Masonic lodges also provided an intense and closed environment for idealistic (and often puritanical) aristocrats who were repelled by the frivolousness of court and salon. They were forerunners of the secret societies that appeared during the latter part of Alexander's reign, and of the intelligentsia circles in the last century of Tsarist rule. The leaders of secret societies discovered that the Masonic lodges would not provide a framework for the kinds of political activity that they contemplated. The activists, those who were seeking something more than self-perfection, carried over into their societies some of the ritual and doctrines of the Masonic movement, but the secular political, social, and economic thought of the eighteenth and early nineteenth centuries was the real doctrinal basis of their movement.

In addition to the Masonic movement, patriotic societies that grew up in the German states and Italy as an outgrowth of Romantic nationalism provided the future Decembrists with rules, rituals, and both organizational and ideological inspiration. The pan-European movement for cultural and political autonomy strongly influenced the Decembrists through the examples of the German *Tugendbund* and the Italian *Carbonari,* as well as through the growing nationalism of the minorities within the Russian Empire.

Literary and philosophical societies also served to bring together idealistic aristocrats. Rarely in the history of modern European culture have the lives of literary men so nearly coincided with their writings. Well-educated, brilliant, and energetic young officers pursued extraordinarily Byronesque careers. Among the future Decembrists were successful duelists, partygoers, and members of leading literary societies. A great deal of their frenetic activity can be attributed to youth, some of it to boredom, and some, no doubt, to the imitation of models discovered in Romantic literature. Literature was still only an avocation for the aristocracy, and poets were just as inclined to express themselves with swords and pistols as with pens. For this reason, Romanticism suited the new aristocratic generation, the last flowering of a decadent *noblesse d'épée,* both as a style of life and as a literary movement. As a consequence of the extended war effort, those who reached full maturity in the 1820s had lived their adolescence in the barracks, field, and officer's club. The peculiar mingling of military and literary traits in individuals, and the cooperation of military and literary types in the conspiracy, made the Decembrist movement unique in the history of the intelligentsia. It was a suicidal combination.

The most prominent writers among the Decembrists, and those who did not belong to the societies but who both influenced and were influenced by the movement, expressed the frustrated patriotism, idealism, and individualism of their generation. Two of the literary giants of the period, Alexander Pushkin and Alexander Griboedev, knew some of the members of the secret societies, and their works of the 1820s are informed by a similar spirit of frustration and victimization. Pushkin's poem, "André Chénier," and Griboedev's comedy, *Woe from Wit,* display this spirit; the former circulated clandestinely under the title "December 14," since the fate of the Decembrist poet Kondrati Ryleev, who was hanged in July 1826 for his part in the conspiracy, was suggested by the poem. Ryleev, Bestuzhev, Wilhelm Kuchelbecker, Alexander Odoevskii, N. I. Turgenev, and others connected the Decembrists with some of the foremost literary and philosophical societies of the period—"The Free Society of Lovers of Russian Literature" (1816–1825), "Arzamas" (1815–1818), "The Green Lamp" (1819–1820), and "The Lovers of Wisdom" (1825)—and their writings appeared in the organs of those societies. The publication most directly associated with the Decembrists was an almanac, *The Polar Star* (1823–1825), edited by Ryleev and Bestuzhev. It is probably not an exaggeration to say that the poetry written by and about the Decembrists was even more significant as an inspiration for future generations than as a revolutionary force in the 1820s.

In sum, all of these modes of association and expression fulfilled a variety of complex psychological and social needs. Looked at from one point of view, they were safety valves, permitting those who saw themselves as virtuous and energetic to demonstrate their virtue to the like-minded and to consecrate themselves to heroic tasks. However, once political action and social reform became the central issues of the secret societies, men of action and daring began to assume leadership. The Masonic lodges and the literary and patriotic societies thus became testing grounds where genuine revolutionaries found each other. After the secret societies formed, a further process of selection occurred, separating radicals from moderates. There was no unanimity about either ends or means, even though two basic goals—establishment of some kind of constitutional government to replace autocracy and the abolition of serfdom—were given assumptions of both radicals and moderates.

The Semenovskii guards regiment was the main incubator of the secret societies. The officers of the Semenovskii regiment had a special relationship to the throne, and evidently an unusually strong sense of mission, which was reflected in the name of their organization, "The Union of Salvation." Alexander Murav'ev, a colonel and member of the guards' general staff, was twenty-four years old when he founded the society. The other initiators were young officers, members of the *dvorianstvo* and well educated. Sergei Trubetskoi was a prince; the others, except for Ivan Iakushkin, belonged to the wealthy, cosmopolitan Murav'ev clan—Nikita Murav'ev, Matvei Murav'ev-Apostol, and Sergei Murav'ev-Apostol. It is not altogether clear what the motives of the first members of the Union of Salvation were, but both the memoirs and the trial testimony of participants suggest that they feared that Tsar Alexander's policies were ruining Russia. Having saved Russia from an external enemy, Napoleon, they now felt that they had to deliver Russia from the enemy within. Foreign advisers, German drill masters, and Count Arakcheev's military colonies seemed to point to the subordination of Russian to foreign interests, especially when contrasted with Alexander's relatively delicate handling of Polish affairs. He had granted Poland, which had fought on Napoleon's side, a Constitution in 1815. This could only enrage Alexander's own officers. In this respect, the Union of Salvation reflected the mentality of a frustrated, patriotric military elite, which felt abused and betrayed by Alexander I.

Within the Union of Salvation appeared the diverging ideological and organizational trends of the movement. From the very beginning, the moderates within the secret societies exhibited an aversion to force, even while conceding that it might be necessary. Above all, they seemed intent upon seeing Alexander carry through reforms that he had encouraged them to expect and, indeed, still hinted at as late as 1818. The Union's goal was a constitutional monarchy and the abolition of serfdom. As early as 1816 some discussed the assassination of Alexander I as a means to their end. But they preferred to operate through the possibilities open to them—by occupying important public offices and exerting influence. At this stage, Masonic ideas were still strong, as both the ritual and the hierarchical organization of the society testify. However, Colonel Paul Pestel, the most systematic thinker in the Union of Salvation, played a major role in writing the society's charter. Pestel soon evolved into a radical republican.

The exact size of the Union of Salvation has not been established, but it probably had between twenty-six and thirty active participants. Disagreements and dissatisfaction with the charter led to its transformation in 1818 into the "Union of Welfare" (also called "The Union of Common Weal"). *The Green Book,* the constitution of the new society, was modeled upon the constitution of the Prussian *Tugendbund.* Ideologically, *The Green Book* expressed traditional views of the centrality of nation, religion, and family. For example, foreigners, non-Christians, and women were not permitted to join the Union. Women were pictured as somewhat idle creatures who were to be diverted to the useful task of raising virtuous children.

Given the times, however, *The Green Book* was a relatively radical document. It professed that the Union was free from prejudice against any condition or estate. Also implicit in the document was subordination of loyalty to the dynasty to duty to society and the nation. And it is quite clear that however much they stressed philanthropic and educational activities in their constitution, the young officers of the Union of Welfare were committed to the destruction of autocracy. They seem to have had great faith in their ability to transform public morality and opinion. By shaping public opinion, leading exemplary lives, and actually occupying important bureaucratic, military, and judicial posts, they believed that they could eventually abolish autocracy and serfdom. They developed no specific plans for revolutionary action, but at least some of the members believed that a rather painless kind of revolution would occur.

The history of the Union of Welfare in some ways repeated that of the Union of Salvation, even though it was much larger (possibly 200 members at its height). The moderates had to fight off the radical element led by Pestel, who continually tried to convert the society into a tightly organized conspiracy with explicit and radical aims. The close connection between organization and ideology became increasingly apparent. The moderates, led by Michael Murav'ev and Prince Trubetskoi, wanted a more or less publicly visible organization, diffused through society as a whole and continually expanding. They did not visualize a sharp distinction between society and the Union. The gradualist and open-ended organizational model was associated with a moderate outlook, a penchant for individualism, and vagueness about revolution.

The period 1820–1821 is the turning point in the history of the secret societies. Until that time, they were not secret in any real sense of the word, and many of the officers who joined the various branches of the Union of Salvation did not believe that they were participating in a political conspiracy. However, both foreign and domestic events completely altered the context in which the Union operated and precipitated a crisis. Revolutions in Spain, Portugal, Naples, Piedmont, and Greece, and, more important still, the mutiny of the Semenovskii regiment and the discovery of an inflammatory proclamation in the courtyard of the barracks of the Preobrazhenskii regiment, induced Alexander to take severe measures. The Semenovskii regiment was dispersed, the other regiments of guards were placed under police surveillance, and units were transferred from St. Petersburg to the western frontier. The government's attitude toward the secret societies—at first permissive because of Alexander's own sense of responsibility for having encouraged liberal thought—became more stringent. Before the events described above, the Union had shown some tendency to drift toward the left. Pestel, who was based in southern Russia, at Tulchin, not only dominated the branch of the Union there but influenced meetings held in St. Petersburg and Moscow as well. In January 1820, at a meeting of the Basic Council (*Korennaia Uprava*) of the Union, he had converted all but one of the members to republicanism. A year later a congress of the Union convened in Moscow. During its entire existence, the Union had not fully committed itself to political conspiracy, although it had planned to gain control over as many army units as possible. The Semenovskii incident and the stirrings in the army that followed it had been neither planned nor inspired by the Union. In January 1821 the delegates knew that the Union could not continue as before. The Moscow congress led to the postponement of any immediate action, by at least ostensibly dissolving the Union. It is not easy to say whether this was primarily a diversionary tactic, aimed at the government, or a genuine repudiation of political conspiracy by most of the delegates. The most plausible explanation is that dissolution of the Union served moderates and radicals equally well, permitting the former to escape from an increasingly uncomfortable association and the latter to regroup and go underground.

After the Moscow congress, what had been a rather amorphous and ineffective association split into smaller but ideologically and organizationally more definite groups. From this moment, one can discern prefigurations of the later attitudes and conflicts of the revolutionary intelligentsia. Pestel in particular evokes comparisons with later figures in what is often described as the Jacobin tradition, Lenin being the heir. Pestel combined authoritarianism, centralism, and organizational zeal with an ideological acceptance of democracy. The idea of a revolution for the masses, but with limited and deferred political participation by the masses, was repugnant to Pestel's ideological enemies, in much the same way that Bolshevism was repugnant to Lenin's opponents. However, most of the Decembrists, like Pestel, shied away from the prospect of mass violence. The question of the role of the revolutionary organization and the role of the masses recurred throughout the history of the revolutionary intelligentsia.

The merging of nationalism with other ideological elements, so characteristic of the entire modern period, is quite prominent in the spectrum of Decembrist ideologies. More specifically, one finds in Ryleev the belief that Russia was in a peculiarly advantageous position to lead Europe toward freedom. The Decembrists attempted to use past and present native institutions as the basis for modern Russia's social, economic, and political transformation. This tendency also reappeared in much more elaborate and developed ideologies, of both the right and the left, in the course of the nineteenth century. Finally, in the writings of Pestel, the foremost ideologue within the Decembrist movement, there is a bias for agrarian socialism, which, in its several forms, became the dominant ideology of the Russian revolutionary intelligentsia.

The organizational difficulties of the Decembrists also anticipated the future of the revolutionary movement. There were actually three distinct organizations, each having a definite ideological tendency. The most aggressive group was Pestel's Southern Society. In March 1821, after a brief internal dispute, Pestel gained control over the Tulchin *uprava* (council). The Southern Society embodied his organizational ideas, his goal of armed revolution, and his republicanism.

Pestel's ideology cannot be described very easily, any more than the man himself. Using the broadest terms, he was more of a rationalist than a Romantic in his love of unified systems based upon a few universal principles or laws. Although he used medieval Russian terms in his constitutional project, *The Russian Law,* his intentions and his spirit were hardly Romantic. The examples of the French Revolution and the North American republic were far more important for the construction of his system than the history of ancient and medieval Russia. In this respect he differed from many of the Decembrists, who believed that ancient and medieval Russia's liberties had been destroyed by autocracy and who thought of themselves as restorers of lost freedoms.

Pestel's political ideas, social thought, and economic thought derive primarily from French and English rationalist schools. Although he was somewhat mercurial in conversation, and although he altered some of his basic opinions about what constituted the best political system for Russia and how to solve the problem of serfdom, his approach to the problems, the style of his writing, and his authorities were rationalist. Among French writers he was influenced most strongly by Destutt de Tracy, but he had also read the Physiocrats and the materialists of the eighteenth century. Pestel had studied both English and French writers on political economy—Adam Smith and J. B. Say—and had been exposed to the more recent economic and social thought of Sismondi, Bentham, and possibly Saint-Simon. His economic thought was eclectic, leading some commentators to call him primarily socialist and others to describe him as an exponent of laissez faire, of bourgeois liberalism. Actually, like later Russian social and economic theorists such as Chernyshevskii, Pestel was searching for a system that would avoid social dislocation and pauperism while at the same time insuring high productivity and rewards for industry and initiative. His search for historical precedents for a common land fund that would serve as a form of insurance against pauperism, and especially his discovery of the Russian peasant commune as a convenient basis for the social sector of his economy, are justifiably assigned to the tradition of Russian agrarian socialism. However, it should be emphasized that nothing can be found in Pestel's writings resembling the mystique with which some of the revolutionary *narodniki* (populists) of the 1870s surrounded the peasants and the commune. Like the more rationalistic populists, Pestel tended to see the peasants as victims, deprived of the opportunity to realize their full human potential and in need of a period of education. Memories of the massacres that had occurred during the Pugachev rebellion (1773–1775) and peasant unrest of the times inspired in the leaders of the Decembrist movement fear of peasant participation in the coming revolution. This too separates the Decembrists from the revolutionary *narodniki,* for whom the peasants were the great instrument of revolution. However much he outdistanced most of his comrades in political, social, and economic radicalism, Pestel was still not willing to see the axe brought into use. Thus, he planned a military revolution and the establishment of a temporary (about ten years) dictatorship, which would in turn establish a centralized democratic republic. Pestel's political goals were quite consistent with his democratic outlook. He wanted to abolish the unequal privileges and burdens of the old estates and to efface traditional cultural and social distinctions. His constitution more nearly resembled the North American than any existing European constitution, except that he was opposed to federalism.

The Southern Society, with Pestel's *Russian Law* its major inspiration, was the pivotal point of the entire Decembrist movement. Pestel's able lieutenants, Sergei Murav'ev-Apostol and Michael Bestuzhev-Riumin, were active proselytizers. The Vassilkov *uprava* to which they belonged (the Kamenka was the third *uprava* of the Southern Society) was responsible for the establishment of an alliance with a secret Polish society (1824) and with a Russian secret society in the Ukraine. The latter was called the "Society of United Slavs." Like the Union of Salvation, it had undergone a number of transformations in the course of several years (1817–1825). However, although military men, the United Slavs were of much humbler origin than the members of the other two segments of the Decembrist movement. They belonged to the gentry class (except for one peasant member with false papers, "P. F. Vygodovskii"), but were junior and middle-grade officers, economically, socially, and culturally inferior to the other Decembrists. In fact, it is best to think of them as a distinct phenomenon, even though they too were influenced by Masonism, European republicanism, and the *Carbonari.* There was something almost juvenile about their cryptograms and their Roman aliases, not to speak of their generous pan-Slavism, which mistakenly embraced the Hungarians. Ideologically, their leader, Peter Borisov, was more democratic than Pestel in that he believed in popular revolution and opposed even a temporary military dictatorship. Borisov never drew up a program as all-embracing as Pestel's *Russian Law,* but he advocated a democratic republican federation of all the Slavs. At the time that they were approached by Murav'ev-Apostol and Bestuzhev-Riumin, the United Slavs were far from the idea of an immediate revolution and certainly were not contemplating the seizure of power that Pestel envisioned. However, Bestuzhev-Riumin so exaggerated the scope and strength of the movement that the United Slavs ceased their opposition to Pestel's program and joined the Southern Society in the autumn of 1825. Once enrolled, the United Slavs proved to be the most zealous group within the Southern Society.

The third subdivision of the Decembrist movement (the Polish Patriotic Society did not really contribute enough to be included), the Northern Society, was, like the Southern Society, a reconstituted fragment of the Union of Welfare. The Northern Society's appearance was somewhat delayed because in 1821 Alexander had transferred the St. Petersburg guards to Lithuania. However, even after returning to the capital in 1822 the leaders of the Northern Society displayed little of Pestel's drive. The constitution that Nikita Murav'ev drew up for the Northern Society does not belong so much to the history of the revolutionary intelligentsia as to the history of Russian liberalism. There was considerable continuity between the moderate tone of the old Union of Welfare and the Northern Society. In 1823–1824 Pestel and his emissaries, even before they gained control over the United Slavs, tried to radicalize the St. Petersburg group, with limited success. Pestel's idea of an interim dictatorship was especially repugnant to the northerners. However, his republicanism and his plan for the assassination of the emperor found some favor with the more radical members of the Northern Society. Between 1824 and 1825, the radicals, led by Ryleev, had tipped the balance in their favor by recruiting more actively. The two groups were converging in the direction of Pestel's program. Both the Northern and Southern societies had enrolled men who were prepared to play the role of a *garde perdue* (suicide squad) in carrying out the assassination of the royal family. Events decided that the Northern Society should begin the actual insurrection.

The planning of the insurrection itself was marked by a great deal of disagreement, confusion, procrastination, and self-deception. The assassination of the emperor was put off until 1826, despite the impatience of the newly incorporated United Slavs. One can only speculate whether or not Pestel would have produced a concrete and workable plan. The historical model that the Decembrists referred to most frequently was the Spanish revolution of 1820, a military revolt led by Colonel Rafael Riego which forced Ferdinand VII to restore the liberal constitution of 1812. (The revolutionary government was crushed in 1823.) Pestel had tried to learn from the successes and failures of Europe's many revolutionary experiments between 1793 and 1823. A swift military rebellion with limited violence did not seem implausible, given Europe's recent history and Russia's own history of successful coups. But Pestel acted too slowly.

Alexander I died while on a stay in southern Russia on November 19, 1825. In the ensuing confusion over the imperial succession, the Northern Society took the initiative. It had been generally understood that St. Petersburg would be the strategic center of revolution. The northerners believed that tens of thousands of men in the Second Army were controlled by the Southern Society, and expected to have a substantial number of units stationed in the capital on their side. The revolution was to occur in the name of Grand Duke Constantine, who was the commander of the armies in Poland and Lithuania. Constantine had renounced his rights to the throne in 1822, and in a secret document (1823) Alexander had named his younger brother Nicholas as heir. However, this document was known to such a small circle and guarded with such strict secrecy that even Nicholas knew about it only through rumors. He himself did not want the throne and was happy to follow the advice of the Governor-General of St. Petersburg, General Nicholas Miloradovich, that he and the guard units in the capital immediately swear allegiance to Constantine in the event of Alexander's death. That is what happened on November 27. To all appearances, Constantine was the new tsar. On December 12, Nicholas received information about the secret societies and decided that it was his duty immediately to accept the throne.

Under Ryleev's guidance, the Northern Society had committed itself to an armed rebellion on the day that they were supposed to take an oath of loyalty to the new tsar, December 14, 1825. However, in spite of the confusion caused by Nicholas's doubtful claim to the throne, the rebels were at a distinct disadvantage. First of all, Nicholas had been informed of the plot and decided to swear in the Senate and most of the guard units very early in the morning. Ryleev had planned to surround the Senate, force it to recognize the revolutionary government, and simultaneously seize the royal family in the Winter Palace. One may conjecture that the disposition of the Senate was not crucial in any event, since the leaders of the insurrection—Prince Trubetskoi and Colonel Alexander Bulatov—lost their nerve. Ryleev, as a civilian, could do little but offer moral encouragement and look picturesque in his battle costume. Alexander Iakubovich, who had been given the responsibility for seizing the Winter Palace, not only refused this assignment—his hate for Alexander I was evidently nontransferable—but deserted the rebels. The few units that did follow the leadership of the officers of the Northern Society drew themselves up in a rectangular formation on Senate Square near Falconet's statue of Peter the Great.

It was eleven o'clock in the morning. They no longer had any strategy to follow, and there was nothing to do but wait and hope that other units would join them. Trubetskoi did not appear on the square to take command. During the afternoon, the Moscow regiment, the first to mutiny, was joined by units of the Naval Guards and Grenadiers. They numbered about three thousand men altogether. Nicholas ordered cavalry units to charge the rebel formation, but the charges failed with few casualties to either side. By three o'clock in the afternoon dusk began to fall. Fearing the darkness, the hostile civilian mob, and the possibility of further desertions to the rebels, Nicholas, on the advice of one of his officers, ordered the artillery into action. Until the canister shot began to deplete their ranks, the rebels did not believe that their fellow soldiers were capable of using artillery against them. After several rounds, the Decembrists' ranks dissolved. Michael Bestuzhev's final attempt to rally his troops on the ice of the Neva River failed when the cannoneers found them. Although the number of troops who were killed was rather small compared to the number involved in the engagement, there were numerous civilian casualties, and the scene on Senate Square and the streets leading to it was bloody and chaotic.

The strange and tragic events of December 14, 1825 revealed that even Russia's alienated military officers could not entirely overcome their conditioned loyalty. The succession crisis and the "reswearing" of the capital to Nicholas created an atmosphere of intrigue and illegitimacy, precisely the kind of atmosphere which Ryleev's scheme demanded. However, Nicholas's military bearing and his evocation of the military discipline of the guards helped, despite his unpopularity, to save the day for him. Even some of the Decembrists, notably Iakubovich and Bulatov, became paralyzed in the presence of the tsar. The younger officers appear to have been less conditioned and less paralyzed, but they realized too late that full responsibility for the insurrection lay with them. It may be that the strange context in which they had to operate destroyed the initiative of the more experienced officers. It may be that the veterans of the Napoleonic campaigns, despite their postwar grievances, could not bring themselves to break discipline before their supreme commander. Whatever the reason for their paralysis, from that day forth the guard regiments no longer played their customary political role.

Events in the south were no less confused and disastrous for the rebels. Pestel was arrested on December 13. On December 25, 1825, Sergei Murav'ev-Apostol received news of the rebellion in St. Petersburg. Having escaped arrest himself, Murav'ev-Apostol assumed leadership of the southern forces, about eight hundred men of the Chernigov regiment. They were decisively defeated on January 3, 1826, in their first engagement with government troops.

The peculiar combination of military men, ideologues, and poets that comprised the leadership of the Decembrist movement gave it the overweening confidence that led to action. But they were for the most part very young men, and in defeat some of them lost not only their confidence but their convictions as well. Under stress, they submitted contritely to the very authorities that they had repudiated. One feels that this resubmission to authority had different significance for men as dissimilar as Ryleev, Pestel, and Trubetskoi, but they all shared the psychological experience of a crushing defeat and total dependency upon their captors.

The investigation that followed the capture of the rebels was supervised by the tsar himself. His psychological victory over them was perhaps the singular achievement of his reign. The inclusion of Michael Speransky, one of the heroes of the Decembrists, in the special tribunal that sentenced the Decembrist leaders was a final cruel touch. Pestel, Ryleev, Sergei Murav'ev-Apostol, Michael Bestuzhev-Riumin, and Kakhovskii were sentenced to quartering, but the tsar generously commuted the sentence to hanging. It was Nicholas's practice to reserve for himself the opportunity to appear clement. Thirty-one of the leaders were sentenced to Siberian exile and hard labor for life, and eighty-five were given less severe sentences. Since they were so young, many of the Siberian exiles survived to enjoy the amnesty granted by Alexander II at his coronation in 1856.

The repression of the Decembrist rebellion had several important consequences. One was to remove from the scene a significant oppositional force—several dozen men who might have had considerable influence in public life, had they chosen to pursue a less radical course. Another was to strengthen Nicholas I's conservatism and rigidity, and leave the field to the traditionalists in both government and culture. An entire intelligentsia generation was forced underground. When in the 1840s a new revolutionary conspiracy began to take shape, it had an entirely different character from that of the Decembrist movement. Unlike the Decembrists, succeeding generations of revolutionaries were to turn to the rural and urban masses for help. But however much their style, their goals, and their strategies differed, each new wave acknowledged that the Decembrists had begun it all. The Decembrists were much more effective as martyrs than as insurrectionaries. Thus, their historical contribution is ambiguous. The direct and overt effect of their activity was reaction and repression. The other momentous consequence was the birth of a revolutionary tradition that survived for a century.

THE INCUBATION OF SOCIALISM

The reign of Nicholas I accomplished almost the opposite of what he had intended. Nicholas wanted to consolidate the position of the *dvorianstvo* in the system of estates. He tried to arrest the processes of cultural differentiation within the *dvorianstvo* and to remold it into a unified, loyal, and fully disciplined military-bureaucratic elite. Nicholas's parade-ground mania, even more marked than Alexander's, was not mitigated by intellectualism or religiosity. He was unambiguously Prussian. While Alexander's ambiguity had encouraged the *dvorianstvo* to speak out and to produce a wide range of civic ideologies, Nicholas's rigidity inspired hatred and forced the psychological withdrawal of significant numbers of the gentry estate. At this period in Russian history, the gentry had few alternatives to state service. Ambitious young men eventually became military officers or civil officials. However, the gentry could remain idle, living off the income from their estates and enterprises. Furthermore, during Nicholas's reign there was nothing resembling the mobilization of gentry manpower that had occurred during the Napoleonic period. Young men spent their entire adolescence in educational institutions, which, although patterned after the barracks in keeping with Nicholas's style, permitted the continuation of the cultural evolution of the *dvorianstvo*. The intellectual and cultural achievements of Nicholas's reign are at least partly attributable to the lessening of the state's demands upon the *dvorianstvo* for active military duty. The much expanded educational system, the professions, literary occupations, or simply dilettantism became increasingly attractive as alternatives to military or government service. Thus, despite Nicholas's intentions, he lived to see the growth of a framework in which the intelligentsia could survive, even as "superfluous men," in the interstices of his system. Social and cultural processes begun long before his reign proved to be irreversible.

The ideological democratization of the gentry had been going on spontaneously during the late eighteenth and early nineteenth centuries. Contact with commoners did not necessarily hasten the process, although this is a frequent assumption of both Soviet and non-Soviet historians. The process of amalgamation of educated gentry and commoners yielded a new social stratum not belonging to the traditional system of estates. Its members usually made their living from writing or from their estates. They were not accumulators in the strict sense of the word. If we use the term "middle-class" to describe the position of a class relative to other classes, then the intelligentsia was a middle class of sorts, although not a bourgeois middle class, since it rejected a number of basic bourgeois values. It did not belong either to the establishment or to the masses.

The intelligentsia, however, did not think of themselves so much as being in the middle as being outside the entire system. They tried to create their own life style. At first, that style reflected the habits of an aristocracy. Even when they began to feel guilty about their privileges, gentry members of the intelligentsia did not see much virtue in the life styles of other estates. As one might expect, they retained a certain amount of snobbishness because of their superior taste, their worldly experience, and their mastery of European culture. Exposure to morally and intellectually superior men from other estates in the gymnasiums and universities sometimes changed their snobbishness into self-abasement, but this did not occur as a significant cultural phenomenon during Nicholas's reign. During this period, 1825–1855, it was more usual for the educated commoner to acquire the outlook and manners of the gentry than for the opposite to occur. In any case, contrary to Nicholas's expectations, the educational system did not produce exclusively docile servants of the state. It became a meeting ground for men of virtue and intellect who rejected Nicholas's epaulets, swords, and militarily proper mustaches. The new generation of intellectuals, frustrated and angered at the attempt to enforce rigid discipline in culture and education, discovered methods of "internal emigration" and self-education characteristic of alienated intelligentsias. The university, although not exempt from official surveillance, was one of the few public institutions where the intelligentsia could express its values.

Nicholas's policy was successful to the extent that it reduced the proportion of commoners in the elite preparatory schools. In spite of this, commoners were admitted into even the exclusive gymnasiums of St. Petersburg, and provincial gymnasiums were frequently quite democratic in their admissions. Furthermore, during the 1840s, more than 50 percent of the student body of the University of Moscow were commoners. In 1849 there were approximately 4,000 students enrolled in Russia's six universities, and 37 percent were commoners.

The needs of the ever-expanding bureaucracy mitigated the effects of the policy laid down by Nicholas and his minister of education, Count S. S. Uvarov (1833–1849). The pressures of maintaining a vast empire and the demands of modernization tended to undermine Nicholas's reactionary educational policy. The absolute number of commoners in the educational system continually increased and, especially at the university level, segregation did not work. Finally, even after the severe reaction to the revolutions of 1848 and the reduction of the student bodies at gymnasiums and universities (1848–1854), the number of students at both levels was still more than twice the number for 1825.

Nicholas's attempt to quarantine Russia ideologically by transforming the university curriculum was an even greater failure. Promising Russian scholars were educated abroad during the 1830s, and they brought back with them the latest European philosophies. They tended to promote the dominance of German thought during the late 1820s and 1830s. Since the faculties of philosophy in Russian universities were closed down in 1826, German idealism was spread in the universities by biologists, physicists, historians, and jurists. The most popular professors did not merely expose their students to the technical knowledge peculiar to their field, but simultaneously propagated a worldview. Young men, both students and teachers, formed discussion circles and study groups where they taught themselves subjects that did not exist in the university curriculum. Thus, despite Uvarov's stress upon classicism, which may seem curious in view of the Decembrists' self-identification with the republican heroes of ancient Rome, university students gained access to all that was current in Europe. Censorship, too, was a qualified failure. Consciousness and sensibility were shaped by forces beyond the control of any official system of watchdogs. Clandestine poetry and essays circulated widely in manuscript and were read at salons.

Furthermore, the censors were not infallible, the most notable incident being their failure to stop publication of P. I. Chaadaev's "Philosophical Letter" in the September 1836 issue of N. I. Nadezhdin's journal, *The Telescope* (Moscow). One of the seminal essays in the history of the nineteenth-century intelligentsia, it was written, ironically enough, by the very army officer who had brought the news of the mutiny of the Semenovskii regiment to Alexander in 1820. Having parted company with the men who joined the Decembrist movement, Chaadaev survived to perpetuate a vision that belonged to the period of Alexander I. Chaadaev's Christian universalism is almost devoid of specific political content, and it is difficult to classify him as a social thinker. His real contribution lies in his philosophy of history, and here he owed a great debt to both conservative and liberal Catholic thinkers such as de Maistre, de Bonald, and Lamennais, although there is a disagreement about the extent to which he was conservative, like the two former writers, or liberal, like

Lamennais. Scholars also dispute Chaadaev's place in the history of the intelligentsia because of seeming ambiguities, or even contradictions, in his ideas about Russia's historical role. But what Chaadaev really meant is not nearly so important for the history of the revolutionary intelligentsia as the questions that he raised and the heated discussions that he provoked. Nothing like his grand, eloquent, and bitter condemnation of Russia's cultural past had ever appeared in the Russian periodical press. Chaadaev approached the problem of distinguishing culture from civilization, but, without the benefit of the more developed historical and anthropological scholarship of the mid-nineteenth century, he was able to express his views only metaphorically. Indeed, he not only asserted that Russia did not have a real civilization, but his argument led to the conclusion that it was not likely to have one in the future either, since it lacked the historical heritage which had permitted other nations to grow, mature, and join the civilized European "family." A painful sense of cultural inferiority is exposed in this luxuriant self-castigation:

> You will therefore find that we all lack a certain assurance, a certain method in our thinking, a certain logic. The syllogism of the West is unknown to us. There is something more than frivolity in our best minds. The finest ideas, for lack of coherence or sequel, dazzle for a moment but are sterile and congeal in our brains. It is natural for a man to feel lost when he is unable to establish a connection with what preceded him and what follows. He loses all certainty, all feeling of consistency. Not being guided by a sense of unbroken continuity, he feels that he has gone astray in the world. There are such lost creatures in all countries, but with us this is a general characteristic. Ours is not the levity which used to be thrown up to the French and which in fact was merely a facility of understanding that did not preclude either depth or breadth of intellect and gave infinite grace and charm to social intercourse. We are scatterbrained; we live without gaining experience or providing for the future; our life is reduced to the ephemeral existence of the individual separated from his species, concerned neither with acquiring glory nor with promoting some cause, nor even with those inherited family interests and the many prospects and prescriptions which, in a society based on a memory of the past

> and an understanding of the future, are the essence of both public and private life.[4]

This passage undoubtedly reveals a great deal about Chaadaev, retired army officer and salon intellectual. There is a brief but brilliant description of Chaadaev in Alexander Herzen's memoirs which confirms the impression that Chaadaev was describing his own wasted life and that of the intellectuals of his generation. In later writings, Chaadaev strongly modified the pessimistic tone of his first "Philosophical Letter," in which he had stated that "while we have some of the virtues of young and not highly civilized peoples, we have none that characterize mature peoples with a high level of culture."[5] The possible virtues of backwardness and of Russia's peculiar cultural heritage were examined in Chaadaev's later essays and correspondence. Although Chaadaev's final goal was always that of a universal Christianity, progressing toward greater unity and perfection according to Friedrich Schelling's vision, his ideas about the means to attain that goal developed in the polemics that followed his "Philosophical Letter." The tensions and ambivalences in Chaadaev's thought foreshadowed the problems of the Westernizers in the Russian intelligentsia. They too looked to Europe for a universal principle of salvation, but sometimes reserved for Russia a very special role in the progressive movement of humanity. Chaadaev's real contribution lay in his dramatic presentation of Russia's backwardness, forcing the issue upon the intelligentsia and opening the debate between the Westernizers and Slavophiles.

However, the very sensation caused by Chaadaev's "Philosophical Letter" in 1836 revealed that censors had attained some control of the periodical press. Most publishers had learned to stay on the good side of the Third Section, Nicholas's political police, but they occasionally failed. N. I. Nadezhdin, publisher of *The Telescope,* one of the most important literary organs of the day, paid for his mistake by seeing his periodical closed. He himself

4 In Marc Raeff, ed., *Russian Intellectual History: An Anthology* (New York, 1966), pp. 165–66. There is an English translation by Raymond T. McNally, *The Major Works of Peter Chaadaev* (Notre Dame, 1969).

5 Raeff, ed., *Russian Intellectual History,* p. 166.

was exiled to Siberia for a short time, while Chaadaev was pronounced mad and placed under surveillance. This was another blow to the most independent and critical element in Russian periodical literature, following as it did the closure of Nicholas Polevoi's *Moscow Telegraph* (1834) and Ivan Kireevsky's *European* (1832). During the earlier part of Nicholas's reign, Moscow was the center of ferment, primarily because of the oppressive closeness at the center of the bureaucracy and police. Toward mid-century St. Petersburg became the center of intelligentsia ferment, *The Contemporary* and *Notes of the Fatherland* being the leading periodicals.

During the 1840s the censors were unable to stop the flow of forbidden books into Russia. Both illegal and legal methods were used to get books past the censors. The importation of foreign books into Russia went on at a grand scale, more than two million foreign volumes entering Russia between 1845 and 1847 alone. One can speculate that tens of thousands of them were forbidden books. In 1849, one St. Petersburg book dealer was caught with 2,581 illegal books, and in the same year 1,105 and 2,035 were discovered in bookstores in Dorpat and Riga respectively.

Finally, by the late 1840s intelligentsia publicists had learned the art of indirect discourse, while their reading public had become expert in the art of inference. One of the most frequent ploys was to display the evils of American slavery, the implications for Russian serfdom being rather obvious. Another was to describe the problems of the working classes in other countries, and in this way to discuss the explanations and solutions of both laissez-faire and socialist theorists. However, the publicists only added fuel to the fire and provided the intelligentsia with issues to debate. The development of the intelligentsia doctrines of the 1830s and 1840s occurred less in this limited type of public discourse than in the circles that formed in the university cities.

There is a very brief and tragic prelude to the history of the circles of the 1830s and 1840s. It consists partly of the stories of abortive provincial attempts to resurrect the Decembrist conspiracy. Such provincial affairs were generally unknown to the intelligentsia of the capitals and thus do not belong to the main stream of the history of the revolutionary intelligentsia. However, they do belong to the martyrology of the revolutionary movement. More important for the history of the intelligentsia were the martyred students and teachers of the 1820s and 1830s. The University of Moscow, the largest of the six universities in the Russian Empire, harbored a number of circles, some of which ran afoul of the authorities.

In some ways the pathetic conspiracies that transpired between 1826 and 1831 repeated the patterns of the Decembrist movement, but in other ways they also belonged to the next revolutionary period. As the center of activity shifted from military garrisons to the dormitories and apartments of rebellious students, a whole new set of conditions, new personnel, and a different approach to revolution gradually emerged.

Aside from the imminent danger of the Third Section, young men of the 1830s and 1840s were beset by serious ideological problems. It is difficult to summarize the complexities of the ideological debates of the second quarter of the nineteenth century. There were several kinds of Romanticism, both revolutionary and conservative. Romantic belles lettres and philosophy were probably the single most pervasive influence during the 1830s. Liberal students assuaged their bitterness and shame for Russia's internal tyranny and conservative role in world affairs by immersing themselves in art and philosophy. Images of antique and medieval heroism, and the literature of Romantic rebellion, especially Schiller's, permitted vicarious enjoyment of what was denied in life. To be sure, the psychological benefits of Romantic literature and its general attractiveness transcended politics. The intelligentsia, however, longed for a unifying vision and did not simply entertain or transport themselves by means of Romantic literature. They formed a conception of the whole human being, unconstrained by narrow and demeaning employments, and totally rejected the philistine world of mean motives and petty actions. They imaginatively shaped a world that would support a new kind of personality. But their satisfying contact with abstractions and idealizations contrasted tragically with the harshness and inflexibility of their immediate environment. The painful gap between an ideal world and the real one is, of course, the source of the tragedy of all historical intelligentsias. But in this period they expressed their alienation through renunciation of action in the social realm and the search for ideologies that would justify their withdrawal.

The intelligentsia of the 1830s and 1840s needed both seclusion and justification for seclusion, and they found them in Romantic literature and German idealism. Thus, they lived intensely in a small world of literary circles and salons, where they engaged in flamboyant verbal tournaments and soul-searching personal relationships. The Stankevich circle (1833–1837) was the most important of these philosophical and artistic groups. N. V. Stankevich, the spiritual and philosophical guide of the circle, displayed to full extent the intellectual integrity, delicacy of manner and motive, and personal weakness characteristic of one of the Russian intelligentsia's several kinds of "superfluous men." Stankevich's personal charm and intellectual gifts permitted him to retain the devotion of men who became bitter antagonists after his circle dissolved. During the years when the Stankevich circle brought together Belinsky, T. N. Granovskii, V. P. Botkin, Michael Bakunin, and several other belles-lettrists and scholars, Moscow was the unchallenged center of intellectual ferment in Russia. Some of the foremost talents of the 1830s and 1840s developed a worldview, or the first elements of one, in Stankevich's or one of the other Moscow circles.

Schelling, Fichte, and Hegel provided them with the cosmic consolation that the concrete world was always tending toward an ultimate order and unity. They felt that they were conscious participants in this process—a kind of spiritual elite. They identified self-expression and self-consciousness with the progress of the spirit. German idealism was translatable into aesthetic, social, political, and scientific thought. More than any other variety of contemporary philosophy, excluding, of course, traditional theologies, German idealism made nature, culture, and history intelligible and benign, but at the same time appealed to the younger generation's sense of drama and personal mission. Like the Masonic movement before it, the Romantic movement in literature and philosophy encouraged moral purity and integrity, but now expressed culturally and in the art of personal relationships rather than in civic activity.

In spite of the tendency for its adherents to become introspective, withdrawn, and civically passive, the Romantic movement and German idealism strongly influenced the revolutionary intelligentsia of the following generation. Three of the major figures in the history of the revolutionary intelligentsia—Belinsky, Herzen, and Bakunin—discovered separate paths out of the enchanted forest of German metaphysics, but each of them carried with him ideas and attitudes acquired along the way. First of all, besides nature and the creative genius, German philosophy offered a splendid array of spiritual vehicles—the folk, the state, and history itself. Second, conflict and struggle, both in Romantic literature and the dialectical vision of Hegel, were part of the system of progress. Third, the ideas of freedom and progress, however much they were hedged in by conservative rationalizations, could not be reconciled forever with political and social systems that resisted change. Of course, the ultimate judgment about progress rested with the individual, as well as the choice to struggle for political and social freedom. Thus, Herzen found the revolutionary implications in Hegel immediately, while others, Belinsky and Bakunin, for example, had to be converted from right-wing Hegelianism, which had encouraged reconciliation with the present order.

Having chosen the path of civic action, the intelligentsia of the 1830s and 1840s could select from many schools of ethical, social, and political thought. Like the Decembrists before them, they were extremely eclectic. In general, the conservative civic ideologies derived primarily from German idealism, while the more radical ideologies were based upon French utopian socialism and communism. The Slavophiles might be called radical conservatives, in that they wanted to reestablish the political, social, and cultural unity that they believed had existed in Russia during the Moscow period in the sixteenth and seventeenth centuries. Slavophilism only obliquely touches the history of the revolutionary intelligentsia. By exaggerating the virtues inherent in native Russian institutions like the peasant commune, by subjecting Europe to devastating criticism, and by establishing Russia's great spiritual mission, the Slavophiles predisposed the radical wing of the Westernizers to think about Russia's unique strengths in a certain way. The later populist belief that the Russian peasant masses possessed unique socialist and revolutionary attributes was not unrelated to the Slavophile vision of the spiritually superior Orthodox peasantry.

The more direct source of the doctrines of the revolutionary intelligentsia was the Westernizers, who were violently opposed to the Slavophiles. The heated debates between the Westernizers and Slavophiles during the 1840s covered a wide ideological spectrum, but only one portion of that spectrum is of special importance for the history of the revolutionary intelligentsia. This position is best described as radical Westernism, a movement steeped in the European revolutionary tradition and the most recent European socialist thought. The radical Westernizers also repudiated the legalistic and gradualistic approach of the liberal Westernizers to the right of them ideologically.

It is impossible to survey adequately and justly the complex ideologies of the Slavophiles and liberal Westernizers here. Suffice it to say that the interaction of these two ideological groupings with the radical Westernizers generated a highly charged intellectual environment during the late 1830s and 1840s. One must mention Chaadaev's "Philosophical Letter," Granovskii's brilliant lectures on European history imbued with the spirit of liberalism, Herzen's early philosophical essays and the enthusiastic circle of Westernizers that formed around him, the debates between Westernizers and Slavophiles held in various Moscow salons, the appearance of literary organs propagating the several ideologies—*The Muscovite* (Slavophile), *Notes of the Fatherland* (Westernizer), and *The Contemporary* (radical Westernizer)—all of which went into the making of "the marvelous decade," as P. V. Annenkov described it in his memoirs.

In belles lettres, writers and critics turned their attention from poetry to prose, and Romanticism yielded to realism. Talents and temperaments as different as those of Nicholas Gogol, Dmitrii Grigorovich, Ivan Goncharov, Ivan Turgenev, Dostoevsky, and Herzen contributed to the formation of what can be described collectively as social literature. Representations of the life of the peasants, the urban classes, and the intelligentsia—whether sympathetic, satiric, or disinterested—permitted Belinsky to create a new kind of social literary criticism.

Belinsky's criticism reflected not only his tortuous ideological evolution but the reemergence during the 1840s of the civic aggressiveness of the intelligentsia. Belinsky taught an entire intelligentsia generation to look for social truths in art and to seek not only the aesthetic qualities but the moral implications of a writer's work. Towards the end of his brief life (1811–1848) he tried to strike a balance in his criticism between the aesthetic and didactic aspects of art, but didacticism assumed the ascendancy. Increasingly Belinsky used the work of art as a means through which social reality could be viewed and evaluated. In Belinsky's criticism social reality came to mean the misery, frustration, and ugliness of Russian life. That is why Gogol's work was so extremely important for him. However, Belinsky failed to distinguish Gogol's ability to portray the bizarre, grotesque, ridiculous, and pathetic from his religious, social, and political views, which were quite conservative. Gogol's seeming acceptance of the official creed of Nicholas and Uvarov in his book *Selected Passages from Correspondence with Friends* (1847) could in Belinsky's eyes only be a monstrous betrayal of everything that Gogol had previously stood for. What Belinsky could not write in his review in *The Contemporary* of Gogol's book (January 1847) he expressed vehemently in a letter to Gogol, written in July 1847. Like Chaadaev's "Philosophical Letter" of 1836, Belinsky's "Letter to Gogol" had an immediate and profound effect upon the intelligentsia. Numerous manuscript copies of the letter circulated clandestinely. There could be no mistaking the meaning of such passages as these:

> Advocate of the knout, apostle of ignorance, champion of obscurantism and reactionary mysticism, eulogist of Tatar customs—what are you doing? Look at what is beneath your feet; you are standing at the brink of an abyss. That you should tie in your ideas with the Orthodox Church I can understand—it has ever been the support of the knout and the toady of despotism; but why do you bring in Christ: What do you think He has in common with any church, and particularly the Orthodox Church? He was the first to teach men the ideals of liberty, equality, and fraternity, and He illustrated and proved the truth of His teaching by His martyrdom. And it was man's salvation only until a Church was organized around it, based on the prin-

ciple of orthodoxy. The Church was a hierarchy, and hence a champion of inequality, a toady to power, an enemy and persecutor of brotherhood among men, and so it continues to be to this day. The true meaning of Christ's teaching was revealed by the philosophical movement of the last century. That is why a Voltaire, who used the weapon of mockery to put out the bonfires of fanaticism and ignorance in Europe, is certainly far more a son of Christ, flesh of His flesh, and bone of His bone, than all your priests, bishops, metropolitans, and patriarchs, in the East as in the West.

. . . When a European, especially a Catholic, becomes possessed by the religious spirit, he turns to denouncing unjust authority, like the Hebrew prophets, who denounced the great of the earth for flouting the law. In Russia, on the other hand, if a man (even a decent man) develops the illness known to the psychiatrists by the name of *religiosa mania*, he at once proceeds to burn more incense to the earthly God than to God in heaven. What scoundrels we Russians are![6]

Aside from his insight into the meaning of active religion, Belinsky revealed here, as in other letters to friends—especially in his correspondence with the liberal Westernizer V. P. Botkin—his affiliation with the French revolutionary tradition.

The exact extent of Belinsky's radicalism is not easy to determine. He was extremely susceptible to French socialism, but he was not a doctrinaire socialist. His last writings reveal the contradictory pressures of the radical (socialist) Westernizers, like Herzen, and the liberal Westernizers, like Botkin. However, the social philosophy of Belinsky's last years cannot be easily classified under headings like "socialist" or "bourgeois-liberal." He was almost universally acclaimed by the intelligentsia for his passionate humanism, his struggle for equality, justice, and human development, and only the most jaundiced critic of the revolutionary intelligentsia will fail to be moved by the authenticity of his quest. Belinsky's occasional expressions of sympathy for Jacobinism in his correspondence are easily misconstrued. He was hyperbolic and theatrical in exposing his latest revolutionary discoveries to his friends, but in his lengthy articles, in which he thought out loud, Belinsky demonstrated a surprising

6 Raeff, ed., *Russian Intellectual History*, pp. 256-57.

capacity for moderation. He died too soon to develop systematically his views about revolution. However, his authentic rendering of the spirit of the French and German ideologies of the left made him the idol of the younger generation. An aura of martyrdom surrounded Belinsky, even though his death prevented the government from imprisoning him.

Alexander Herzen, considerably less of an influence on the younger generation than Belinsky during the "marvelous decade," was the fixed point of radical Westernism throughout this period. Herzen and his lifelong friend and intellectual partner, Nicholas Ogarev, had pledged themselves while still schoolboys to continue the work begun by the Decembrists. Toward the end of his studies at the University of Moscow, and as a postgraduate (1831–1834), Herzen had gathered about him a circle of radical youths and even had planned to publish a periodical that would embody the rather elevated Saint-Simonian socialism that Herzen had assimilated to his Schellingian worldview. However, the authorities intervened, and Herzen spent the next few years in internal exile. When he returned to Moscow in 1840, he was dismayed to find that conservative ideologies were prevalent among the intellectual vanguard, and that even Belinsky had been converted to passive Hegelian "Buddhism," as he later called it. Herzen was largely responsible for destroying Belinsky's temporary (1839–1841) fascination with the right-wing Hegelian theodicy and restoring his characteristic activism. During the next few years in both salon debates and in his writings, Herzen helped to drag the intelligentsia back to earth. In the process of attacking the prevailing quietism, he demonstrated profound insights into the mission and meaning of the intelligentsia as opposed to intellectual workers and pure thinkers. The series of articles that Herzen wrote for *Notes of the Fatherland* between 1843 and 1846 established a philosophical basis for intelligentsia activism. Repudiation of pure form, the merging of art and science with life—these are typical intelligentsia aims. Herzen expressed them with great power in his essay "Buddhism in Science" (1843), where he wrote:

> We concur with the formalists in that science is *superior* to life, but this very superiority testifies to its onesidedness. What is

> concretely true cannot be either beneath or above life; it must lie in the nodal center, like the heart in an organism. And just because science is above life, its sphere is abstract and its *completeness is incomplete*. . . . In science, thought and being are reconciled, but the terms of peace are the doing of thought, and the full reconciliation lies in the doing. "Doing is a live unity of theory and practice," said the greatest thinker of the ancient world more than two thousand years ago.[7]

Herzen's own study of Hegel revealed to him the revolutionary implications of the dialectic, which he called "the algebra of revolution." Exposure to the writings of the Young Hegelians, and especially to Ludwig Feuerbach's *Essence of Christianity* (1841), reinforced Herzen's interpretation. Thus, in Herzen two streams of radical ideology—French utopian socialism and German left Hegelianism—combined in a highly developed philosophical radicalism. Fully in keeping with realism in literature, the new radical tendency in philosophy and social thought reintroduced the intelligentsia to the miseries of the flesh, to concrete suffering and material solutions to human frustration. It is therefore not surprising that Herzen displayed a strong bias for materialism and scientism during the mid-1840s. French social thought, especially Pierre Proudhon's, completed his ideological evolution toward revolutionary socialism. By 1848 one could see in Herzen some of the distinctive attitudes of the later *narodnik* movement.

The experiences of his first years abroad, his Italian journey and his presence in Paris during the revolution of 1848, both justified and clarified the revolutionary and antibourgeois sentiments that Herzen had expressed in debates with the liberal Westernizers before his departure in 1847. His antibourgeois, antiliberal attitudes in some ways brought him closer to the Slavophiles than to the Westernizers. Europe, especially that most European nation, France, now seemed corrupt and decadent to him. The term "Westernizer" was always somewhat ambiguous when applied to the radical Westernizers, for they had internalized the most critical and revolutionary European doc-

---

7 James M. Edie, James P. Scanlan, and Mary-Barbara Zeldin, eds., *Russian Philosophy*, 3 vols. (Chicago, 1965), I, p. 335.

trines which, in effect, repudiated Europe's contemporary bourgeois civilization. Both radical Westernizers and Slavophiles deplored the philistine, urban-commercial civilization implied by the term "bourgeois." Herzen's sensibilities, like those of the Slavophiles, were aristocratic, Romantic sensibilities, even though he emphatically rejected their image of Russia's historical, spiritual, and social endowment. After 1848 Herzen himself began to propagate the idea of Russia's special path.

In Herzen's case, his action is attributable to some extent to a kind of defensive patriotism evoked by the condescending attitude of European intellectuals toward Russia. Like Chaadaev, Herzen employed the metaphor of organic growth and pictured Russia as a young, vigorous, and promising nation which might contribute to the general progress of mankind. But, in addition to the fact that his universal principle (once again, borrowed from Europe) was socialism instead of Christianity, Herzen went further than Chaadaev by assuming the decadence of the West. Since Europe seemed unable to tear itself free from its medieval past, Herzen believed that youthful Russia might actually arrive at socialism first, skipping the decadent phase of bourgeois civilization. It did not occur to Herzen, who had never had much interest in economics, that the wealth and technology created by the bourgeoisie might be a prerequisite for socialism. Furthermore, after the suppression of the proletarian insurrection in Paris (June 1848), Herzen repudiated bourgeois republicanism for anarchism.

In short, Herzen invariably drew the most radical conclusions from his study of Hegel, the left Hegelians, and the French socialists. His experiences of 1847–1848 confirmed his radicalism and converted him temporarily into a revolutionary anarchist with a nationalistic bias. The Russian peasant commune became the object upon which Herzen projected his longings for an anarchistic variety of socialism. Despite his remarkable critical intelligence, Herzen drew up a simple formula which united progress with nationalism. To be sure, Herzen's conception of progress was rather complex and did not resemble the old linear conception of progress. In *From the Other Shore,* a collection of philosophical dialogues written in 1848–1849, Herzen had subjected existing theories of progress to ruthless criticism. However, Herzen was incapable of carrying out the program of "existential egoism"[8] suggested in the dialogue. Instead, he allied himself with a "progressive" European theory, anarchistic socialism, and indulged both his aristocratic snobbery and his patriotism with a hopeful vision of the Russian peasant commune—a living historical relic which would presumably permit the Slavs to achieve socialism first.

Except for rare moments, Herzen always found himself a note higher or lower than other Russian social and political thinkers. During the late 1840s and early 1850s, he was far more radical than the other Westernizers, except Bakunin. By the 1860s a more mature Herzen had moderated his views and found himself cautioning the younger revolutionary generation and his émigré colleagues in much the same way that Granovskii had cautioned him. But it was Herzen who engaged in the first systematic attempt to reconcile socialism with Russian backwardness, and in that respect he is a progenitor of the long line of theoretical development that ends with Trotsky and Lenin.

Like Herzen, Bakunin was a product of the Romantic period. A member of the Stankevich circle during the 1830s, Bakunin was the most neurotic and extreme ideologist to emerge from that pleasant and vaporous environment. During his conservative phase he had tutored Belinsky in right-wing Hegelianism. His own conversion to left Hegelianism occurred at the beginning of the 1840s, while he was traveling in Germany. Bakunin was probably the first Russian to study the writings of the Young Hegelians—David Strauss, Arnold Ruge, Bruno Bauer, and Ludwig Feuerbach. They were drawing radical conclusions from the Hegelian dialectic and transforming Hegel's conservative idealism into revolutionary materialism. Bakunin's article, "The Reaction in Germany," appeared in their journal in 1842 and attracted Herzen, who was independently reading and thinking along the same lines. The article appeared in German (over a French pseudonym), foreshadowing Bakunin's later wanderings as a cosmopolitan revolutionary exile, and in a way symbolizing the uprootedness of his generation.

---

8 Malia, *Alexander Herzen*, p. 382.

Between 1842 and his arrest in 1849, Bakunin was a member of the growing community of exiled revolutionaries who congregated in Paris, London, and Switzerland. Much more than Herzen, Bakunin sought out the company of prominent socialists and communists during these years—one might even call his wanderings a kind of pilgrimage. Wilhelm Weitling, the German communist,[9] and Proudhon were the two most important influences on Bakunin. While Herzen remained a somewhat detached observer and commentator, Bakunin plunged into the revolutionary movements of the late 1840s. During the period 1847–1849 Bakunin became increasingly attracted to the Slavic revolutionary movements. In 1848 in Paris, Herzen, the former Francophile, was becoming a Francophobe and extolling the virtues of Russian peasants. Almost simultaneously, at the Slav Congress in Prague, Bakunin, the former Germanophile, was becoming a Germanophobe and discovering the revolutionary potentialities of the Slavs. So pervasive was the spirit of nationalism in 1848 that it transformed two of the most cosmopolitan members of the intelligentsia into special pleaders for their own backward but "youthful" people.

But Bakunin's ideas were developed for a different audience than Herzen's. The latter derived a certain pleasure from shocking the intellectual community around him and from smashing the idols of those who thought themselves progressive. Bakunin was actually involved in the business of creating revolutionary programs and was already displaying considerable flexibility in considering the agencies and means that would bring about the revolution. The Russian peasantry, with their tradition of mass violence and incendiarism, became increasingly attractive to Bakunin. For Herzen, the peasants' primary attraction lay in their communal institutions, while Bakunin was most impressed by their capacity for violence. Herzen's brief fascination with revolutionary destruction proved ultimately to have been part of a passing mood, while Bakunin's was an expression of his entire personality.

---

9 Weitling (1808–1871), a communist of Christian inspiration, was influential in Switzerland in the 1840s.

Thus, by 1848 Herzen and Bakunin had sketched the theoretical outlines of Russian revolutionary populism. Together with Belinsky, they formed the ideological vanguard of the revolutionary movement in Russia. Their anarchism was a logical conclusion of Romantic and dialectical thought and was assimilable to a number of existing socialist doctrines. By 1848 their views corresponded rather closely to Proudhon's. On the other hand, Belinsky had not broken decisively with the liberal Westernizers. At his death in May 1848, before the European revolutions ran their course, he was still carrying on his task of enlightenment, and one can only speculate whether or not he would have followed Bakunin and Herzen in their evolution toward revolutionary anarchism.

Neither Belinsky, Herzen, nor Bakunin had developed a consistent revolutionary strategy. At one time or another, all of them had entertained Jacobin or Blanquist ideas.[10] However, only Bakunin seemed serious about Blanquism, just as only he really seemed to look forward to the prospect of mass violence. It remained for new generations of revolutionaries to test revolutionary strategies and establish the relationship between the intelligentsia and the masses.

The history of the revolutionary intelligentsia of the 1840s would not be complete without the tragic story of the Petrashevskii circle (1845–1849). Its history runs parallel to that of the radical Westernizers. In one sense, the *Petrashevtsy* were students of the radical publicists, since they were on the average ten years younger than Belinsky and Herzen; but in another sense they were younger colleagues, reading Saint-Simon, Fourier, Feuerbach, and other authorities, as well as Belinsky's and Herzen's stimulating essays. The circle became an important part of the cultural ambience of the 1840s. There were at least ten circles connected with the main one in St. Petersburg, and they existed in such remote places as Tambov and Kazan. Perhaps as many as 800 persons belonged to the network.[11]

---

10 "Blanquism" is the doctrine of revolutionary conspiracy, an outgrowth of Jacobin practice and theory, created by the French revolutionary socialist Louis Auguste Blanqui (1805–1881).

11 J. H. Seddon, "The Petrashevtsy, a Reappraisal," *Slavic Review* 43 (1984): 435.

Petrashevskii himself was a minor bureaucrat in the Ministry of Foreign Affairs, having graduated from the Lycée at Tsarskoe Selo in 1840 and completed the requirements for the degree of *Kandidat* in law at the University of St. Petersburg in 1841. Petrashevskii maintained his connections with the Lycée, an elite preparatory school, and had wide academic ties; but the circle that grew up around him was a cross-section of the lower and middle ranks of young, educated St. Petersburg society, containing bureaucrats like Petrashevskii, military officers, writers (some of whom became prominent), teachers, and students. Petrashevskii's guests included M. F. Saltykov-Shchedrin, who became one of Russia's greatest satirists, N. Danilevsky, later an influential pan-Slavist, and Dostoevsky. Their presence suggests the diverse talents gathered by Petrashevskii. His soirées and his large library of forbidden books provided the occasion for the exercise and nurture of minds stifled by official society and chafing with resentment.

Petrashevskii has been described by one of his contemporaries as a "born agitator." Although this designation fits Bakunin well, it fails to capture Petrashevskii's dotty subversiveness. Hardly a conspiratorial type, during the eight years between his graduation and arrest, Petrashevskii never ceased to try to reform society by direct civic action. In 1844 he applied for a teaching post as instructor of law at the Lycée, and for a short time he ran a legal aid office for indigent clients with A. N. Baronovskii. Petrashevskii also ran unsuccessfully for the positions of secretary to the St. Petersburg city council and Gentry Assembly.

However, Petrashevskii did find some legal outlets. In 1845–1846 he helped edit the *Pocket Dictionary of Foreign Words Commonly Used in the Russian Language*, a guide to the mass of foreign expressions appearing in Russian periodicals. Having full editorial control over the second installment of the dictionary, he carefully selected words that permitted him to write oppositional articles. During the early 1860s, Peter Lavrov was to imitate Petrashevskii by using the same ploy as editor of the *Encyclopaedic Dictionary*. Methods of this sort point up the kinship between the French *philosophes* of the mid-eighteenth century, who propagandized their ideas by means of Diderot's *Encyclopédie*, and elements in the Russian intelligentsia who thought of themselves primarily as enlighteners. There is no question of the socialist and materialist bias in Petrashevskii's essays, which frequently cite the works of Feuerbach, Charles Fourier, Saint-Simon, Louis Blanc, Étienne Cabet, and other "dangerous" writers from earlier centuries. The *Pocket Dictionary* was confiscated and burned by the authorities once its character was discovered, but a number of copies circulated among the intelligentsia and were received with both astonishment and appreciation.

The doomed *Pocket Dictionary* contained in brief form an idea with vast importance for the future of Russian socialism. Petrashevskii noted that the Russian peasant commune had characteristics in common with the phalanstery, the ideal communal society propagated by his favorite social thinker, Fourier, and suggested that, thanks to this *obshchina* (commune), Russia might immediately move to a socialist order. Not only Petrashevskii but several members of his circle propagated the idea before Herzen made it a systematic part of populist theory, and even before the appearance of Baron August von Haxthausen's influential book of 1847 extolling the virtues of the Russian peasant commune.[12] Indeed, Petrashevskii himself decided to create a Fourierist phalanstery on his estate in 1848, with tragic results. His peasants, not ready for the passage from their *obshchina* to utopia, burned down the building that was to house them.

Petrashevskii's Friday evening gatherings featured open discussion of history, religion, economics, politics, and society. The members of the circle were attracted to Fourier's social ideas, Saint-Simon's historical optimism, and Feuerbach's materialism. They appreciated industrialism and technology, but were critical of traditional political economy. One of Petrashevskii's guests, V. Miliutin (whose older brothers Dmitrii and Nicholas were prominent officials during the reigns of Nicholas I and Alexander II) wrote several articles for *Notes of the Fatherland* and *The Contemporary.* Although pro-industrial, his articles revealed the problems of capitalistic industrialism.

---

12 Ibid., p. 441.

His most important work, *The Proletariat and Pauperism in France and England,* appearing in the first four issues of *Notes of the Fatherland* (1847), contained outlines of solutions which very closely resembled those of Fourier, Saint-Simon, and Blanc. Although Miliutin's articles were not the official socio-economic platform of the Petrashevskii circle, they provide a good picture of the kind of critique of modern industrial capitalism at the end of the 1840s that was characteristic of the circle. In this respect, Petrashevskii's circle was closer to the next generation than Herzen and Bakunin, neither of whom appreciated industrialism. Indeed, there is a direct tie between the socioeconomic ideas of the *Petrashevtsy* and those of Nicholas Chernyshevskii, the ideological leader of the revolutionary intelligentsia of the 1860s. Towards 1848, as the discussions and presentations of the circle became better organized, concrete proposals for the abolition of serfdom and the transformation of Russian government and society aroused controversy.

The real character of Petrashevskii's Friday evening gatherings has been somewhat obscured by the differentiation of the circle into moderates and radicals in the period 1848–1849, and especially by the appearance of S. F. Durov's circle. Both Herzen and Dostoevsky, the latter actually a member of the Durov circle, emphasized in their memoirs the somewhat pathological and sinister character of the young men who fell under the influence of Nicholas Speshnev, the foremost exponent of a revolutionary conspiracy among the *Petrashevtsy.* Looking back twenty-five years, Dostoevsky in his *Diary of a Writer* described the Petrashevskii circle as the prototype of the bizarre and destructive conspiracies of the 1860s. Whatever truth there may have been in Dostoevsky's perception of men like Speshnev, who literary historians believe was a model for Stavrogin in *The Possessed,* it is wrong to let the shadow cast by Speshnev/Stravrogin obscure the character of the larger circle. The desire to form a revolutionary conspiracy was confined to a small clique. Petrashevskii himself feared the reaction that would inevitably follow an attempt at revolution. Speshnev, who was a communist following Dezamy and Weitling, wanted to create a central committee composed of exponents of several revolutionary strategies.[13] In some ways, Speshnev's categories of revolutionary strategy anticipated the strategies that were actually followed in the 1870s, when peaceful propaganda, agitation, and terror were all employed by Russian revolutionaries. Speshnev had drawn up plans for a highly disciplined revolutionary organization as early as 1845. He had also planned to use his connections abroad to print a journal that could be smuggled into Russia. Unlike Petrashevskii, who in 1848 worked on projects that would convince reasonable, calculating men of both the rationality and justice of freeing the serfs with land and creating a democratic, federal republic of Fourierist communes, the small group of men, primarily writers, who gathered at S. F. Durov's "literary-musical" salon during February and March 1849, dreamed of a vast peasant revolution. The proponents of violent revolution focused their attention upon the regions that in the past had been the centers of large-scale peasant rebellions. N. P. Grigor'ev wrote an agitational pamphlet, *Soldier's Talk,* that was meant to arouse the army against the government, while P. N. Filippov produced an agitational piece for the peasants entitled *The Ten Commandments.* The Durov circle actually went so far as to acquire a printing press, although they were arrested before it could be put to use.

Only the embellishments of I. P. Liprandi, the government agent responsible for surveillance of the Petrashevskii circle between March 11, 1848, and April 23, 1849, could make the circle look like a real center of revolutionary activity. The investigation that was conducted during the spring and summer of 1849 revealed that rumors circulating in St. Petersburg about its size and activities were gross exaggerations. High officials were relieved to discover that the vast majority of the members of the circle were not prominent, highly placed, or from well-known families. However, the severe reaction of the Russian government to the revolutions of 1848–1849 in western and central Europe created an unfavorable atmosphere for the trial, and the penalties were extraordinarily severe. Out of a list of 252 suspects, 123 were investigated, more than sixty were arrested, and

13 Théodore Dezamy (1803–1850) was a French communist active in the 1840s. He is sometimes considered a forerunner of Marx.

twenty-three were tried by a military tribunal which sentenced twenty-one of them to death. The death sentences were commuted by Nicholas to penal servitude in Siberian mines and convict labor gangs, and to impressment into the ranks. Those sentenced to death, Dostoevsky among them, were cruelly treated to a confrontation with a firing squad and a last-minute reprieve. Petrashevskii himself received the severest penalty—an open-ended sentence to the mines. Other sentences of penal servitude ranged from fifteen months to two years. The distant Siberian province of Irkutsk became Petrashevskii's new arena. Throughout his life, even after amnesties granted by Alexander II, he continued to attack the Siberian administration. Petrashevskii died in Siberia in June 1866 at the age of forty-five, the only member of his group remaining in exile. Some of the amnestied members of the Petrashevskii circle (they were still in their twenties and thirties) later played significant roles in public life, literature, and the revolutionary movement.

The intelligentsia of the 1830s and 1840s spent themselves in ideological debate. Only a handful finally became serious socialists or communists, and of these not all were revolutionaries. However, Belinsky, Herzen, Bakunin, and the *Petrashevsty* presented the new generation with fully developed radical ideologies. The radical style of the new generation was at least partly an extension of the literary realism and philosophical radicalism of the mid- and late 1840s. However, in many ways the next generation's philosophical and literary achievements were qualitatively inferior to those of the preceding generation, possibly because they did not generally experience the older generation's agonizing wanderings through Romanticism and idealism. All of Herzen's and Belinsky's careful qualifications of philosophical materialism and literary realism were swept aside. Herzen survived to be attacked by the wrathful young men of the 1860s. Bakunin lived to see his doctrines translated into disastrous revolutionary experiments, while Belinsky thankfully died at the height of his appeal. Finally, the radicals of the 1840s, and many of the liberals as well, initiated the exile communities that served as centers of antitsarist propaganda, published organs of revolutionary parties, and later became essential havens and way stations for revolutionaries.

Thus, the lost generation of the 1830s and 1840s prepared the ground for the radicals of the 1850s and 1860s. A number of them died young in prison or in exile. Some of them sojourned in the twilight world of émigré revolutionaries, while the vast majority lived out their lives in the state of spiritual emigration characteristic for "superfluous men." The death of Nicholas, the accession of Alexander II, and the reform movement that followed the Crimean War revived them during the late 1850s, but their time had already passed. Leadership of the revolutionary intelligentsia had passed to new hands.

3 / THE PERIOD OF NIHILISM 1855–1869

THE RAZNOCHINTSY *AND NIHILISM*

The fierce reaction that set in after 1848 made the earlier part of Nicholas's reign seem moderate by comparison. Even Count Uvarov, who despite his conservatism was an honest scholar and educator, opposed the severe measures taken against the universities and was forced to resign in October 1849. Although the universities were not closed as Uvarov had feared, their autonomy was further limited, "dangerous" subjects such as philosophy were removed from the curriculum, fees were raised, and the number of students was arbitrarily restricted. However, Count D. P. Buturlin's committee on censorship, which shaped the new policy, appears in retrospect to have been the last reflex of a system of suppression that had never really worked.

The image that was often used to describe Nicholas I and his regime—a long, ice-bound winter followed by a thaw—is not unfamiliar to modern readers, since it is the same image that was evoked in the mid-1950s in the aftermath of Stalin's reign. However, the nineteenth-century thaw began even before Nicholas's death (March 1855), during the Crimean War. There was a definite improvement in the position of oppositional groups during the military campaigns of 1854–1856, when the incompetence of the civil and military bureaucracy was unmasked on a large scale. The government failed diplomatically and militarily. Before the Crimean War there had been widespread belief in Russia's military invincibility. Although no consolation to the radical intelligentsia, the sense of belonging to the world's greatest continental power was important to the psychology of the masses and a large segment of educated society. Deep in the national psyche was the belief that sacrifices for Russia's national greatness were justifiable. The tsars were seen as defenders of the Russian land and the Orthodox faith. This may seem strange in view of the character of Russia's rulers after Peter the Great, but the myth had been revitalized by Alexander I's defeat of Napoleon. Military success had always been an important method of strengthening the position of the regime. However, during the late eighteenth century rumors had begun circulating in the countryside that the tsars would reward peasant soldiers for fighting in Russia's wars by freeing them with land. This seemed perfectly logical, since the *dvorianstvo* had been freed, in a sense, in 1762. By the mid-nineteenth century, rumors of this sort accompanied every military campaign, and during the massive effort of the Crimean War they were prevalent. Like earlier tales of kidnapped tsars, these rumors were simply forms of self-deception or rationalization that the peasants used in order to legitimize their own aspirations. The rumors were accompanied by dramatic increases in the number of disturbances in the countryside, especially after peasant recruits returned home from the bloody campaigns of the Crimean War.

The utter failure of the government in the Crimean War and the increase in peasant discontent encouraged all elements within the intelligentsia to speak out for reform. The opposition could now propagate their liberal program in an atmosphere of frustrated nationalism. Between 1855 and 1861 Alexander II's government permitted greater discussion and freer criticism. Although censorship was still strict until 1858, public opinion was expressed in widely circulated letters, petitions, and poems, often addressed to the tsar. The years immediately following Alexander II's accession to the throne were also marked by a temporary unification of the intelligentsia. Sectarian struggles were pushed into the background. The cry for liberation of the serfs, for civil liberties, and for freedom of expression came from all sides, from Westernizers and Slavophiles, moderates and radicals alike. In those years few looked forward to violent revolution.

Both the government and enlightened society feared a peasant uprising, and during the first year of his reign Alexander made it clear that in order to avert social revolution he would abolish serfdom. Rarely has an "autocrat" reflected more faithfully the pressures of his environment. The social stratum upon which the autocracy rested was a highly differentiated body, with different and often opposing regional outlooks, economic interests, and social and political philosophies. The tsar could not have carried out any kind of program against a united *dvorianstvo*, but the clash of opposing forces within the court, the bureaucracy, and the committees of the gentry estate created to advise the government yielded a historically momentous compromise in 1861. It was historically momentous because, while on the one hand it accomplished its aim of averting immediate revolution, on the other it confirmed the radical intelligentsia in its belief that the tsars were simply agents of the *dvorianstvo*.

The fleeting unity of oppositional forces broke down between 1858 and 1861, largely over the question of the way in which the serfs would be liberated. From that moment forth, the intelligentsia was divided into groups that spent almost as much time and energy attacking one another as in criticizing the autocracy. Some causes of friction were ideological, while others issued from the changing style of the intelligentsia.

One tendency in the historical literature describing this period attributes the rather clear generational conflict that Turgenev depicted in his novel *Fathers and Sons* (1862) to an influx of educated commoners into the intelligentsia. In the 1870s the populist literary critic and theorist Nicholas Mikhailovskii sketched out a typology of the intelligentsia. The terminology that he employed passed into usage, and with it some of his ideas about social psychology. He used the term "*raznochintsy*" to describe the educated commoners, often of humble, provincial background, who became prominent writers and ideologists during the late 1850s and 1860s. The term had had other meanings before Mikhailovskii popularized it, and it acquired new meanings during the late nineteenth and early twentieth centuries. Lenin used it adjectivally to describe the middle phase in the history of the revolutionary movement (1861–1895), bounded on the one side by the gentry phase (1825–1861), and on the other by the proletarian phase (1895–1918), which was still in progress when Lenin formulated this periodization in 1914. However, Mikhailovskii's use of the term "*raznochintsy*" is most significant, for it is a symptom of the mature awareness within the intelligentsia of clashing styles and varying degrees of radicalism. The term "intelligentsia" itself was not commonly employed as a collective noun to signify a distinct social entity until the 1860s.

There is an unfortunate tendency, especially among Soviet historians, to attribute the prominence of the *raznochintsy* to their rise in the system of higher education. Actually the proportion of *raznochintsy* in higher education shrank relative to that of the nobility toward the middle of the nineteenth century, partly because of Nicholas's policies and partly because of the internal evolution of the *dvorianstvo* estate. Furthermore, this was not just a short-term tendency confined to Nicholas's reign. The numbers of university students from all estates increased absolutely during the new reign, but the *raznochintsy's* proportional strength continued to decline. Another misleading assumption is that the *raznochintsy* were more radical and democratic than the *dvorianstvo* because they had climbed out of the lower strata of Russian society. Some historians have believed that the *raznochintsy* therefore had to reflect the aspirations of these strata which, by definition, were more radical and democratic than the *dvorianstvo.* Finally, quite a few historians have been attracted to the idea that the former seminarians among the *raznochintsy,* who were frequently sons of provincial priests and who played conspicuous roles in the ideological struggles of the 1860s, imparted to the radicalism of that period a peculiarly Russian Orthodox character. The latter two hypotheses, like those about the relationship of the social psychology of the *dvorianstvo* to radical ideologies, are supported by only superficial evidence.

One can make, however, strong arguments for assigning the *raznochintsy* a central role during the nihilist phase of the movement. First of all, they were the cutting edge, so to speak, of the socialist intelligentsia. Aristocratic rebels of the 1840s found the *raznochintsy* tedious, unpleasant, devoid of the intellectual grace and personal warmth that pervaded the circles of the 1830s and 1840s. The *dvorianstvo* circles of that period had displayed all of the sensibility, warmth, and largeness of spirit that the intellectual climate of Romanticism had encouraged. Aristocratic breeding and substantial financial resources permitted such cultural largesse. The first prominent critic from the *razno-*

chintsy was Belinsky, who became a kind of mascot in *dvorianstvo* circles, but both his personal and literary style distinguished him from his aristocratic comrades. His somewhat squalid and lonely life, his financial difficulties, and his moral passion set him apart. In the 1830s and 1840s it was difficult to know that the increasing participation of the *raznochintsy* in literature was more than a temporary phenomenon. By the 1860s there was a growing fear that the *raznochintsy* were undermining art and philosophy by their didacticism, anti-aestheticism, and vulgar materialism. Personal contact between members of the aristocratic intelligentsia who had reached maturity in the 1830s and 1840s and the new generation of critics and writers of the 1850s and 1860s only aggravated the conflict between cultural generations. Finally, the fear during the 1860s that political and social radicalism would unleash destructive forces and endanger the progressive movement of Russian society estranged the older intelligentsia generation from the new one.

However, in spite of the stylistic and personal asperities of the *raznochintsy,* their moral zeal and uncompromising commitment to agrarian socialism forced the earlier proponents of agrarian socialism either to follow suit or to seem insincere. The two foremost plebian critics, Nicholas Chernyshevskii and Nicholas Dobroliubov, repelled liberal Westernizers like Turgenev and antagonized fellow socialists like Herzen but became the leaders of a new generation of aristocratic rebels. Their truculence was fully in keeping with the new polemical style in European social philosophy, their bitterness and righteousness a logical aftermath to the failures of 1848 and 1861. It is best to think of them as a group whose social background and personal experience had prepared them to unmask, accuse, exhort, preach, and prophesy like their counterparts in the European socialist intelligentsia.

To say that the *raznochintsy* were best equipped to forge the new radical style is easy enough. To explain why they were best equipped is open to interpretation. Their psychological and stylistic extremism has been attributed to their clerical upbringings, their humble origins, their social uprootedness, their inability to form "diffuse affective attachments"—in a word, to a number of sociopsychological or psychosociological factors.[1] A suicidal element in their psychological makeup has been noted by both contemporaries and historians. Lean, bespectacled, ascetic, humorless, high-strung, insulting, uncompromising, impatient—all of these come to mind when one conjures up a picture of the radical *raznochinets.*

Liberal historiography of the *raznochintsy* has tended to be unsympathetic to them, not only because of their extremism and vindictiveness, but also because of their subordination of art and science to political and social ends. Soviet historiography has extolled them for precisely the same traits. Both liberal and Soviet historians understand that the *raznochintsy* of the 1860s were ancestors of Bolshevism. Lenin was a great admirer of Chernyshevskii and Dmitrii Pisarev (the latter was not a *raznochinets*), the two leading radical publicists of the period, and their importance, especially Chernyshevskii's, for Lenin's ideological development was perhaps greater than Marx's. Thus, historical discussions of this group have frequently been either unctuously reverent or bitterly accusatory. Even the supposedly clinical sociological and psychological discussions of the *raznochintsy* are not neutral. Whether speaking sympathetically (they were victims) or unsympathetically (they had innate defects), the clinicians agree that there was something pathological about the *raznochintsy.*

However one explains the mentality of the radical *raznochintsy,* and whether one finds them repellent, attractive, or pitiable, the fact remains that they played a central role at a crucial moment in the formation of the revolutionary intelligentsia. They helped to create a new and distinctive radical style out of European and Russian materials—a style that suited the mood

---

1 Their inability to form "diffuse affective attachments" is discussed in Vladimir C. Nahirny, "The Russian Intelligentsia: From Men of Ideas to Men of Convictions," *Comparative Studies in Society and History* 4 (1962): 403–35, and in *The Russian Intelligentsia, From Torment to Silence* (New Brunswick, N.J., 1983).

For a study of the changing meanings of the word *raznochintsy* see C. Becker, "*Raznochintsy:* The Development of the Word and of the Concept," *American Slavic and East European Review* 18 (1959): 63–74. For a more recent attempt to specify the role of the *raznochintsy,* see Robert J. Brym, "A Note on the Raznochintsy," *Journal of Social History* 10 (1976–77): 354–59.

of the new generation of radicals, whether gentry or nongentry, who entered the universities in the early 1860s. Indeed, the widespread appeal of the new style was an indication of a further blurring of the cultural and social lines that had previously separated the *dvorianstvo* from the *raznochintsy.* In the 1860s the *raznochinets'* sense of moral superiority still created some friction between the two groups. By the 1870s this was less of a problem, although the *raznochintsy* enjoyed some moral leverage over their comrades from the *dvorianstvo,* who often worked quite hard at being common.

The coalescence of these and other social elements during the 1860s and afterward was facilitated by the shared experience of university life, exposure to the radical publicists writing for the literary periodicals of the capitals, and acceptance of scientism and materialism. The peculiar position of the student in Russian society inspired a sense of elitism in *raznochintsy* and *dvoriane* alike. A government commission formed to investigate the student riots of 1861 concluded:

> Russian society has instilled in the student a conception of his own high status the like of which does not exist in any other country. In other countries, where education is widely disseminated and has sent out deep roots, students attain a natural place in the social structure. In Russia they became the sole representative of education, and, at the present moment every Russian deeply feels the need for education as the natural way out of the social ills which oppress him.[2]

Thus, the universities, technical institutes, and gymnasiums became the recruiting grounds for the radical publicists who delineated a system of values, a way of life, and concrete tasks for the "developed individuals," "thinking realists," "rational egotists," "new people," and "critically thinking individuals" in the student body. Science worship attracted both aristocrats and plebians; and when the new intelligentsia generation moved from words to action, from the idea of a scientific ethic, socialism, to its realization through revolutionary propaganda and ag-

---

2 M. N. Pokrovskii ed., *Istoriia Rossii v XIX veke,* 9 vols. (St. Petersburg, 1907–1911), 4, p. 189.

itation, idealistic young men and women from a wide range of social strata sacrificed their personal careers to the cause.

The stylistic changes of this period derived from the new radical critique of the political and social order, which had seriously eroded the Romantic worldview by the early 1840s. Radical materialists, especially after 1848, unmasked bourgeois society, revealing the brutal economic relations "underlying" its institutions and ideologies. For the Russian intelligentsia, this entailed a vigorous repudiation of their former absorption in philosophical and aesthetic problems, and immersion in economics, the natural sciences, and the nascent discipline of sociology. To many young people, especially during the late 1850s and early 1860s, the development and display of a correct radical style in dress, speech, and general attitude were possibly as important as allegiance to a substantive doctrine. The term "nihilist" was widely used to describe the new style. It included, among other things, condescension in conversation and a casual attitude toward dress and appearance, if not downright eccentricity. The effect was usually one of austerity, especially for nihilist women, whose short hair, drab clothing, spectacles, and cigarettes were symptoms of the drive for feminine equality that began in Russia during this period. Nihilists denied not only the traditional roles of women but also the family, private property, religion, art—in a word, all of the traditional aspects of culture and society. Their improprieties were greeted with a storm of abuse from the conservative press, and satirical or critical portrayals of nihilism appeared in belles lettres.

Conservative society was justifiably alarmed, for it was witnessing a cultural movement of profound historical significance. Nihilism represented a much sharper break between generations than anything that had preceded it. The Romantic rebels of the 1830s and 1840s had dressed, dined, and amused themselves in much the same way that their parents had. Even while feeling a spiritual distance between themselves and polite society, young Romantics had mingled in the salons and at balls with the older generation. The nihilists tried to sever all ties between themselves and their elders. They sometimes lived with comrades of both sexes in communes, whose organization reflected the views of their favorite ideologues. In order to escape cloistered lives, nihilist women entered marriages of convenience with their comrades. There were even instances of *ménages à trois,* in keeping with the nihilist belief in rational egoism. By the 1860s the universities and technical institutes and the cultural environment of St. Petersburg were supporting a highly developed and distinctive radical subculture over which the older generation exercised little or no control. For a great many young men and women of this period, as is true for youthful rebels in other times, the new radical life style was little more than an assertion of independence, an experiment that entailed small exertion and ended as soon as they had to commit themselves seriously to a cause. Some did not even trouble themselves to examine at first hand the ideologies that were the foundation of their style. For others, exhibition of the style was a manifestation of their total commitment to the ideas of the radical publicists.

THE LITERATURE OF NIHILISM

The term "nihilism" is less useful when applied to the ideologies of the leading publicists—Nicholas Chernyshevskii, Nicholas Dobroliubov, and Dmitrii Pisarev. Pisarev's ideology is perhaps closest to the term "nihilism" and its connotations, because he emphasized the need to destroy the nonscientific and nonutilitarian aspects of culture and society and did not represent a distinct school of social thought (as did Chernyshevskii and Dobroliubov). The latter two, together with Herzen, not only provided a systematic critique of the traditional government, society, and culture, they also presented a clear alternative—an immediate transition to socialism by means of Russia's peasant commune and workers' *arteli* (cooperative associations).

Herzen, more than any single radical publicist in the years immediately after 1855, presented to the Russian reading public a clear picture of the vast problems facing the Russian government and the range of solutions being offered by enlightened bureaucrats, reactionary nobles, liberals, Slavophiles, and socialist publicists. He was able to play this role for both practical and ideological reasons. Practically, he was financially able to create the Free Russian Press in London, to maintain connections with a great variety of Russian informants, and to smuggle his publications into Russia. Herzen's wide connections with insiders and outsiders gave his publications, especially *The Bell,* an omniscient character. Ideologically, Herzen had undergone an important evolution. Although still a devoted socialist, he had developed a strong antipathy for violent revolution. He expressed it in his hopefulness, indeed wishfulness, about reforms from above. During the years 1855–1857, Herzen's publications *The Polar Star* and *Voices from Russia* were rallying points for the most catholic demands for reform. Between 1857 and 1861 his highest journalistic achievement, *The Bell,* expressed the hopes and fears of the increasingly hostile intelligentsia camps that were forming during the debates about the projected reforms. Herzen rejected the cautious, legalistic, bureaucratic rationalism which, both within and without the government, was the guiding spirit of the reform. But he also wanted to avoid a revolution, which the radicals believed was inevitable and necessary in view of the government's inability to liberate the serfs in accordance with their vision of a just and rational social order. Before the reform era ended, Herzen had antagonized all factions, and his unaccustomed role as unifier gave way to a more customary loneliness.

Although Herzen ushered in the new era, two journals in St. Petersburg, *The Contemporary* and *The Russian Word,* propagated the most characteristic radical ideologies of the period. However, censorship did not permit writers to express radical social and political views in a systematic programmatic or ideological statement. Much had to be inferred by the reader from oblique or cryptographic references to tyranny, injustice, and the inevitability or desirability of revolution. As in the 1830s and 1840s, literary criticism and reviews of foreign publications were the most important vehicles for radical thought.

Much more than Belinsky had, the radical writers undermined aesthetics by studying novels and stories as sociological, psychological, or ideological sources rather than as works of art. A work of art, no less than a scientific treatise, was measured by its realism and its utility—its consonance with and applicability to real problems. Chernyshevskii was the leader of the new school of criticism in that he established its theoretical basis in a master's dissertation, *The Aesthetic Relations of Art and Reality* (1855), and shorty thereafter became the literary critic for *The Contemporary.* However, Chernyshevskii's major interests were not literary, and his protégé, Nicholas Dobroliubov, took over the journal's literary section in 1857, permitting Chernyshevskii to write about the social, economic, and philosophical issues that engrossed him. Dobroliubov carried on with considerable flair and succeeded in even further estranging Herzen, Turgenev, Tolstoy, and other important literary figures, some of whom severed their connections with *The Contemporary.* The battle over aesthetics was closely associated with personal antipathies, and both sides resorted to personal attacks.

The other prominent radical literary critic, Dmitrii Pisarev, wrote for *The Russian Word.* Pisarev's nihilism had a more individualistic than civic character, but, like Chernyshevskii and Dobroliubov, he proselytized for science and expressed hope that through science and utilitarian ethics larger civic aims of material abundance and social justice would be achieved. While Soviet historians tended to emphasize the social and revolutionary aspect of Pisarev's writings, it is probably more correct to stress his impact upon individual morality and life style. And, since social action was still carried out on only a very limited scale in the 1860s, there was little visible difference between Pisarev's program and the actions of radical students during the mid- and late 1860s. This does not necessarily mean, as some authors believe, that the youth of the 1860s placed self-development ahead of civic action, and that Pisarev's variety of nihilism was more popular than Chernyshevskii's and Dobroliubov's socialism. But Pisarev was unquestionably a powerful influence, beginning his career shortly before *The Contemporary* suffered the loss of Dobroliubov—he died in 1861 at the age of twenty-five—and of Chernyshevskii through imprisonment (1862). Although Pisarev himself was imprisoned in 1862, *The Russian Word* continued to print his articles.

The doctrinal bases of Russian nihilism—whether expressed on a personal or civic level—were materialism, utilitarianism, and scientism. There was a range of materialisms to choose from in the 1860s: Chernyshevskii was an exponent of Feuerbach's human-centered materialism (anthropologism), while

Pisarev popularized the "vulgar" materialism of Jacob Moleschott, Ludwig Büchner, and Karl Vogt. Philosophical idealism and agnosticism were considered to be symptoms of a conservative or compromising worldview, and the complex epistemological questions raised by idealists and agnostics were summarily dismissed. In fact, the nihilists tended to see philosophy as a waste of time, since they believed that materialism had settled once and for all that spiritual phenomena were ultimately reducible to matter in motion. The philosophical discussions of Chernyshevskii, Dobroliubov, Pisarev, and their collaborators or imitators invariably touched upon the natural sciences. Two of the seminal articles of the period, Chernyshevskii's "Anthropological Principle in Philosophy" (1860) and Pisarev's "Nineteenth Century Scholasticism" (1861), are excellent examples of this kind of literature. Chernyshevskii's anthropologism is expressed in the following paragraph:

> That part of philosophy which deals with questions of man, just like the other part which deals with questions of external nature, is based on the natural sciences. The principle underlying the philosophical view of human life and all its phenomena is the idea, worked out by the natural sciences, of the unity of the human organism; the observations of physiologists, zoologists, and medical men have driven away all thought of dualism in man. Philosophy sees in him what medicine, physiology, and chemistry see. These sciences prove that no dualism is evident in man, and philosophy adds that if man possessed another nature, in addition to his real nature, this other nature would surely reveal itself in some way; but since it does not, since everything that takes place and manifests itself in man originates solely from his real nature, he cannot have another nature.[3]

Pisarev used materialism as a weapon in the struggle for human liberation:

> It is only against theory that materialism is waging a struggle; in practical life we are all materialists and are always at odds with our theories. The whole difference between the idealist and the materialist in practical life is that to the former the ideal is a standing reproach and a constant nightmare, while

3 Edie, et al., *Russian Philosophy,* 2, p. 29.

> the latter feels at liberty and in the right so long as he is not doing actual evil to anyone.[4]

It perplexes students of philosophy that materialism should have been associated with human freedom, for materialists accepted the doctrine of mechanical determinism. Human actions presumably issued from the working of vast, impersonal, and immutable laws of nature, and were therefore mechanical and involuntary gestures. Seen in this light, materialism would seem to encourage quietism or a kind of cosmic pessimism. However, the enthusiasm with which materialism was embraced as a doctrine of liberation cannot be explained by philosophy. Inappropriate as it may have been from a philosophical point of view for a theory of freedom, in the social and cultural context of the 1850s and 1860s materialism became a central feature of the radical life style. Young radicals felt that they were freeing themselves from false theories, ghostly forms that impeded them from developing fully, from coming to grips with reality. They believed that acceptance of materialism brought with it power over matter—over human ethical problems as well as over nature external to man. Nature and society were to be workshops in which enlightened people could exercise their reason and will.

The utilitarianism of the nihilists accorded well with their materialism. Jeremy Bentham and John Stuart Mill were their authorities, and the pleasure principle was the foundation of their ethical philosophy. However, just as they employed materialism as a weapon in the struggle for liberation, Chernyshevskii and Dobroliubov in particular converted the pleasure principle into a doctrine of honest labor and civic responsibility. Dobroliubov launched a major attack upon the idleness of the nobility and its consequences for their human development. Several of his major articles are studies of the harmful effects of the Russian social system upon the bodies and minds of both serf owners and serfs. Chernyshevskii offered a portrait of utilitarian ethics in operation in his novel *What Is to Be Done?* (1863). Pisarev's utilitarianism had a more hedonistic quality, but even he reconciled

---

4 Ibid., p. 71.

the selfish interests of "new people" with the larger interests of society.

The scientific and anticlerical worldview propounded by the nihilists had a much more confident rationalistic character than that of the Russian left Hegelians of the 1840s. Auguste Comte and Thomas Buckle provided the rebels of the 1860s with a grand historical vision of the march of science. The increasing volume of discovery in the biological sciences and in chemistry, largely a consequence of German scholarship, excited the Russian *philosophes* in much the same way that Newton's discoveries had excited Voltaire and the French *philosophes* in the eighteenth century. It is not difficult to understand why the nihilists of the 1860s identified themselves with the Encyclopedists.

However, Chernyshevskii, Pisarev, and Dobroliubov were confronted with a broader problem than had faced the earlier *philosophes*—that of assimilating much more advanced scientific scholarship to ethical and social thought. More specifically, they had to cope with Darwinism. The idea of the struggle for existence does not, at first glance, lend itself readily to the idea of social solidarity and cooperation; but N. D. Nozhin, provoked to action by a review article in which V. A. Zaitsev, Pisarev's collaborator on *The Russian Word,* seemed to suggest that the black race was inferior, first formulated what was to become a characteristic Russian socialist interpretation of Darwin. Nozhin, a biologist, in 1865–1866 developed a theory that although different species struggled against one another for existence, members of a given species naturally cooperated with one another in order to survive in the struggle against other species. Thus, out of the struggle for existence he arrived at the principle of social solidarity. But the difficulty presented by Darwin did not escape Chernyshevskii, who was vehemently anti-Darwinist. Pisarev, the most ambiguous figure in Russian nihilism, was an ethusiastic exponent of Darwin, and there are occasional signs of social Darwinism in his essays. In general, the nihilists' response to Darwin revealed their need to make it consistent with "rational egoism."

The radical thinkers did more than create a new style of social thought out of materialism, utilitarianism, and scientism. They also conveyed to their audience an image of the life style of the men and women who accepted the new thought. In this task, they were aided by Russian novelists and playwrights, whose heroes, heroines, and antiheroes were discussed as psychological and social types rather than as merely literary creations. Dobroliubov proved to be equally adept at projecting onto fictional characters motives and attitudes of the men and women of the future and at unmasking the social sources of the malaise of antiheroes. Turgenev's Bazarov, the nihilist hero of *Fathers and Sons,* became the center of considerable controversy within the nihilist camp, the critics of *The Contemporary* rejecting him and Pisarev enthusiastically accepting him. The differences between Pisarev and the other nihilist critics are often explainable by the former's enthusiasm for eccentricity. Even despite Dobroliubov's gift for satire, there was a deadly earnestness about *The Contemporary* that offended Pisarev's sensibilities. For his part, Pisarev sometimes frivolously exaggerated his own utilitarianism, provoking even the *raznochintsy.* Very basic differences in personality underlay these style preferences. Pisarev was an aesthete and (though largely defeated by severe neuroses) a *bon vivant* who despised austerity, yet helped to promote it. Chernyshevskii and Dobroliubov were pedants and puritans desperately trying to liberate the flesh, but unable to overcome their basic asceticism. One might say that there were clear elements of self-repudiation in the lives of the three major nihilist ideologues, but that they all needed the image of a "positive hero," a masterful man (quite unlike themselves) whose life exhibited a perfect consonance of thought and deed.

In Chernyshevskii's novel *What Is to Be Done?,* which he wrote in 1862 while in prison, there is a detailed picture of "rational egoists" at work and play, organizing and operating Fourierist enterprises, rationally resolving love conflicts, and dreaming of an even better future. Nihilist men displayed their new morality by helping rather than exploiting the new women seeking both enlightenment and meaningful work. One of them, however, stood out. Rakhmetov, the positive hero in the novel, thrives on a diet of raw meat, recalling Feuerbach's dictum, "Man is what he eats." (Feuerbach believed that the English maintained their superiority over the Irish because they ate beefsteak while the Irish ate potatoes.) By following a strict physical and intellectual regime, Rakhmetov achieved an extraordinary level of human development in a short period of time. This was no doubt a great source of his appeal to the impatient youth of the 1860s and 1870s. With science and discipline anything seemed possible, and quickly. Although there is no indication that Rakhmetov's feat of sleeping on a bed of nails was widely imitated, youths could emulate his hard-headed intellectual regime—a kind of intellectual purism in which all frivolous or second-rate books were ignored. They could also duplicate the free and rational love relationships described in the novel. Vera Pavlovna, the novel's heroine, was a model emancipated woman. Chernyshevskii's heroes and heroines inspired a multitude of imitators. Communal enterprises, often publishing ventures, became popular during the mid-1860s.

Pisarev, who welcomed both Rakhmetov and Bazarov, offered scientific labor as an antidote to the old life style of the intelligentsia. He challenged his audience to abandon the "satin and rosewood" world of aesthetics for useful work in laboratories and industries. The models that he placed before them were physiologists, chemists, and industrial entrepreneurs. The youth responded eagerly by flocking to the biological sciences and studying medicine, which had always been popular among Russian students. Instead of spending ecstatic nights under the stars discussing poetry and philosophy, as their parents had, the new people holed up in attics and basements, laboring by candlelight over the severed members of laboratory specimens. Pisarev's idea of science as social medicine became characteristic of the youth of the period. It is therefore not surprising that the Medico-Surgical Academy in St. Petersburg became a center of student radicalism and the focal point of so many student uprisings in the 1860s and 1870s that the chief of gendarmes asked Alexander II to remove it from the capital.

The figure that emerged from the combined propaganda of Chernyshevskii, Dobroliubov, and Pisarev can be variously described as ethical scientist, social engineer, or social surgeon, who would help to cure society of its moral and physical ills by an exemplary life of useful work. Rational egoism was really a form of puritanism based upon the discipline of scientific work and a "scientific" ethic. Because of the emphasis upon scientific study, especially in Pisarev's essays of the mid-1860s, a large segment of the younger generation assumed that by training for a professional career in the sciences they were fulfilling the program of rational egoism. But, curiously enough, their withdrawal into the life of science and into closed circles of new people repeated the isolationism of the Romantic rebels of the 1830s and 1840s. Some of Pisarev's followers during the late part of the 1860s were no less removed from an active movement to revolutionize the peasants than their predecessors had been. For this reason, it is important to distinguish Pisarev's nihilism from that of Chernyshevskii and Dobroliubov.

One might call *The Contemporary's* brand of nihilism evangelical. Alongside Chernyshevskii's rationalistic and rather dry propaganda for science, industry, and socialism, *The Contemporary* offered Dobroliubov's moral passion for the peasantry. Dobroliubov pictured the peasants as a great reservoir of vital force. Chernyshevskii's and Dobroliubov's program, like Herzen's, tended to focus the hopes of the younger generation upon the peasant masses. Although there is some justification for calling their program populism rather than nihilism, there are even stronger arguments for calling it evangelical nihilism. First of all, the nihilists emphasized the tutelary role of the educated elite of new people. Theirs was, on the whole, a rather sober view of the countryside. They visualized it as an arena for the activity of the new men and women, a grim world to be transformed by a heroic, rationalistic elite. To be sure, Chernyshevskii, like Herzen, believed that the peasant communes and workers' *arteli* might serve as a framework for socialist development, and that Russia might avoid an extended period of bourgeois exploitation. He too believed in the virtues of backwardness, but only as part of a catholic and unsentimental vision of historical change, in which backwardness could provide the basis for a great leap forward. There may have been wishfulness in Chernyshevskii's doctrine, but not Romantic nostalgia for agrarianism; neither his, Dobroliubov's, nor Pisarev's rationalism betrayed any ambivalence about identity and role that agonized the populists of the mid-1870s. Evangelical nihilism meant going to the people to teach them, to transform them, and to revolutionize them—not to learn from them, and certainly not to submerge one's identity by living in the villages.

The radical publicists of the 1860s, therefore, concentrated their efforts upon definition of the intelligentsia's role as a scientific and ethical vanguard. The evangelical note, sounded by Dobroliubov and, in a somewhat different spirit, by Herzen, was still somewhat muted. The radical publicists presented no clear programs of revolutionary action vis-à-vis the peasants, no developed strategies. They created, however, an atmosphere of ideological extremism, stimulated the younger generation's moral outrage, and encouraged them to discipline themselves for action, on the model of Rakhmetov. All of this could as well be applied to the formation of underground revolutionary parties as to communes and study circles. Thus, the revolutionary movement of the 1860s was intimately associated with the publicistic activity of Chernyshevskii, Dobroliubov, and Herzen.

Besides formulating ideologies, the publicists of the 1860s were involved in illegal pamphleteering. While socialism and science could be taught through the monthlies, the burning issues of the day demanded a more immediate and direct mode of expression. Herzen's émigré publications were outlets for views on the state of the reforms. Radicals in Russia could anonymously express revolutionary views in *The Bell,* which became a biweekly publication (1858–1867). Although Herzen tried to moderate the radicals, he did not censor their views. He himself stood behind reforms from above only so long as they seemed to be possible. In Russia, Chernyshevskii very quickly concluded that the throne would protect the interests of the *dvorianstvo,* and that revolution was the only solution to Russia's social and economic problems. All speculations about the reforms occurred against a background of increasing peasant violence, so that the matter was in a large part one of wanting either to avert or to promote a revolutionary situation that already existed. While Herzen hoped that a bloody revolution could be averted, Chernyshevskii, after a brief period of elation in 1858, concluded that revolution was the only solution to Russia's social and economic problems. Indeed, once the terms of the emancipation were announced in February 1861, many radicals were convinced that revolution was imminent.

THE RADICAL INTELLIGENTSIA AND SERF REFORM

As had been expected, the serf reform was surrounded by misunderstandings, defeated expectations, and violence. The government was fully prepared and firmly suppressed the rebellions that preceded and followed the emancipation. However, in the period 1861–1863 one threat followed another in rapid succession. The countryside was only one aspect of the revolutionary situation. Revolutionary pamphlets, student revolts, the petitions of gentry liberals, mysterious fires in the capital, and, finally, the Polish rebellion in 1863 provoked a severe reaction. Of these events, the Polish rebellion was probably the most important, for it aroused sufficient chauvinism to permit the government to carry out repressive measures. However, even before the events of 1863, the government had begun to arrest subversive writers and to close down radical periodicals.

There were no really effective centers of revolutionary organization and activity during the period 1861–1863. Herzen, Ogarev, Chernyshevskii, M. I. Mikhailov, Nicholas Shelgunov, Nicholas Serno-Solovevich, and Peter Zaichnevskii were probably the most important figures in the upsurgence of activism. Like earlier figures in the Russian revolutionary movement, they were more important as ideologists and martyrs than as leaders or strategists in a direct confrontation with the forces of the old order. As revolutionary forecasters or plotters, they had to rely upon fragmentary information, which often consisted of exaggerated rumors about peasant unrest. In retrospect, historians can see, except for the outbreak of peasant rebellions in the months immediately following the reforms, a sharp downward dip in the graph of agrarian violence during the period 1861–1863. Thus, the revolutionary intelligentsia miscalculated the strength of the antigovernment forces. As a consequence, they planned and, to some extent, created a conspiratorial superstructure without a mass basis in the countryside or in the cities. The government sometimes had to call out troops to cope with the agrarian unrest, but there was nothing approaching the dimensions of the Pugachev revolt, even at the height of the disturbances.

In the cities a flood of pamphlets and leaflets addressed the tsar, the progressive forces in the intelligentsia, the restless masses in the countryside, and the troops. The most radical pamphlets expressed revolutionary socialist programs reflecting Chernyshevskii's ideas and influence. Soviet historiographers of this revolutionary upsurge have showed a strong tendency to picture Chernyshevskii as the central figure in an elaborate revolutionary organization, but most of the evidence of Chernyshevskii's activity is indirect; and, although he was without a doubt an ideological leader, his activities as a participant in the short-lived conspiracy "Land and Freedom" (1862–1863) are only vaguely established. The real leaders were students in the university cities. They sometimes sought the advice and enlisted the aid of respected ideologues from the older generation whose radicalism was proven beyond question. Thus, Ogarev, a reluctant Herzen, and Chernyshevskii encouraged them to form conspiracies, and Ogarev especially demonstrated acumen as a conspiratorial theoretician, but the students seized the initiative.

In 1861–1862 a large-scale student movement flourished independent of the nascent conspiracies, and the pamphleteers soon realized that the students were the most fertile soil for propaganda. Student unrest had been growing thoughout 1860. By 1861 the universities were filling up with indigent and semi-indigent students (and nonstudents) who were able to continue their studies only with the aid of stipends and funds from student banks. The student banks were only one aspect of the rich and varied corporate life that university students led during the first years of Alexander II's reign with little or no interference from university officials or the government. Quite to the contrary, university administrations had encouraged student self-government. However, as the students became more intransigent in their demands, and as it became increasingly apparent that nihilism was their guiding spirit, the government became alarmed. In the spring and summer of 1861, new university regulations were issued abolishing student assemblies and subjecting student banks, libraries, and other formerly autonomous institutions to university supervision. Furthermore, the access of indigent students to the universities was all but cut off by severe restrictions on the number of nonpaying students admitted to lectures. By this last measure and others the government tried to clear the lecture halls of the radical elements that had begun to play such a significant role in the university communities.

When the students returned to the universities in late September 1861 and learned of the new regulations, large numbers rebelled. Proclamations and manifestoes denouncing the government's action immediately appeared, and many students refused to matriculate under the new rules. Some of the participants in the student movement—Eugene Mikhaelis and Nicholas Utin, for example—injected the larger political and social issues of the day into the protest against the government's infringement of academic freedom. Students from other institutions in St. Petersburg joined the university students in street demonstrations on September 25 and 27. After the first demonstration, some of the student leaders were arrested. The second major demonstration was dissolved when the military governor-general of St. Petersburg arrayed a battalion of troops against the protesters in the university courtyard. The agitation continued, and on October 11, 1861, when the university reopened (it had been closed since September 24), a new struggle began. On October 12, a large number of students clashed with troops of the Preobrazhenskii regiment. This time more than 100 students were arrested (estimates range from 130 to 170), and their comrades challenged the police to arrest them as well. Eventually, almost 300 students were arrested for participation in the disturbances around St. Petersburg University on October 12. The authorities were forced to close the university again in December 1861. After a promising beginning, a Free University established by students and liberal professors in January 1862 collapsed two months later. The government prevented some of the students' favorites (Chernyshevskii and Lavrov) from lecturing. The Free University's collapse is usually attributed to the inability of students and professors to form a solid front and suspend lectures to protest the arrest of Platon Pavlov, a liberal professor, on March 2, 1862.

Contemporary observers felt for a moment that a revolution was imminent in the capital. The government moved quickly to destroy the incipient revolutionary movement by arresting radical pamphleteers and publicists. M. I. Mikhailov, a radical poet who had brought Nicholas Shelgunov's proclamation "To the Younger Generation" to Herzen and Ogarev for printing and had then smuggled copies into Russia, was arrested on September 14, 1861, even before the beginning of the student rebellion. Indeed, Mikhailov's arrest was a catalyst for the formation of oppositional opinion. Sentenced to penal labor, he died in Siberia in 1865, thus becoming the first literary martyr of the 1860s. (Dobroliubov, who had been severely ill for over a year, had died in St. Petersburg on November 17, 1861.) However, the government was still reluctant to move against the radical press in the face of liberal public opinion. The authorities needed some clear provocation to justify large-scale repression. Justification was soon forthcoming.

Peter Zaichnevskii, a model activist, organized a radical circle at the University of Moscow, printed illegal materials, spread propaganda in the countryside, and was arrested for his activities in July 1861. Like many radicals imprisoned or exiled during the 1860s, Zaichnevskii was able to smuggle his writings out to his friends. His inflammatory "Young Russia" was the most radical and alarming document of the "era of proclamations." It appeared in St. Petersburg in May 1862. The bloodthirsty character of "Young Russia" dismayed both Herzen and Chernyshevskii, who anticipated the kind of reaction that it would provoke. The pamphlet was the first conspicuous sign of Jacobinism in the revolutionary movement of the 1860s. The socialist program outlined by Zaichnevskii reflected the influence of French socialism, adapted to Russia by Herzen and Chernyshevskii. The *obshchina* and its assembly were the basic social, economic, and political units in his proposed federal republic. However, Zaichnevskii provided for a strong National Assembly with wide powers in several areas—foreign policy, taxation, appointment of provincial officials, and resolution of disputes between provinces. Most important, he assumed that the revolutionary party seizing power would have to preserve the centralized political structure.

> The party must retain a dictatorship in its hands and not let anything interfere with it. Elections in the National Assembly

> must proceed under the influence of the government, which must take pains to assure that supporters of the present regime are not admitted (if they indeed survive). What nonintervention of a revolutionary government in elections leads to is demonstrated by the French assembly of 1848 and . . . the election of Louis Napoleon as emperor.[5]

Zaichnevskii's Jacobin program is another instance of the recurring theme of revolutionary dictatorship in the radical movement. "Young Russia" also reveals his vision of the putative revolutionary forces in Russia—the peasant masses, especially the millions of religious schismatics with special grievances against the government, the army officers, and above all, the younger generation, as the title of the proclamation suggests.

However, the call for violent and ruthless slaughter of the "imperial party" and the royal family was too much of a provocation, and "Young Russia" helped to destroy whatever tolerance there was in educated society for the students and their leaders. Furthermore, the document referred to a Central Revolutionary Committee, and an alarmed and credulous capital began to believe that a vast revolutionary plot was afoot when, almost simultaneously with the appearance of "Young Russia," a number of conflagrations swept through St. Petersburg between May 14 and May 30, 1862. The cause of the fires has never been determined, but, in the tense atmosphere following the student rebellions and the proclamations, more and more citizens of the capital hoped that the government would take forceful measures against the "nihilists."

By the spring of 1862, the government was fully prepared to act. The Third Section had prepared a list of fifty leading suspects and a number of "extraordinary measures" to be taken in case of a crisis. The primary targets were the radical journals, *The Contemporary* and *The Russian Word;* the Sunday school run by idealistic students and teachers for illiterate workers; and organizations such as the Chess Club and the Literary Fund, where many prominent liberals and radicals debated issues, cir-

---

5 The quotation is taken from a slightly abbreviated version of "Young Russia" appearing in B. P. Koz'min, ed., *Istoriko-revoliutsionnaia khrestomatiia* (Moscow, 1923), 1, pp. 57–58.

culated petitions, and raised money for colleagues and students who had been arrested.

Pisarev was one of the first major victims of the full-scale reaction. He had written a pamphlet defending Herzen against a devious attempt by the Third Section to discredit him. The pamphlet, aimed at an agent of the imperial government writing under the pseudonym Shedo-Ferroti, was written for an underground student press discovered by the Third Section in June 1862. Pisarev's open attack upon the government and dynasty contained some rather uncharacteristically revolutionary statements, and he was arrested on July 2, 1862.

Chernyshevskii, who had been extremely careful to avoid involvement in the underground student groups, nonetheless had ties with some of their leaders, and with Herzen and Ogarev. One of Chernyshevskii's associates, Nicholas Serno-Solovevich, was a central figure in the student underground. Herzen injudiciously sent a letter to Serno-Solovevich in which he proposed that Chernyshevskii avoid the inevitable reaction by transferring *The Contemporary* to London. (It should be noted that Herzen had resumed his former position as revolutionary leader, despite the rancor aroused by his earlier hopes for reforms from above.) The courier was intercepted, and the letter was used as a pretext for arresting both Serno-Solovevich and Chernyshevskii on July 7, 1862. Thus, by the summer of 1862, most of the leaders and ideological heroes of the younger generation in Russia had been arrested.

In June 1862, the workers' Sunday schools in St. Petersburg and throughout Russia were closed down as centers of sedition. The Sunday school movement was the first large-scale attempt by the intelligentsia to make direct contact with the masses. The movement began in Kiev in 1859, but St. Petersburg soon had the largest system of schools. In March 1862, the founder of the Sunday schools, Platon Pavlov, formerly a professor at the University of Kiev, was arrested for a speech delivered before the Literary Fund. In addition to becoming a *cause célèbre* among the intelligentsia, his arrest, followed by the events of May and the discovery that several teachers and workers in two of the schools were spreading subversive propaganda, served as an excuse for closing down the entire system. Its closure was a symptom of the spreading public and government alarm in 1862, and of the growing reactionary trend. The Chess Club, which had been founded in January 1862 by some of the leading literary figures in the capital and was described by an agent of the Third Section as a center of sedition, was also closed in June 1862. Finally, *The Contemporary* and *The Russian Word* were forced to suspend publication for eight months beginning in June. Thus, in June and July 1862 the government had severely damaged the radicals by removing their public platforms, such as they were.

The revolutionary movement did not collapse all at once during the summer of 1862. Indeed, an underground organization of young revolutionaries began to take shape in the autumn of that year. The real founders of the Land and Freedom organization were Ogarev and Serno-Solovevich. Ogarev was far more attuned to the conspiratorial outlook than Herzen and helped to formulate the strategic basis for a revolutionary conspiracy. Bakunin, who had recently escaped from Siberia, also joined the discussions. Ogarev's article, "What Do the People Need?" published in *The Bell,* July 1, 1861, became the program of a small group of St. Petersburg students and provided them with a slogan, "Land and Freedom." In August 1862 Land and Freedom became the official title of the organization itself. At this time, the young revolutionaries expected a peasant uprising of vast dimensions in the summer of 1863. They hoped to prevent a repetition of the bloodbath that had occurred in earlier peasant rebellions in the seventeenth and eighteenth centuries by creating a solid front with the peasants against the government. Although Herzen was skeptical about the strength of the organization, which A. A. Sleptsov had exaggerated in an attempt to tie *The Bell* to Land and Freedom, Ogarev supported it enthusiastically. Actually, Herzen's instincts about the weakness of Land and Freedom proved to be sound, but, in view of the revolutionary situation taking shape at the end of 1862, he felt that it had to be supported. Thus, *The Bell* announced the existence of Land and Freedom, and Ogarev wrote a number of programmatic articles for it.

In retrospect, despite evidence of the existence of widely scattered cells (groups of five members), there is no indication that Land and Freedom ever developed beyond the stage of propaganda, most of which was prepared and published with the help of the émigrés. The appeals of the young radicals were more moderate in tone than "Young Russia." In some respects, they echoed the demands of the group of radical liberals in Tver province who had issued a resolution in February 1862 demanding, among other things, the convoking of a National Assembly. The call for a National Assembly made up of representatives of all the people was part of the political atmosphere in 1862. There were precedents in Russian history for such assemblies, although the intelligentsia tended to exaggerate their democratic character, just as they tended to idealize a number of ancient and medieval Russian "democratic" institutions. The Tver liberals, of course, had much more limited goals than the radicals of Land and Freedom, but in 1862 and the early part of 1863 the idea of a National Assembly provided a possible rallying point for oppositional groups. However, Alexander II had no intention of dissolving his government in favor of a constitutional system, and the signers of the Tver resolution were arrested.

The belief that the autocracy and its bureaucratic apparatus were no longer capable of carrying out the reforms necessary to save Russia from internal dissolution was a common assumption of all oppositional groups. Land and Freedom was in some ways a desperate effort to repair the damage done to the revolutionary front by "Young Russia" and the St. Petersburg fires. Under the pressure of circumstances, it appeared for a moment that the conflicting camps within the intelligentsia might draw together. The revolutionary socialists, although bitter ideological opponents of liberalism, tried to attract liberal elements in order to gain an immediate objective. This strategy of Land and Freedom foreshadowed the attempted and real alliances that occurred in later cycles of the revolutionary movement.

However, in 1863 it was too late to effect an alliance. The final blow to the revolutionary movement in 1863 was the Polish rebellion. Polish nationalism had grown increasingly militant since 1860. In February 1861 Russian troops had been used in Warsaw to suppress demonstrations. Concessions to the Poles by the imperial government did not change the situation. Russian socialists supported Polish demands in keeping with their belief in local self-determination. Herzen was a prominent spokesman for the Polish cause, and both *The Bell* and Land and Freedom promised to aid the Polish revolutionaries in any way that they could. The Russo-Polish revolutionary alliance that formed late in 1862 was largely responsible for Herzen's reluctant decision to make *The Bell* an affiliate of Land and Freedom. Actually, as Herzen sensed throughout the entire episode, the revolutionary forces were not sufficiently strong in 1862 to liberate Poland or set off a general uprising in Russia. The contrary occurred. The Polish rebellion in the winter and spring of 1863, and the diplomatic intervention of England and France in particular (several other nations and Pope Pius IX also took the side of the Poles), touched off a wave of anger and alarm in Russia. Whatever chance there might have been for a solid oppositional front against autocracy—and it was a rather remote chance to begin with—disappeared. The radicals were isolated. *The Bell* became an object of scorn, and Herzen never recovered his position as a leader of the opposition. The peasant uprisings that had been predicted for the summer of 1863 never materialized. Land and Freedom simply dissolved. By the end of 1863 the victory of the government over the revolutionaries was complete and devastating.

THE DECLINE OF NIHILISM

During the middle and late 1860s young nihilists feverishly attempted to fulfill the programs of their favorite theorists. Although Alexander's government was carrying through an ambitious program of modernizing judicial reforms and was creating a more democratic species of local administration (the *zemstvos*), which later served as an important arena for the intelligentsia, the failure to free the serfs socially and economically and the unwillingness of the government to reform itself limited the extent of progress.[6] The moral aberrations of the young nihilists of this period are at least partly attributable to their sense

6 The *zemstvos*, established in 1864, were provincial and district assemblies whose members were elected by individual landowners, peasant communes, and propertied urban groups. Despite liberal pressure, the *zemstvos* were limited to educational and what can be broadly classified as welfare functions.

of utter frustration after the events of 1861–1863. Whatever frail ties had existed between nihilist youth and Russian society were broken. Unlike the youth of the early 1860s, the nihilists of the new breed had no patience with higher education. They were more extreme in their interpretation of Chernyshevskii, Dobroliubov, and Pisarev than their predecessors had been. The cultural and moral anarchism implicit in Pisarev's writings, and the ascetic, evangelical socialism of Chernyshevskii and Dobroliubov were sometimes carried to logical extremes. Dostoevsky's *Crime and Punishment* and *The Possessed* suggest that murder, suicide, madness, and destruction were the natural consequences of nihilism. The lurid conspiracies of the middle and late 1860s should not be viewed as the most typical expression of nihilism, but rather as a phase in the revolutionary movement when aberrant types moved to the center of the stage. They prefigured later characters in the revolutionary movement and espoused a violence and criminality that seemed to negate the ideas of the mainstream intelligentsia. They lived in a state of perpetual crisis. The conspirators of this period were in complete harmony with views expressed by Zaichnevskii in "Young Russia":

> Soon, soon the day will come, when we will unfurl the great banner of the future, that red banner and with a great shout: Long live the socialist and democratic Russian republic! we will march on the Winter Palace to destroy those who live there. It might happen that the whole business will end with only the destruction of the royal family, that is, of some hundred or so people, but it might also happen—and the latter is more likely—that the entire imperial party, to a man, will stand behind the sovereign, because here the question will arise, will they themselves survive or not.
>
> In the latter case, with complete faith in ourselves, in our strength, the people's sympathy with us, in the glorious future of Russia, which has come forth as the first to realize the great moment of socialism, we shall give forth one shout: "to the axes,"—then . . . smash the imperial party . . . smash them in the squares, if those dirty swine dare to enter, smash them in their houses, in the narrow alleys of the city, on the broad streets of the capital, in the countryside and villages.

> Remember, that at this time, he who is not with us is against us; he who is against us—is our enemy; and enemies must be destroyed by any means.[7]

The nihilists in Russia in the 1860s ended by mutilating themselves rather than the regime. Historians who stress the resemblances between the nihilists and the Bolsheviks have a good grasp of the conspiratorial outlook and all-or-nothing radicalism uniting both groups. The nihilists, however, remained rank amateurs, with little of the professionalism and methodical preparation for both survival and the exercise of power one finds in figures like Lenin.

If the revolutionaries of 1861–1863 had been mistaken about their ability to mobilize and unite the discontented social groups around them, the new groups made them seem almost reasonable by comparison. Nicholas Ishutin's Moscow circle (1865–1866) is the most historically significant example of evangelical nihilism of the period. In keeping with Chernyshevskii's program in *What Is to Be Done?* they formed their own cooperatives, lived communally with emancipated women, and tried to spread the revolutionary socialist gospel through contact with workers and as school teachers. Their "rational egoism" was a true rendering of Chernyshevskii's nihilism. Despite inevitable lapses, they lived lives of self-denial, creating a little community of saints. Chernyshevskii's social and economic ideas were their scriptures. However, Ishutin was also a student of conspiratorial methods. Techniques of underground organization were widely discussed, and students who had been connected directly or indirectly with Land and Freedom had acquired some basic ideas about organizing cells, maintaining secrecy, and communicating with a central guiding cell. By 1865 Ishutin expressed impatience with communal enterprise and propaganda and diverted his comrades (a hard core of about eight, supplemented by several converts) to the formation of a revolutionary conspiracy. Ishutin called his group "The Organization." Their primary goal was the fomenting of a social revolution by means of terror. For this pur-

---

7 Excerpt from "Young Russia" in Koz'min, ed., *Istoriko-revoliutsionnaia khrestomatiia,* I, p. 59.

pose, Ishutin intended to establish a kind of central committee called "Hell."

During the course of contacts with I. A. Khudiakov, an early populist and leader of a St. Petersburg circle of more moderate leanings than The Organization, Ishutin was led to believe that a "European Revolutionary Committee" had formed. It is not clear what group Khudiakov described to Ishutin in August 1865. Khudiakov may indeed have learned about a group of European revolutionaries in Geneva during a stay there. On the other hand, Ishutin may have embellished an account of the newly formed International. In any case, Ishutin used Khudiakov's information as an excuse to press for the use of terror, telling his comrades that they were part of an international conspiracy. Khudiakov himself, some of his followers, and even members of Ishutin's circle believed that a social revolution would be premature, and hoped instead for political democracy. Therefore, they believed that it was essential to carry on their propaganda to help prepare society for a socialist future. The bitter struggle in the Moscow and Petersburg circles between the proponents of terror and immediate social revolution and those of gradualism is correctly seen by historians as a foreshadowing of the struggles between Bakuninists, Lavrovists, and Tkachevists (followers of Peter Tkachev, perpetuator of the Jacobin tradition in Russian revolutionary thought) in the 1870s. Conflicts of this sort were inevitable in view of the fact that the revolutionary intelligentsia attracted men and women with varying amounts of impatience and adventurousness and who felt different degrees of urgency. Disagreements over revolutionary strategy revealed more about clashing personalities than about the possibility of revolution in 1865–1866.

Dmitrii Karakozov, Ishutin's cousin, was a miserable and suicidal person, one of those who place their self-destructive impulse in the service of some larger cause. When Ishutin's group discussed assassinating Tsar Alexander II, Karakozov took it to heart. Between February and April 1866 he reached a psychological point of no return and evidently carried some of his comrades with him. Shortly before his attempt, he wrote and distributed a proclamation in St. Petersburg justifying his contemplated action and expressing his hopes for the liberation of the masses. Although the government learned about Karakozov's proclamation, no special precautions were taken to protect the tsar. On April 4, 1866, Karakozov aimed a pistol shot at Alexander II near a royal garden in St. Petersburg. The shot missed, but the attempt aroused an even greater wave of public anger than that provoked by the events of 1862–1863.

The incident brought both long-term and short-term consequences to the revolutionary intelligentsia. The immediate effect was the arrest of Karakozov and thirty-four of his associates. Karakozov became the first Russian revolutionary since the Decembrists to be executed. Besides arresting those immediately involved, General M. N. Murav'ev used the Karakozov affair as an excuse for detaining and prosecuting numerous radicals and liberals who had been under police surveillance for several years.[8] *The Contemporary* and *The Russian Word,* which had survived the first reaction, were now suspended for good. Michael Katkov, who had been a liberal Westernizer during the 1840s, led the attack against nihilism through his journal, *The Moscow Gazette.* He and others convinced Alexander that stronger men were needed to keep the students in hand. A. V. Golovnin, the liberal minister of education who had repaired some of the harm done to the universities in 1861–1862 by issuing a new, liberalized university charter in 1863, was dismissed and replaced by Count D. A. Tolstoy, an archreactionary in educational policy. Tolstoy's repressive measures made revolutionary activity a reasonable alternative to higher education. Many teachers and students who were arrested in the investigations of the period, or expelled for protesting the reactionary measures, became revolutionary propagandists. Thus, the period 1866–1869 was highly significant for the formation of a nucleus of professional revolutionaries and for the government's "white terror" that produced an effect quite unlike the one intended.

By the late 1860s the revolutionary intelligentsia had acquired the critical mass to maintain a self-perpetuating movement in the face of the strictest police measures and censorship. Self-education circles grew up in university cities and even in second-

8 M. N. Murav'ev was a member of the family which had contributed several men to the Decembrist movement.

ary schools. Expelled students who were exiled to the provinces, often to their homes in European Russia, sometimes indoctrinated schoolboys. There always seemed to be a village atheist about who had read Chernyshevskii, Dobroliubov, and Pisarev. Liberal or radical gymnasium instructors sometimes read socialist literature to the students. Inquisitive and adventurous students joined study circles where they read much the same kind of literature that their older brothers in the universities were reading. One memoirist describes the way radical styles of thought percolated down to students in the lower classes. Having read Vogt's physiology, a neophyte was examined by an older student in this vein:

> ". . . In order to benefit fully from reading books of this sort you have to know how to apply what you've read. Tell me, when you read, for example, about the digestive processes and nourishment, didn't something about the Irish people occur to you?"
>
> "No—nothing."
>
> "I thought so. Well there's a direct correlation. You only need to remember that the potato is in large part starch, which has little nutritional value, and that the Irish exist largely by means of the potato, and you are led to conclude that the Irish people must die out. . . ."[9]

This anecdote also demonstrates the way in which scientific and social thought could be crudely combined. Furthermore, by the end of the 1860s one can detect the beginnings of a shift of emphasis from knowledge to morality, and from scientific study to social action. Ishutin's group was an early sign of this shift. The intelligentsia's role as the vanguard of science, as a corps of teachers, was deemphasized in favor of roles as organizers and agitators. Bakunin emerged as a leader because his anarchism satisfied the mood of some of the frustrated and angry young intellectuals. Pisarevism in the late 1860s (Pisarev died in 1868) was not so much social as personal in impact, whether interpreted in a positive sense as an affirmation of science, or in a negative sense as a repudiation of culture. A handful of the youth proba-

---

9 N. A. Morozov, *Povesti moei zhizni*, 2 vols. (Moscow, 1962), 1, p. 47.

bly needed justification for direct expression of revolutionary action, however criminal or devious, as much for personal as for ideological reasons. In every major period of the revolutionary movement, ideologies appeared to consecrate courses of action that were developing spontaneously. In the period 1868–1869, Sergei Nechaev set out on a course of action that achieved the status of an "ism," while Bakunin supplied the ideology. In addition to his uncompromisingly radical ideology, Bakunin had in his favor a foreign base of operations and, after 1868, the glitter of membership in the First International. The veteran gave his blessing to the most extreme forms of revolutionary action. His Romanticism made him especially susceptible to the most flamboyant members of the new generation and, to his great folly, he consecrated the efforts of a ruthless young man named Nechaev.

Sergei Nechaev has become a symbol of revolutionism without conscience, an embodiment of the notion, now repudiated by the Russian intelligentsia, that the end justifies the means. Nechaev's career inspired Dostoevsky to write *The Possessed* and to portray wildly pathological elements of the revolutionary movement. More recently, Michael Shatrov presented Nechaev as a premonition of Stalin in his play *The Dictatorship of Conscience,* which distinguishes healthy revolutionism from pathological terrorism. In their efforts to demonize Nechaev and make him, not without justification, an early warning signal of twentieth-century totalitarianism, his critics have lost sight of a more complex personality. He resembled Dostoevsky's Raskolnikov in *Crime and Punishment* more than he did the demonic Verkhovensky in *The Possessed.* The gifted child of a bartender and waiter in the mill town of Ivanovo-Voznesensk, Nechaev was discovered by populist teachers who recognized his ability, cultivated him, and encouraged him to seek higher education. He decided to become a teacher himself. After his arrival in St. Petersburg and exposure to student radicals, he abandoned those plans and transformed himself into a kind of revolutionary whirlwind. He quickly distinguished himself in the student movement of 1868–1869, formed to resist new university regulations designed to cripple nihilism. Nechaev continued, yet dramatically altered, the tradition of Zaichnevskii, Ishutin, and Karakozov.

Nechaev used deception and outright extortion to enhance his reputation and power in the student milieu. He was also an astute psychological manipulator, who understood that his humble origins, feverish activity for the cause, and rhetoric of self-sacrifice gave him leverage over the more privileged, guilt-ridden students. Assuming the role of popular avenger (naming his organization, in fact, "The People's Revenge"), he made his fellow students bow to him as an authentic man of the people, and the most committed forgave his domineering, intimidating style of leadership. Similar forms of psychological manipulation worked equally well with the aging émigrés; Nechaev lied about an imprisonment and escape from the Peter and Paul Fortress and appeared in Switzerland and England in March 1869, seeking their help. He manufactured the persona of the young hero, risking danger and bringing word of fresh, new revolutionary forces. Bakunin and Ogarev, too, forgave Nechaev's roughness and surrendered considerable resources to him, although Herzen did his best to avert the catastrophe that he foresaw before his death in 1870. The dynamics of the revolutionary subculture gave the tough, plebian members of the movement a special mystique and if, like Nechaev, they knew how to use that mystique, they might go far. In this respect, Nechaev prefigured Stalin, and his relationship with Bakunin in some ways resembled Stalin's with Lenin.

The rhetoric Nechaev used in his publications and his dealings with his comrades suggest a paranoid personality. However, even in the earlier stages of the revolutionary subculture, rhetoric about embattled victims of heroic stature, about spies and traitors and vigilant conspirators, seemed pertinent and apt. Furthermore, the grandiose aspirations of revolutionary movements and their clandestine operations typically generated rhetoric that might inspire both dedicated, self-sacrificing idealists and paranoid power-seekers. Worse still, the aspiring paranoid dictator and self-sacrificing idealist sometimes coexisted in a single personality. Nechaev's authentic dedication to the cause was one side of the coin; on the other side was a vengeful power-seeker and megalomaniac. The life of Nechaev reveals with great clarity that revolutionary subcultures, like many other kinds of subcultures, cannot always easily detect and defend themselves against pathological personalities. Even when warned, revolutionaries often refused to believe the worst and failed to repudiate proven comrades in the cause who exhibited dangerous symptoms. Moreover, such people at times seemed very useful to the cause, especially when dirty jobs had to be done or when an energetic personality was needed to galvanize a stalled movement. Only later, when pathological individuals had overstepped their roles as hired guns and endangered the movement did their sponsors realize how destructive they could be.

In 1868 Nechaev, with a small number of co-conspirators, among them Peter Tkachev, a talented publicist and Blanquist, feverishly began to plan for a revolutionary explosion to occur in 1870. Like the earlier groups who had chosen 1863 as a target date, they had great faith in the revolutionary potential of the peasants. The conspirators of the early 1860s had expected the peasants to rise up when the land inventories, determined between 1861 and 1863 in connection with the first stage of emancipation, became operative. The uprisings did not occur. Equally hopeful, Nechaev and his fellow conspirators believed that the critical moment would come in February 1870, when the peasants had to accept either reduced land allotments or a system of redemption payments that would force them into forty-nine years of indebtedness and dependency upon their former masters. Nechaev, Tkachev, and the others estimated that the uprisings would occur in the spring of 1870 and worked out an organizational plan and timetable for the revolution in a brief but detailed document, "A Program of Revolutionary Actions." It included plans to enlist the aid of revolutionaries based abroad and to formulate a set of rules, or catechism, for the organization.

These and other revolutionary dreams were shared in the smoky atmosphere of student apartments in St. Petersburg and Moscow in 1868. Nechaev attended meetings, burning with resentment at the privileged youths that he met there and longing to subject them to his will. However, when student disorders did erupt in March 1869 in an attempt to reestablish the student assemblies and corporate institutions, the authorities dealt firmly with them. The circles with which Nechaev was connected were decimated by expulsions and arrests. Tkachev was arrested in

March 1869. While all of this was going on, Nechaev was in Geneva and London, trying to enlist the support of Bakunin, Ogarev, and Herzen. (Once again, the events of 1861–1863 are called to mind.) Ogarev and Bakunin became the major collaborators with the young man who represented himself as a delegate from the "Russian Revolutionary Committee." Bakunin, still involved in his latest intrigue to transform the First International into a Proudhonist rather than Marxist organization, had alienated the Russian émigré community by his organizational escapades. He had even lost control of his journal, *The Popular Cause,* whose first issue had strongly influenced the growing populist mood of the younger generation in Russia. Always quick to put another iron in the fire, Bakunin did everything possible to help Nechaev. It was an interesting case of mutual deception, each man enrolling the other in a fictitious revolutionary organization. However, Nechaev derived very concrete benefits from his association with Bakunin, while Bakunin's reputation was gravely damaged by *l'affaire Nechaev.* The pamphlets that Bakunin composed during the spring and summer of 1869 suggest that the older man worked almost as a subordinate to Nechaev. Bakunin and Ogarev also transferred to Nechaev a large sum of money, their share of a fund jointly held with Herzen for *The Bell* (by then defunct).

The pathetic mistakes of the émigrés are not attributable to personal failings alone. Dependent upon reports of youthful activists, who almost invariably exaggerated the possibilities of revolution in Russia and who demanded that the émigrés extend themselves and their resources for the revolutionary cause, the older revolutionaries were at a considerable disadvantage. Bakunin, however, zealously collaborated with his "boy" and during 1869–1870 became a willing accomplice in his own humiliation. Although Bakunin's admirers have tried to salvage some of his reputation by denying his co-authorship of the notorious "Catechism of a Revolutionary," the evidence weighs strongly against him.

The coded document that became known as the "Catechism" came to the public's attention at the trial of the Nechaevists in 1871. It instantly became a symbol of revolutionary Machiavellianism and of the betrayal of the ideals of the movement. Yet it also fascinated a small portion of Russian revolutionary youth and continues to inspire terrorist movements far beyond Russia's borders to this very day. The "Catechism" dramatically reveals the extent to which the intellectual aspect of the revolutionary intelligentsia's identity could be reduced, repudiated, or subordinated to revolutionism. The first three paragraphs of the "Catechism" fairly well describe Nechaev's creed.

> The revolutionist is a doomed man. He has no personal interests, no affairs, sentiments, attachments, property, not even a name of his own. Everything in him is absorbed by one exclusive interest, one thought, one passion—the revolution.
>
> In the very depth of his being, not merely in word but in deed, he has broken every connection with the social order and with the whole educated world, with all the laws, appearances and generally accepted conventions and moralities of that world which he considers his ruthless foe. Should he continue to live in it, it will be solely for the purpose of destroying it the more surely.
>
> The revolutionist despises every sort of doctrinairism and has renounced the peaceful scientific pursuits, leaving them to future generations. He knows only one science, the science of destruction. For this and only for this purpose he makes a study of mechanics, physics, chemistry, and possibly medicine. For this purpose he studies day and night the living science of human beings, their characters, situations, and all the conditions of the present social system in its various strata. The object is but one—the quickest possible destruction of that ignoble system.[10]

This was not nihilism. It was a symptom of the decline of nihilism. In some ways it was a challenge to the nihilists. However, the emphasis upon centralized conspiracy distinguishes Nechaevism from the mainstream of the populist movement of the mid-1870s. Bakunin, a true leader of the populist movement, was not so much interested in forming a conspiracy as in unleashing the healthy destructive forces residing in the masses. This glorification of the peasants and of peasant brigands was still that of a Romantic. Although Nechaev's ultimate goals were those of

---

10 In Max Nomad, *Apostles of Revolution* (Boston, 1939), p. 228.

Bakunin's revolutionary anarchism, the means that he advocated and practiced were Blanquist, with his own amendments. In him, one finds the combination of organizational authoritarianism and democratic purpose whose contradictions and evil consequences (the phenomenon has been called "totalitarian democracy") were anticipated by Dostoevsky in *The Possessed.* It is difficult to find anything appealing in Nechaev's association with the Moscow underworld, or his own criminal ventures, including blackmail and murder. Dostoevsky brilliantly expanded his perception of Nechaevism into a vision of a political and social order organized on Nechaev's principles.

Nechaev, having exploited the Genevan community to the fullest, decided to return home with his new credentials, cash, and revolutionary pamphlets, among them the "Catechism." He evidently believed in the timetable of the "Program of Revolutionary Actions" and returned to Russia in August 1869 in order to organize his revolutionary cadres. By this time, Nechaev had acquired some notoriety. The incipient populist groups in Russia, especially in St. Petersburg, did everything that they could to combat his influence. Nechaev found a more congenial atmosphere in Moscow, where he settled in the autumn of 1869. He organized several cells. In November 1869 he and four members of his organization murdered I. I. Ivanov, another member who may have threatened to expose Nechaev's duplicity and form a new association. Whatever Nechaev's motives for murdering Ivanov, the act itself was extremely important for determining the character of the revolutionary movement for several years.

Nechaev's activity did not end with the murder of Ivanov. In December, while his organization was collapsing because of dozens of arrests, Nechaev fled abroad again. Bakunin and Ogarev remained under his spell. After Herzen died in February 1870, Nechaev acquired the remainder of the money in the joint fund mentioned earlier. He issued a stream of pamphlets again, in a last furious effort to transform his fantasy into a genuine revolutionary movement. He and Ogarev even published several issues of *The Bell,* shifting their rhetoric in order to appeal to liberal elements. They drafted manifestoes for almost everybody, written in the name of fictitious councils or brotherhoods.

Ideologically, Nechaev repudiated Bakuninism for communism. By the summer of 1870 Bakunin realized the mistake he had made and repudiated Nechaev. The latter moved to London for a short time, then back to the Continent. The moment of revolution had passed. Nechaev could find no support among the émigrés. Finally, in August 1872, he was arrested in Switzerland and deported to Russia, where he was tried and imprisoned in January 1873. The tsarist regime violated its extradition treaty with Switzerland and its own judiciary by secretly isolating Nechaev in a dungeon in the Peter and Paul Fortress, but his plight became known to members of The People's Will. In a truly extraordinary episode demonstrating his charisma, Nechaev converted some of the guards in the Fortress to the revolutionary cause, made contact with The People's Will in January 1881, and tried to collaborate with them in their campaign to assassinate Alexander II. The campaign's success in March 1881 did not help him. The authorities discovered his organization among the guards in November 1881 and isolated him, once again. He died, possibly by suicide, in November 1882 in the Fortress.

More than Nechaev's apprehension and incarceration, the trial of seventy-nine young men and women in the summer of 1871 who had aided or abetted his activities exposed to public view the sordid character of Nechaevism. Although the defendants could not but evoke sympathy, the revolutionary movement and especially the conspiratorial strategy were discredited. By carrying the Blanquist or Jacobin strategy to such sordid extremes, Nechaev promoted a reaction in the intelligentsia against this and similar techniques of recruiting and organizing revolutionary circles. In this regard, he strengthened the nascent populist movement, whose growth his own movement had both obscured and impaired. Nechaev had purposely implicated populists in his conspiracy, while they had done everything possible to fight his influence. The collapse of Nechaevism left the field open to the populists.

The Nechaev episode exposed the vulnerability of the revolutionary movement to brutal, aberrant personalities who might turn against the very intelligentsia that had nourished them. Even so, The People's Will, many of whom had distanced themselves from Nechaevism, rehabilitated Nechaev when they discovered that he had been martyred in Peter and Paul Fortress, as did the Bolsheviks, who saw him as a hero. Hence, the legacy of even the most ruthless extremists was far from unambiguous to the intelligentsia community.

4 / POPULISM

THE ETHICAL SOCIOLOGISTS

Like nihilism, Russian populism was not so much a systematic ideology as a style of thought and an emotional orientation common to a large segment of the intelligentsia. The desire to skip the phase of bourgeois capitalism by means of the peasant commune did not alone make a person a populist, nor did great sympathy for the suffering peasant masses. Populism was a peculiar response to a variety of frustrations, both strategic and emotional, that involved several degrees of rejection of the nihilist's rationalistic elitism. Evangelical nihilism, as noted earlier, resembled populism because it established the dependency of the intelligentsia upon the vital strength of the peasant masses. The attitude of the radical intelligentsia toward the peasants began to change in the 1860s as historians, folklorists, and publicists, often under the direct or indirect influence of Slavophilism, extolled the virtues of the masses. It has been convincingly shown that the new image of the peasants influenced the attitude of a significant group within the radical intelligentsia in the 1870s, as well as its strategies.[1]

In theoretical terms, populism can be described as a resolution of the problem of the role of the intelligentsia and the role of the masses in favor of the masses. That is, the contributions of the intelligentsia and the peasants to the new social order were reassessed, with the role of the intelligentsia, at least theoretically, forever diminishing, and that of the masses forever increasing. In its purest form, populism demanded that the intelligentsia merge with the peasants and learn from them rather than teach them. Ideologically, Bakunin's revolutionary Romanticism was much more suited to populism than the rationalistic and positivistic doctrines of the late 1860s. In Baku-

1 See Richard Wortman, *The Crisis of Russian Populism* (Cambridge, U.K., 1967).

ninism, science and rational calculation were subordinated to instinct and passion.

Since the masses were to absorb the intelligentsia rather than the intelligentsia transforming the masses (as in nihilism), populism often signified a kind of self-repudiation on the part of the intelligentsia. More than a mere renunciation of privilege and status, it issued from a much more profound self-ambivalence which had been frequently expressed by the nihilists in personal dramas. Chernyshevskii's almost pathological self-subordination to his frivolous wife is an example of this phenomenon. Dobroliubov's adventures with prostitutes and the fascination with abomination revealed in the pages of his diary (Chernyshevskii destroyed some of the most shocking passages) reveal a similar psychology. Private expressions of ambivalence were excluded from the public discussions of the nihilists. Sometimes populists ran to the opposite extreme—that of repudiating their own propensity for intellectualism and fondness for high culture. Turgenev captured the populists' painful self-ambivalence in his novels. In *Virgin Soil*, a young poet, Nezhdanov, discovers that he is incapable of reshaping his personality to fit the circumstances of life in the villages and commits suicide. The populists rarely achieved in life what they advocated in theory, not even those who were better adapted to the squalor of the villages than Nezhdanov. Thus, the populists' formula for revolution and social transformation was no less unrealistic than the nihilists'. While the nihilists had placed too much faith in their ability to transform reality by virtue of superior reason and discipline, the populists staked their lives on an unrealistic vision of the peasants' socialist instincts and revolutionary passion.

Finally, like nihilism, populism tended to break down into submovements, reflecting the different responses of its adherents to their experiences in the countryside, to the government's persecution, and to their changing historical environment. A variety of revolutionary tactics corresponding to their discoveries, frustrations, and reorientations emerged. Since nineteenth-century rebels generally imitated or recreated a few basic modes of revolutionary expression, populism too gave birth to tactics involving either long-term educational and organizational activities or short-term agitational and conspiratorial actions.

No less than previous intelligentsia generations, the generation of the 1870s needed an all-embracing theory to justify, explain, and guide its actions. Although populism was essentially a Romantic doctrine, in its initial phase it was quite rationalistic, little more than a philosophical modification of evangelical nihilism. The most prominent theorists of the late 1860s and early 1870s, like their predecessors, professed an anthropocentric philosophy of action in the cause of progress by means of science. However, while the nihilists had been materialistic and objectivistic, the new theorists, Peter Lavrov and Nicholas Mikhailovskii, were phenomenalistic and subjectivistic.

The acceptance by the new generation of the more sophisticated epistemology of the new school of thought was probably a symptom of a shift of interest away from epistemological questions, rather than a sign of the greater intellectual maturity of the youth of the 1870s. Early in the 1860s Lavrov's expression of similar epistemological views had irritated the materialists of *The Contemporary* and *The Russian Word,* who had no patience with Kantianism in any form. To the youth of that period, materialism was an essential feature of the radical worldview. As a consequence Lavrov had been dismissed as a well-intentioned but muddled thinker, something less than a radical. Many young radicals were surprised when he was arrested in April 1866 after Karakozov's attempted assassination. Actually, although he sympathized with revolutionary socialism, Lavrov had not joined any conspiracies. His arrest and exile to a remote province near the White Sea is an example of the government's brutal handling of academicians in the late 1860s.

While in exile Lavrov wrote a series of articles for a St. Petersburg journal, *The Week*. After serial publication in 1868–1869, the articles were issued in a single volume, *Historical Letters,* in 1870. However abstract *Historical Letters* appears to the contemporary reader, it was received with great enthusiasm. It offered alternatives to a lonely withdrawal into the natural sciences on the one hand and amoral Nechaevism on the other, by providing convincing answers to the theoretical problems that the intelligentsia continued to pose—problems of determinism and free will, the relationship of science to morality, the nature of progress, and the role of the intelligentsia. Lavrov's newly found cogency (he had been publishing philosophical articles for about ten years before *Historical Letters* appeared) issued from a combination of utilitarianism, left Hegelianism, Proudhonism, and Kantianism. In many conclusions and in his basic orientation Lavrov resembled Herzen, and in some ways in his later career as an émigré revolutionary publicist (1873–1900) he took over Herzen's role.

Lavrov believed that the illusion of free will was an inevitable phenomenon of human consciousness, and that people had to act *as if* they chose some of their goals freely. Although historians of ideas feel much more comfortable about Lavrov's peculiar doctrine of free will than they do about Chernyshevskii's determinism as the basis for an anthropocentric worldview, one should remember that the determinism of the nihilists had not prevented them and their followers from displaying a profound sense of responsibility for the fate of their fellow human beings, nor had it turned them into passivists. Lavrov, no less than the nihilists, felt obliged to stress the scientific character of ethical and social thought. According to him, the theories of progress of "developed" people at each successive stage in history, though subjective, were nonetheless scientific. These people, whom Lavrov called "critically thinking individuals," are best described as ethical sociologists. The term "ethical sociology" is preferable to "subjective sociology," the usual designation for Lavrov's school of thought, because the latter expression places an undue emphasis upon Lavrov's idea that theories of progress are not absolute but the product of a changing historical environment. The central concern of his thought is the duty of the scientist, particularly the social scientist, to humanity. Just as Lavrov believed that people had to act as if they were free, he encouraged them to act as if they were right. This open-mindedness may seem peculiar for a man who spent almost thirty years of his life as a dedicated revolutionary socialist; yet, despite occasional doubts, he remained firm in the conviction that socialism was the correct ethical sociology for his time.

Perhaps the most striking illustration of Lavrov's subjective approach to the scientist's progressive role is his conclusion that if two scientists achieved identical results, but one was motivated by mere curiosity or love of science, while the other was contemplating the applications of his work and its wider social consequences, then only the latter really participated in progress. In effect, he distinguished amoral or pure intellectuals from the intelligentsia. The best, most highly developed people in society were meant to do more than merely acquire scientific skills. Lavrov wanted them to exhibit a higher ethical consciousness and to raise the ethical level of the entire society. The astute reader of *Historical Letters* knew that Lavrov was telling the intelligentsia to perfect their knowledge of socialism and to spread the "scientific" socialist ethic (not to be confused with Marx's classification of socialist thought) to the masses. Thus, his formula for progress combines the idea of individual development and social action: "The physical, intellectual, and moral development of the individual; the incorporation of truth and justice in social institutions. . . ."[2]

The most compelling argument in support of a new evangelical socialism was Lavrov's idea of the intelligentsia's debt to the masses, which he set forth systematically in *Historical Letters*. He demonstrated that the "critically thinking minority" had developed only at the expense of the toiling masses, who had provided them with the wealth and leisure necessary for higher development, and that the developed minority therefore owed a debt to the masses. Lavrov, a mathematician, put everything in clear quantitative terms, but despite his utilitarian calculus an impassioned plea for social justice breaks through:

> Every comfort which I enjoy, every thought which I had the leisure to acquire or work out was purchased by blood, by the suffering or labor of millions. I cannot correct the past, and no matter how dearly my development cost, I cannot renounce it. It is the source of the very ideal which stirs me to action. . . . Evil has to be righted, insofar as possible, and it has to be done during one's lifetime. . . . I remove from myself responsibility for the bloody cost of development if I use this very development in order to lessen evil in the present and in the future. If I am a developed man, then I am obliged to do this, and it is quite an easy duty, since it coincides with that which is a source of pleasure for me—searching for and disseminating greater

2 Edie, et al., *Russian Philosophy*, 2, p. 134.

> truth, clarifying for myself the most just social order. And in striving to realize it, I increase my own pleasure and at the same time do everything that I can for the suffering majority in the present and in the future.[3]

Thus, while Chernyshevskii and Pisarev had claimed that it was natural for rational egoists to work for the betterment of society, Lavrov argued that it was their *duty* as well. He called for the formation of a disciplined intelligentsia party as the preliminary task. Afterwards, they would convert the Russian masses to a scientific worldview and to socialism. Lavrov developed these ideas more fully after escaping from Russia in 1870 and becoming the editor of a revolutionary socialist journal, *Forward!,* in 1873, when he translated his ideas about the role of the intelligentsia into the revolutionary strategy that was called Lavrovism or "preparationism." At first, preparationism seemed to imply an extended period of scientific self-education on the part of future socialist propagandists, followed by an indeterminate period of propaganda work among the peasants. However, under the pressure of impatient young radicals, and in the course of polemics exchanged with Bakunin and Tkachev, Lavrov continually modified his thinking. In a way, he became a barometer of the *narodnik* movement, adjusting his own views to the revolutionary trends in Russia. *Forward!,* which became a biweekly publication and moved from Zurich to London in 1874, was the most dignified Russian émigré journal of this period, containing a wealth of information about the international labor movement, social and economic evils, and the programs for social change developing in the socialist camp.

Within Russia, views similar to Lavrov's were expounded by Nicholas Mikhailovskii in the journal *Notes of the Fatherland.* Mikhailovskii's long-term influence was probably greater than that of any populist or populist-oriented thinker. He was a talented literary critic, popularizer of social and scientific thought, social philosopher, and heir to the central role played by Belinsky, Chernyshevskii, Dobroliubov, and Pisarev in the legal press. Mikhailovskii embraced the entire tradition of the Rus-

---

3 Peter Lavrov, *Izbrannye sochineniia,* 4 vols. (Moscow, 1934), 1, pp. 225–26. The translation is mine.

sian intelligentsia. He displayed both the aristocratic sensibilities of the generation of the 1830s and 1840s and the scientism of his immediate predecessors. Like most populist theorists, he was a follower of Proudhon.

Mikhailovskii's major theoretical contribution was his critique of positivism and social Darwinism. Auguste Comte and Herbert Spencer were extremely popular in Russia during the 1860s and 1870s. Following Lavrov, Mikhailovskii believed that positivism was basically amoral and could not serve as the basis for an ethical sociology. Both Lavrov and Mikhailovskii, in their attempt to uphold a scientific worldview without repudiating advanced scientific thought, found Herbert Spencer's sociological adaptation of Darwin's and Karl Ernst von Baer's theories of natural and organic evolution a challenge to their belief in socialism. According to Spencer, increased specialization and an increasingly complex division of labor in society was progressive, just as development from homogeneity to heterogeneity was progressive in individual organisms. Lavrov, while accepting the validity of comparing society to an organism, demanded that the sociologist, on the basis of an understanding of human pleasure and pain and personal ideals (arrived at critically), determine whether or not the transition from a primitive, more homogeneous social order to a more complex one involved more or less pleasure for individuals and more or less justice. Mikhailovskii, in his famous essay, "What Is Progress?" went even further, denying the validity of Spencer's analogy. He cited recent reports about factory organization to demonstrate that an extreme division of labor led to monotonous work at a highly specific task and to a reduction of human intellectual capacity, concluding that

> . . . if society makes a transition from homogeneity to heterogeneity, then the process of integration in the citizens which corresponds to this transition must proceed from heterogeneity to homogeneity. In short, individual progress and social evolution (on the model of organic evolution) are mutually exclusive, just as the evolution of organs and the evolution of the whole organism are mutually exclusive. . . .

> . . . In an organism it is the whole that experiences pain and pleasure, not the parts; in society it is the parts that experience pain and pleasure, not the whole.[4]

Mikhailovskii's own formula for progress, with which Lavrov disagreed, was an attempt to translate correctly into social thought the biological theories of von Baer and Ernst Haeckel. The Russian biologist N. D. Nozhin and the American chemist and historian John William Draper were his scientific authorities, but the vision that predisposed him to think in terms of the whole human personality belongs to the Romantic tradition. Mikhailovskii's attempt to balance the demands of science with a basically Romantic vision of human self-fulfillment recalls Herzen's earlier struggle. Thus, he believed:

> Progress is the gradual approach to the integral individual, to the fullest possible and most diversified division of labor among man's organs and the least possible division of labor among men. Everything that impedes this advance is immoral, unjust, pernicious, and unreasonable. Everything that diminishes the heterogeneity of society and thereby increases the heterogeneity of its members is moral, just, reasonable, and beneficial.[5]

The early phase of Russian populism (1868–1874) embodied to a significant extent this theoretical compromise between rationalism and Romanticism.

Mikhailovskii's social thought, once again in Herzen's tradition, reflected an unwillingness to submit to a system of industrial "progress" in which an extension of human misery played a necessary (even if temporary) role. Populists were attracted to theories offering the most direct and immediate solution to human suffering. For this reason, they attacked both the laissez-faire liberalism of the social Darwinists in the 1860s and 1870s and, later, the industrial socialism of the Russian Marxists. Mikhailovskii and the populist thinkers who became known as "legal populists" offered a middle road to the intelligentsia. They exhorted the intelligentsia to go to the people, not for the

---

4 Edie, et al., *Russian Philosophy*, 2, pp. 180, 181.
5 Ibid., p. 187.

purpose of bringing about a revolution, but in order to teach them and help them improve their lives. Like earlier Russian socialists, they believed that the peasant commune was a potentially progressive institution. Mikhailovskii, given the intellectual climate of the late 1860s and early 1870s, justified his wishful thinking about the commune in evolutionary terms. He tried to demonstrate that the commune, based upon progressive principles of cooperation and solidarity rather than upon exploitation and competition, was a superior *type* of social organization, even though it existed at a relatively primitive *stage* of development.

There were disagreements within the ranks of the nonrevolutionary populists about strategy, but they were in essential agreement about both the necessity and the desirability of helping the peasants to raise the commune to a higher stage of development. Two of their economic theorists, N. F. Danielson and V. P. Vorontsev, adduced sophisticated arguments to demonstrate that this was the only moral and economically feasible approach to contemporary problems of Russian economic development. It is difficult to do full justice to the wide range of revolutionary and nonrevolutionary populist theories and strategies. Suffice it to say that they reflected the continuing frustrations of the intelligentsia over the dismal circumstances of the Russian countryside. The populist intelligentsia regarded themselves as servants of the people, bitterly opposing the groups that they believed were increasing the misery of the peasants, and forming temporary alliances with a number of governmental cliques, oppositional movements, and revolutionary parties during the several decades between the inception of populism and the consolidation of Bolshevik power.

Educated and idealistic Russians growing up in the cultural and social environment of the late nineteenth and early twentieth centuries who did not at one time or another gravitate toward one or another variety of populism must have been unusual indeed. They could find in the writings of Lavrov and Mikhailovskii a very complimentary picture of themselves as the motive force of progress. Or, if they were disenchanted with intellectualism, they could turn to I. I. Kablits's demand that the intelligentsia subordinate themselves to the real agency of social progress—the instinctively socialistic peasants. If they were in a revolutionary mood, they could select from the strategies offered by Lavrov, Bakunin, or Tkachev. Losing confidence in revolution, they could follow the advice of Ia. V. Abramov and dedicate themselves to a life of "small deeds" in the countryside as teachers, agronomists, statisticians, or doctors in the *zemstvos.* Although the populist theorists were forced to amend their doctrine in order to maintain cogency in a climate of rapid industrialization and nationalism, one should not assume that populism was simply an aberration on the part of some of the intelligentsia who happened to fix upon the peasant commune as their vehicle for socialism. The fundamental condition that had fostered populism in the 1860s and 1870s continued to exist in the twentieth century. This condition was modernization under the auspices of a relatively inflexible old regime that inflicted the cost of industrialization upon a huge and impoverished peasant population.

GOING TO THE PEOPLE

From the point of view of the Russian revolutionary movement, the varieties of populism that deserve special attention are Lavrovism, Bakuninism, and Tkachevism. Of these, only Bakuninism consistently emphasized the role of the peasants, and therefore Bakuninism is the truest form of revolutionary *narodnichestvo,* which should be distinguished from "revolutionary populism." The latter term has been widely used to describe the whole range of ideologies and strategies that had as their goal an immediate transition to socialism by means of the peasant communes and workers' *arteli. Narodnichestvo* will be discussed later.

There was an incipient populist movement before the appearance of the aforementioned strategies, which did not exist as well defined alternatives until about 1874. It was inspired by the same moral outrage and impatient desire to set things right in the world that moved thousands of students into the countryside in the period 1874–1876. Even though Bakunin's revolutionary anarchism had immediate emotional appeal—the first issue of *The People's Cause* had attracted wide attention in 1868—Bakuninism was held in abeyance until the student movement acquired its critical mass in the spring of 1874. In the period 1869–1874 young populists were actually carrying out the strategy of "preparationism"—forming self-education circles, charging their moral impulse with the most "advanced" social thought of the times, and creating the basis for the revolutionary parties of the period 1876–1881. They studied the theoretical and historical works of Lavrov, Mikhailovskii, Louis Blanc, Ferdinand Lassalle, John Stuart Mill, Karl Marx, and others. The literature of the nihilists still had great appeal for them, especially Chernyshevskii's *What Is to Be Done?* The belles-lettrists whose stories and novels appeared in *Notes of the Fatherland* provided them with images of both the degradation and the dignity of the peasant masses. The inspirational poems of N. A. Nekrasov, and the fiction of F. M. Reshetnikov, N. N. Zlatovratskii, D. L. Mordovtsev, M. E. Saltykov-Shchedrin, G. I. Uspenskii, and others were avidly discussed and examined. The youth searched for and found in this literature both devastating portrayals of the evils of the old order and new "positive" images of "live" men and women working in the countryside to uplift the peasants.

A growing body of data collected by populist scholars reinforced literary descriptions of peasant life. V. V. Bervi-Flerovskii, a former bureaucrat in the Ministry of Justice, gathered together a large number of anecdotes and descriptions of the life of the laboring classes in European Russia, both agricultural and industrial. On the basis of his book *The Position of the Working Class in Russia* (1869), he instantly attracted a wide following. At the request of the Chaikovskii circle (to be discussed below) he produced another book, *The Alphabet of the Social Sciences* (1871), which confirmed his popularity. Although not a theoretical thinker of any real stature, Bervi-Flerovskii's frank and direct exposé of the concrete conditions in the countryside, and his equally candid attack on the social, political, and religious foundations of exploitation, made him one of the central influences of this period. Later, populist statisticians launched much more systematic efforts to learn about the life and economy of the peasants. In effect Lavrov's ethical sociologists made their appearance in the 1870s. They were not always revolutionaries, but their sense of obligation to the peasants compelled them to abandon their life of solitary scientific work in the cities.

The uneven, but nonetheless substantial growth of the Russian educational system was a major precondition of the large-scale intelligentsia movements of the mid-1870s. Although the universities did not grow at a rapid rate, the number of students in secondary schools more than doubled between 1864 and 1875. There were more than 5,000 university students in Russia in 1875, and more than 78,000 gymnasium students, including 27,470 women students. Russia's thirty-four seminaries contained 1,847 students. After 1869, in both St. Petersburg and Moscow, higher courses for women were offered. Several hundred women attended. The limited opportunities available in Russia, however, failed to satisfy hundreds of young women influenced by the radical subculture. In the early 1870s they sought education abroad, mainly in the natural sciences. In Switzerland, they not only pursued science but formed circles devoted to the study of socialist thought, to the Russian government's alarm. In May 1873, shortly before they were called home by the government, 104 women were studying in Zurich. The government, choosing to have the women home where they could be more easily policed, finally gave in to the pressure of the women's demand for higher education by approving a special curriculum, the "Bestuzhev courses," which appeared later in the decade.[6] Lenin's sisters Anna and Olga attended the Bestuzhev courses in St. Petersburg, as did his revolutionary co-worker and wife, Nadezhda Krupskaia. One may surmise that the introduction of higher education did little to slow the entry of women into revolutionary activity.

Finally, a number of specialized institutions of higher learning—the Medico-Surgical Academy (St. Petersburg), the Technological Institute (St. Petersburg), the Petrovskii Agricultural Academy (Moscow), and the Mikhailovskii Artillery School (St. Petersburg)—became centers of student activism to an extent quite out of proportion to their size. For example, although the Medico-Surgical Academy had approximately the same num-

---

6 R. Stites, *The Women's Liberation Movement in Russia* (Princeton, N.J., 1978), pp. 82–83.

ber of students as the University of St. Petersburg in the mid- and late 1870s, it contributed more than twice the number of recruits to the populist movement. The Technological Institute, which had considerably fewer students than the university during the same period, provided almost the same number of recruits.[7]

Students who returned to Russia from Zurich in 1874 exhibited an extraordinarily high degree of participation. St. Petersburg, Moscow, and the Ukrainian university cities (Kiev, Khar'kov, and Odessa) together provided more than 90 percent of the advanced students involved in the movements of the 1870s. A. V. Nizovkin, a student who turned informer after being arrested in 1874, on the basis of his experiences in St. Petersburg in the period 1870–1874 divided the student body into several categories according to degrees of activism, concluding that "...the democratic part of the student body is comparatively small compared to the entire mass of St. Petersburg students, which...generally is distinguished by varying degrees of liberalism. ..."[8] Nizovkin found that the students in the lower (first and second) courses were more liberal than those in the upper courses. He identified two groups of democrats, distinguishing them by their methods for carrying out the populist program. The larger group he categorized as followers of Lavrov, while the smaller he labeled Bakuninists.

There is no question but that the young were the driving force behind the intelligentsia movements of the 1870s. The figures gathered by the Third Section provide a very clear picture of the youthful tenor of the movement in the 1870s. The ages of 1,665 participants in the populist movement during the period 1873–1879 were determined and grouped into five-year intervals beginning at age 21. It was found that 87.2 percent of the activists were below the age of 30. The largest single group, comprising 38.4 percent of the total, fell between the ages of 21 and 25. There were a considerable number of youths below the age of 21 in the

7 B. S. Itenberg, *Dvizhenie revoliutsionnogo narodnichestva* (Moscow, 1965), p. 376. One can find here a good breakdown of the numbers by institution.

8 B. S. Itenberg, ed., *Revoliutsionnoe narodnichestvo*, 2 vols. (Moscow, 1964), 1, p. 248.

movement—27.5 percent of the total known.[9] According to contemporary observers, the year 1876 was a low point for the recruitment of activists. Many of the revolutionaries of the period 1876–1881 began their activities between 1870 and 1874.

The problem of determining the social composition of the revolutionary movement during this period is somewhat more complicated. Soviet historians, in keeping with Lenin's periodization, generally minimized the role of the gentry and tended to exaggerate that of the *raznochintsy*. However, it is quite clear that young noblemen and noblewomen were a leading element in the movement, so much so that the decade of the 1870s is thought of as the era of "repentant nobles." Next to the gentry, young men of the clerical estate were the most numerous group. However, the revolutionary movement of this period was not dominated by any estate or any peculiar outlook attributable to an estate. It was a movement of students and teachers, distinguished primarily by their attainment of a high degree of literacy, their youth, and their idealism. In short, it was an intelligentsia movement.

The self-education circles of the period 1869–1874 were the organizational bases for the "Going to the People" of 1874–1876. The most important of these began as a "book circle," ostensibly a book cooperative for students of the Medico-Surgical Academy. Mark Natanson and V. M. Alexandrov, both medical students, were the founders. This circle and its affiliates were a living reproach to Nechaevism. There was no hierarchy, no catechism, no elaborate organization of conspiratorial cells. Members were bound together by common moral and intellectual goals and mutual respect. They demanded of each other moral integrity, intellectual honesty, and personal dedication. A potential recruit or member who displayed signs of vanity or self-indulgence was likely to be judged harshly by the circle. Despite the lack of an elaborate ritual of initiation, recruits were fully aware of the grave consequences of joining. N. A. Charushin, who was recruited in 1871, described in his memoirs his attitude toward joining:

---

9 Itenberg, *Dvizhenie revoliutsionnogo narodnichestva*, p. 377.

> Giving my consent I of course knew that in doing so I left my Rubicon behind, that there could be no retreat and that from now on all my modest energies must inevitably be placed in the service of the circle, and that the fate awaiting me would not be a crown of laurels but prison and exile. Perhaps it would be something far more cruel. But all this hardly disturbed me, since I was already sufficiently prepared for this by my previous course of development. The present political reality did not militate against my earlier conclusions, which I had arrived at quite gradually, but, quite to the contrary, by incessant arrests and exiles, by systematic suppression of the written word, by open mockery of the aspirations of Russian society, and to top it all, by its panicky fear of life itself and of any sort of spontaneous social movement, closed, so it seemed, all paths for legal action and pushed any person who was even barely alive onto the illegal path. The actual transition to this course of action was quite easy.[10]

The young men and women who were drawn into the populist movement by such recruitment proved to be abler, more resourceful, more reliable, and, in a limited sense, more successful than any previous generation of activists.

By the end of 1871 there were twelve men and three women in the "book circle." After Natanson's arrest in November 1871, N. V. Chaikovskii played a leading inspirational role, and the Petersburg organization became known as the Chaikovskii circle. The period 1872–1873 was one of successful recruitment in which twenty-one new members were enrolled. Altogether, about fifty men and women were associated with the Chaikovskii circle in one capacity or another at this time. Furthermore, the *Chaikovtsy* in St. Petersburg had ties with similar groups in the major cities of European Russia. It is no exaggeration to say that this network of self-education and propaganda circles was the framework in which revolutionary *narodnichestvo* developed. Many of the future leaders of Land and Freedom and "The People's Will" (to be discussed below) began their careers in the St. Petersburg circle or one of its affiliates.

---

10 N. A. Charushin, *O dalekom proshlom* (Moscow, 1926), pp. 84–85.

The relatively moderate aims of the *Chaikovtsy* at the outset of the movement are best explained by the peculiar historical environment of the early 1870s. Despite their total commitment to the idea of social justice, the young people were pessimistic about the chances for revolution. Thus, they studied socialist literature, learned about the needs of the masses, converted fellow students, and finally, began to spread propaganda among the masses—in the case of the *Chaikovtsy*, among the factory workers of St. Petersburg.

The other important circle of the period of preparationism was named for its founder and central figure, A. V. Dolgushin. Unlike the Chaikovskii circle, Dolgushin's circle began as a Siberian *zemliachestvo*—one of the many mutual aid societies with a regional basis that existed in Russian institutions of higher education. Dolgushin was an auditor in the Technological Institute at the time that his circle began to form in 1869. They were tangentially involved with Nechaev's conspiracy in the autumn of 1869, and several of them, including Dolgushin, were arrested in January 1870, but they were released for lack of evidence in the autumn of 1871. When the circle revived a year later the members displayed a much more impatient temperament than the *Chaikovtsy*. They immediately began to prepare to spread propaganda among the workers and peasants. Like the *Chaikovtsy*, they turned to Bervi-Flerovskii, who obliged them as well with a proclamation, "About the Martyr Nicholas and How a Man Must Live according to the Law of Truth and Nature." Dolgushin wrote his own proclamation, "To the Russian People," and after the most active members of the circle moved to Moscow and established a printing press, the circle printed another proclamation, "To the Intelligentsia." For the *Dolgushintsy*, knowledge and preparation were secondary to the business of stirring the masses into revolution. The existence of two kinds of circles once again demonstrates that in every revolutionary period there was only relative dominance, not uniformity. Although the term "preparationism" fairly well describes the period 1869–1874 relative to what followed, the Dolgushin circle belonged more clearly to the Bakuninist tradition, and their pilgrimage to the villages in 1873 was an early variant of the Bakuninist strategy of *buntarstvo* (the attempt to ignite the revolutionary instincts of the peasants).

Actually, by 1873 the advocates of preparationism, or Lavrovism, were already on the defensive within the Chaikovskii circle itself. Lavrov's programs, which he modified as he developed a clear idea of the nature of the revolutionary movement, no longer seemed up to the moment. The first issue of *Forward!* disappointed many of the *Chaikovtsy,* while Bakunin's *Statehood and Anarchy,* also printed in Switzerland and smuggled into Russia, was warmly received. Bakunin was less of an active force at this time than his young followers in Switzerland, especially M. P. Sazhin, who led a bitter struggle against the Lavrovist faction in Zurich in 1872 and 1873. Bakunin and Lavrov had little to do with the creation of these factions within the youth, and Lavrov did everything possible to draw closer to Bakunin without abandoning his fundamentally rationalistic outlook. The two middle-aged ideologues were really used by the new generation, just as Bervi-Flerovskii was, rather than the other way around.

Peter Kropotkin, who had witnessed the struggles of the two factions in Zurich, returned to Russia and became the leader of the Bakuninist element in the *Chaikovtsy's* St. Petersburg circle, where they were already on the defensive. Lavrov had left many practical questions unanswered. His opponents took advantage of this by claiming that he demanded an extended period of study on the part of the propagandist. Even after he clarified his strategic position in later issues of *Forward!,* Lavrov and those who purported to be Lavrovists were resented by students who felt compromised by the comfort of their earlier lives and the relative security of academic life. Of the response of a group of young revolutionaries gathering in Kiev, Paul Akselrod wrote:

> In general, it seemed that Lavrovism turned them away from the true revolutionary path, that by its constant reservations it put off revolutionary activity for an indefinite time, while we wanted to give all of our strength immediately. Undoubtedly, Bakunin intoxicated us, especially with his revolutionary phraseology and flaming oratory.[11]

---

11 Paul B. Akselrod, *Perezhitoe i peredumannoe* (Berlin, 1923), 1, p. 111.

The difference between Lavrovism and Bakuninism, preparationism and insurrectionism, can best be explained in psychological terms. Bakuninism could never be much more than an expression of revolutionary optimism, of passion and enthusiasm, and of the young revolutionaries' desire totally to repudiate their past. They placed themselves in a state of complete dependency on the revolutionary instincts of the masses. Lavrovists refused to let the heart dictate to the mind and frequently chose to spread their propaganda among the urban workers, who were more receptive than the peasants. They did not try to repudiate their past or change their manners or modes of dress. Their relative cautiousness and restraint, not to speak of their speech and dress, were seen as defects rather than virtues in the emotional atmosphere of the intelligentsia circles. G. V. Plekhanov's assessment of Lavrovists in the late 1870s probably reflects the attitude which prevailed among the Bakuninists. He described them as

> . . . a rather high-minded group of sectarians, stubbornly and monotonously condemning everything that caused the hearts of the "radicals" of those days to beat faster: student uprisings, strikes, demonstrations of sympathy for political prisoners, mass protests against the administration's arbitrariness, etc.[12]

Curiously enough, Lavrov himself kept on making concessions to the more impatient and passionate elements in the movement, and ended by being estranged from and alienating his own former followers in 1876. This was at least partly a consequence of his desire to unite all revolutionary populists and to diminish the influence of Tkachev, who had set himself up as an opponent of the other revolutionary strategies by propagating "political" methods—meaning a swift seizure of power by a disciplined elite—in his émigré journal, *The Tocsin.* Tkachev believed that failure to act quickly and decisively at the political level would permit Russia's incipient capitalism to develop, and the chance to skip the bourgeois stage and achieve socialism immediately would be lost. Lavrov and Bakunin believed in *social* revolution, which would overthrow the power of the state rather than appro-

---

12 Sh. M. Levin, *Obshchestvennoe dvizhenie v Rossii v 60–70 e gody XIX veka* (Moscow, 1958), pp. 378–79.

priate it. Although Lavrov did not believe that the state could disappear all at once after a social revolution, he protested that the revolution had to occur by and for the people—a conviction shared by Bakunin and his followers. The readiness of the masses for revolution was the real strategic issue between Lavrov and Bakunin. The apoliticism of the Russian socialist movement had been long established; the revolutions of 1848, the regime of Louis Napoleon, and the Paris Commune of 1871 only reinforced it. Fear of the reestablishment of a dictatorial and repressive power made the populists wary of "political" revolutionary strategies. This, plus the unsavoriness of political plots, made Jacobinism the least popular of all revolutionary strategies in Russia, and its adherents during each phase of the Russian movement were a mistrusted and even despised minority.

Although Lavrov's conviction that the masses had to be thoroughly prepared *before* the social revolution in order to insure the development of a stable socialist order seems reasonable from the point of view of ultimate aims, in retrospect it was not a very sound program of revolutionary action. Lavrov's hopeful picture of a considerable army of revolutionary proselytes multiplying at a rapid rate (in 1876 he determined that at the end of six years 100 propagandists from the intelligentsia could gain almost 36,000 converts), the role of the intelligentsia forever diminishing and that of the masses forever increasing, simply did not accord with the realities of the movement. On the other hand, although Tkachev's belief in the inability of the peasant masses to produce a socialist revolution without intelligentsia control was astute, his faith that a revolutionary elite could wield power on behalf of the masses, educate them to socialism, and then relinquish power was not borne out by Russia's subsequent revolutionary history. The populist fear of Jacobinism was well founded. But the populists wanted to bring about the kind of revolution that had never occurred, a social revolution. Such an event would put an end to oppression and exploitation by dissolving the framework for power—the modern state—that might permit injustice to reemerge in some new form. Tkachev, and those in the Jacobin tradition, believed in the necessity of seizing power and concentrating it in the hands of those who clearly understood socialist aims. For him, this kind of revolution was, in any case, the only kind of socialist revolution possible in Russia in the 1870s. Tkachev's respect for power and emphasis upon organization, so repellent to the populists in 1874–1875, was later repeated by Lenin, whose belief in the need for a revolutionary elite to guide the masses resembled Tkachev's. Ironically, dedicated populists themselves were forced to come to grips with the question of power and organization. This was not a consequence of Tkachev's influence, but rather a series of adjustments based upon the experiences of 1874–1876.

It is not clear how and why the self-education and limited propaganda activities of the period 1869–1873 evolved into the famous "Going to the People" of 1874. One gets the impression from the literature that the young intelligentsia of this period created such a successful and satisfying subculture of mutually reinforcing idealists that a compromise with the old society became increasingly difficult. Peter Kropotkin, the future anarchist leader and one of the most active propagandists among the *Chaikovtsy,* captured the spirit of their subculture:

> The two years that I worked with the Circle of Chaikovskii, before I was arrested, left a deep impression upon all my subsequent life and thought. During these two years it was life under high pressure—that exuberance of life when one feels at every moment the full throbbing of all the fibers of the inner self, and when life is really worth living. I was in a family of men and women so closely united by their common object, and so broadly and delicately humane in their mutual relations, that I cannot now recall a single moment of even temporary friction marring the life of our circle. Those who have had any experience of political agitation will appreciate the value of this statement.[13]

In the spring of 1874 life in the universities and the cities no longer seemed possible to these activists. Throughout the school year the populist circles had multiplied in the university cities. Although many of the circles had been depleted by arrests, literally hundreds of young activists remained still at large, feverishly debating the problems of going to the peasants. Indeed, individual reconnoitering had been going on for some time.

---

13 Peter Kropotkin, *Memoirs of a Revolutionist,* ed. James Allen Rogers (Garden City, N.Y., 1962), p. 210.

Every shade of politicism and apoliticism, preparationism and insurrectionism was discussed at these meetings, but always with the peasants' welfare the central issue. How were the young pilgrims to prepare themselves? What were the most useful skills to learn? What kind of clothes, what kind of speech were appropriate? Given the character of the Russian countryside, these questions were of great moment. In a culture that was barely emerging from a system of estates that had been almost a caste system, it was extremely difficult for a person simply to pack up belongings and move from the city into the countryside. Life in the villages was relatively isolated and unchanging. The appearance of a stranger was something of an event. One could not simply walk into a village and expect to be received with open arms. Indeed, as events bore out, being identified as a student could lead to real physical danger. Hadn't a student tried to kill the tsar? Despite all of the difficulties that they knew would face them, students by the hundreds chose to go to the people. The religious character of the movement has been well established. Many young populists felt very much like early Christians. In the last analysis, the evangelical impulse that urged them into the countryside was little governed by rational restraints, and their preliminary discussions were often more in the nature of spiritual preparation than real planning. Ultimately, not only socialist revolutionaries but a large number of students of simpler faith and equally good intentions filled out the ranks. The upper estimate of the total number who participated is 3,000.

Sometimes, in the process of discovering the mentality of Orthodox peasants, the young propagandists rediscovered the appeal of Christianity, and the anticlerical, "scientific" socialism which they had embraced was rendered trivial by comparison. Once again, there was a correlation between the degree of rationalism or Romanticism, or Lavrovism or Bakuninism, and the extent to which a populist was likely to embrace the peasant mentality. Furthermore, in periods of "active religion," especially when young people are involved, conversions from one creed to another are not uncommon. In an atmosphere of new religious dedication and hope, the essential meanings of old religions were rediscovered. Some populists converted to a pacifist religious doctrine founded by a former law student, A. K. Malikov, who had been involved in Ishutin's organization. Malikov made a small number of converts, the most prominent of whom was Chaikovskii. The pacifist mood of the religion of "God-manhood" did not appeal to most populists of this period, but its appearance alarmed and dismayed the activists. More important was the widespread use of Christian symbols and the language of the gospels by populist ideologues and propagandists. Although in many cases these were rhetorical devices, in others they were probably a sign of the religious ambivalence described above. The later popularity of Lev Tolstoy's doctrine of nonresistance to evil among the Russian intelligentsia, including many populists, is thus understandable. The balance between reason and faith, between a commitment to science and a desire to draw near to the masses, was difficult to sustain.

The wandering populists who traveled from village to village in the summer of 1874 carried in their knapsacks propaganda for the peasants that was much more advanced than anything previously written. Twenty-three brochures for the period 1873–1875 have been found. Materials were printed on secret presses in Russia and on émigré presses. Most of this new propaganda was in the form of stories about peasant life written in colloquial language, with a clear message of injustice through exploitation and an exhortation to armed rebellion. The propagandists also taught the peasants revolutionary songs, which sometimes spread through a wide area. Some of the pamphlets and songs of this period were used by later revolutionary generations with even greater success. Although those arrested as propagandists would, under interrogation (and later in their memoirs, for different reasons), emphasize their own naiveté and the lack of receptivity accorded them by peasants, they were often quite competent at concealing their identities and adapting to their circumstances and had at least limited success with the peasants. In some instances, the peasants did listen sympathetically and tried to protect them.[14] On the whole, however, the propagandists of the period 1874–1875 were frustrated in their efforts to turn the peasants into socialist revolutionaries. The peasants

---

14 Dan Field, "Peasants and Propagandists in the Russian Movement to the People of 1874," *The Journal of Modern History* 59 (1987): 423.

had a very vivid memory of the force employed by the government in crushing past peasant uprisings, and even those who sympathized with the aims of the populists had no confidence that their own people had sufficient mettle to carry through a large-scale revolt. Many of the peasants could not grasp the idea of a system of government without a higher authority, and could not imagine how a vast area like Russia could be ruled by the people. Some revealed a shockingly exploitative mentality during discussions of the disposition of the land after the revolution, and the populists themselves noticed that the villages were already infected with the inequalities and exploitativeness of bourgeois society. Those propagandists who were actually able to read their pamphlets and stories to the peasants in respectful but unreceptive gatherings were successful compared to many who were expelled from the villages, beaten, and turned over to the local authorities.

Ultimately, the greatest obstacle between the propagandists and the peasants was the latter's image of a benevolent tsar who intended to give the land to the peasants but was prevented from so doing by the landlords. The peasants had their own interpretation of the Emancipation of 1861. It had confirmed their belief that, eventually, the tsar would give them the land that they needed. Thus, however astute the populists were at communicating with the peasants, they were never able to change entrenched ideas, a precondition necessary for a revolutionary socialist program.

Some of the most dedicated populists severed all ties with their former lives, even losing contact with their comrades, and lived as hired laborers in the villages. They worked as joiners, smiths, cobblers, and, at least in one case, as a *burlak* hauling barges along the Volga. In order to understand the extent of the sacrifice of this young *dvorianin,* D. M. Rogachev, one has only to look at Repin's famous painting of the Volga barge haulers. Before venturing into the countryside, the same Rogachev had worked as a stoker in the Putilov metal works in St. Petersburg. He traveled through the Volga region, searching for a peasant leader who might become a new Stenka Razin or Pugachev, without success.[15]

---

15 Razin was the Cossack leader of a vast peasant rebellion in the Volga region (1667–1671).

The traditionally violent areas of Russia, the Ukraine and the Volga basin, attracted large numbers of insurrectionaries. The middle region of the Volga, embracing seven provinces, was especially attractive, for there the peasant leaders of the seventeenth and eighteenth centuries had found their greatest support. Furthermore, in 1873–1874 a great famine struck one of the seven middle-Volga provinces, Samara. The Samara famine evoked both anger and hope among the populists, who saw it as a possible jumping off point for a peasant uprising. However, on the whole the propagandists in the Volga region were no more successful than those in other regions. At best, they created sympathy for themselves and a frail, but nonetheless definite infrastructure for the neopopulist resurgence at the turn of the twentieth century. Recent studies of the activities of revolutionary populists in Saratov province on the Volga, for example, show the extent to which they sank roots in certain areas.[16]

Even while engaging in a variety of attempts to organize the movement and to disseminate propaganda more efficiently, the young revolutionaries had to admit to themselves that they had been mistaken about the revolutionary potentialities of the masses. The insurrectionists no less than the preparationists were forced into propaganda activities that rarely bore fruit. Thus, the populists throughout the entire period of revolutionary populism remained a relatively isolated and vulnerable group in the countryside. The large number of arrests made during the period of the Going to the People is a clear symptom of their failure. If the estimate of the number of active participants in the movement of 1874–1876 is put at about 2,500, then the authorities were quite successful in discovering them, for more than 1,600 arrests were made between the middle of 1873 and the end of 1876. Most of the arrests were made during the "mad summer" of 1874 and the autumn of the same year. Despite its continuation during 1875, the spontaneous movement of the intel-

---

16 For some excellent scholarship on the movement in Saratov, see Rex A. Wade and Scott J. Seregny, eds., *Politics and Society in Provincial Russia: Saratov, 1590–1917* (Columbus, Ohio, 1989). The chapter most relevant for this period is Pamela Sears McKinsey's "Populists, Workers, Peasants, and the Beginning of Worker Organization in Saratov," 49–72.

ligentsia into the countryside had failed as a revolutionary strategy, whether the individuals or groups considered themselves to be propagandists or insurrectionists, and whether they practiced "flying" propaganda (conducted quickly, from place to place) or "settled" propaganda and agitation in the villages.

The question of organization became imperative as the young populists experienced all of the difficulties associated with the maintenance of an active movement. They had created a tenuous network of way stations on the most traveled routes into the areas of European Russia where most propagandists and agitators were concentrated. Sympathetic landowners, relatives, and the provincial intelligentsia, although not active participants in the movement, often lent material support. Some of the activists in the university cities maintained apartments that became meeting places and communication centers. Nonetheless, it was a very loose kind of communication, and propagandists often found themselves without books, brochures, or the means to carry on their work. Thus, despite their antipathy for anything that remotely resembled Nechaevism, the populists were forced to reconsider their ideas about organization. They were encouraged in this by Lavrov's *Forward!*, which called for the formation of a unified and secret party of both intelligentsia and working-class elements.

In this respect, some early progress had been made in the cities, where several groups concentrated their efforts among the growing urban proletariat. As noted earlier, both the Sunday school movement of the 1860s and a group within the Chaikovskii circle had pioneered intelligentsia–working-class contacts. The workers' interest in education facilitated the propagandists' work, much of which was still in the nature of "enlightenment" tasks, carried on primarily by Lavrov's followers. The first significant organization that went beyond reading and discussion circles was E. O. Zaslavskii's "South Russian Workers' Union" (1874–1875), which began as an educational and cultural association, with its own legal printing press, a cooperative bathhouse, a fund, and a library. The workers of two large factories in the Black Sea port of Odessa were the nucleus of the organization, which expanded to include other workers in Odessa. Although Zaslavskii was a Lavrovist and distributed *Forward!* among the workers, during the course of 1875 they were also exposed to *The*

Worker, a Bakuninist journal published by Z. K. Ralli, N. I. Zhukovskii, and A. L. Elsnits in Geneva. Both *Forward!* and *The Worker* tried to inspire in the Russian working classes a sense of solidarity with the international workers' movement and contained information about the strategies of workers in other nations as well as exposés of capitalist exploitation. The *ustav,* or rules of the Union, expressed in no uncertain terms the idea of the struggle against capitalism. During the course of 1875, this idea was carried over into action, and the Union became involved in strikes. Although the growth of Russian industry during the 1860s and 1870s had been accompanied by strikes, in this instance the strike movement was directly associated with an intelligentsia-inspired organization. The South Russian Union, with a leading cadre of about fifty members, was crushed by the authorities in late 1875 and 1876.

Simultaneously with the appearance of the South Russian Workers' Union in Odessa, another organization with a grander set of objectives took shape in Moscow. "The Pan-Russian Social-Revolutionary Union" was formed by a group of students who had returned from Zurich in 1874. They were also known as the "Muscovites," because Moscow was the base of their activities. The Muscovites were somewhat unusual, in that a large number, perhaps the majority of the organization, were women. The leading members were called the Fritschi, after the name of their boardinghouse in Zurich. Vividly illustrating the quest of aristocratic young women for both science and social justice, the Fritschi were high-minded and self-disciplined to the point of asceticism. Among them were Vera Figner and Sofia Bardina, later to become revolutionary luminaries. The other element that went into the formation of the Muscovites was a group of Caucasian students whom the women had met in Switzerland. In the autumn of 1874 the organization began to take shape in Russia. Arrests were decimating the ranks of the populists. Still, resistance to centralization of the revolutionary movement and to any kind of hierarchy was strong, and the statutes of the Pan-Russian Social-Revolutionary Union reflected the continuing fear that the movement would degenerate into Nechaevism. The contradictory lessons of the conspiracies of the 1860s and the spontaneous intelligentsia movement of 1874 forced a rather unsatisfactory compromise upon the Muscovites. They established a central administration *(upravlenie),* at first composed of three members, which was to conduct the day-to-day business of the organization. For this purpose, the members were to be freed from their ordinary duties for a period of one month, after which a new administration would be appointed. The workers who were enrolled in the organization shared administrative duties with the intelligentsia members. Most of the members of the circle worked in the industrial centers of European Russia—Moscow, Tula, Ivanov-Voznesensk, and Kiev—in the Ukraine. Although they did establish contact with other populists, nothing emerged resembling an effective and coordinated union of the dimensions suggested by the title of the organization.

Spiritually, the Pan-Russian Social-Revolutionary Union was Bakuninist and affiliated with the group that published *The Worker.* The Union members concentrated their efforts on textile workers, who were more traditionalistic and closer to a peasant mentality than the metal workers. The populist image of the workers as peasants in an urban setting was true for a significant percentage of the labor force, since many of them returned to the villages after a brief sojourn in the cities. The populists believed that the urban peasants could be a link between them and the villagers. However, the Pan-Russian Social-Revolutionary Union never was more than a rather small group of activists whose several working-class members were no less vulnerable and detectable than the populists themselves were. Life in the factories, like life in the villages, was too monotonous and well regulated for any unusual person or activity to pass unnoticed. The populists' efforts among urban factory workers proved to be no more fruitful than those among the peasants. The first arrests of members of the Pan-Russian Union began in April 1875, and further arrests in August and September destroyed it. Its stable membership had never been much more than twenty.

Thus, the year 1875 marked a low point in the movement. The "failures" in the villages had been followed by failures in the factories. None of the organizational problems had been successfully resolved. The prospects for social revolution were bleak, even to the most sanguine populists. Those who wanted to carry on the struggle were forced farther in the direction of "political" aims and centralized organization. Given the fundamental assumptions of populism, the turn to political strategies was an admission that social revolution could not be achieved directly. In view of the number of arrests in 1874 and 1875, and the considerable decline in the number of new recruits noted earlier, the period 1876–1881 can be viewed as a phase in which the remnants of the earlier movement regrouped and formulated new tactics based upon a new perception of what was possible in both the countryside and in the cities. The bitter experiences of the Going to the People only hardened the determination of the activists, many of whom had sold their property and converted it into liquid assets for use in the revolutionary organizations. There was no turning back for them. These remnants formed the first potent organization of professional revolutionaries in the history of the Russian revolutionary movement. A combination of circumstances and their own impatience induced them to concentrate upon the destruction of the Russian government by striking the first blow themselves.

FAILURE IN SUCCESS

In Russian history the period 1878–1882 in many ways resembled the period of crisis that had occurred after the Crimean War. Although the Russian government did not suffer a decisive military defeat in the Turkish war of 1877–1878, the cost inflicted by the war and the diplomatic defeat suffered in Berlin generated an atmosphere of crisis. During this period too, the internal opponents of autocracy acquired public platforms, partly because of the government's clumsiness in handling the mass trials of the populists who had been arrested during the Going to the People. The return of peasant recruits from the war, rumors about the partition of the land, the growth of the strike movement and labor organization, the revival of militant liberalism in this climate of unrest, and the final gathering together of the remaining forces of revolutionary populism for a blow against the old order led a leading Soviet historian to describe the period beginning in the spring of 1878 and ending in the summer of 1882 as a "crisis of the autocracy."[17] The extraordinary measures that the government was forced to take against oppositional movements in this period and signs that it might yield concessions to the liberals in view of the threat from the left are seen as clear symptoms of this crisis. For a brief time it seemed as though the liberals would be the beneficiaries of the turmoil.

However, parallel to the crisis of the autocracy one can speak of a crisis of revolutionary populism. The ideologies of the movement had been subordinated to tactical problems to such an extent that positions that had been anathema to the populists in the earlier phases of the movement were reluctantly accepted. At the moment when they achieved their greatest power as an organized oppositional force, the populists were furthest from their own ideological bases. Their willingness to moderate their demands and to accept political change as a progressive step is another symptom of their pessimism about the possibilities of social revolution. However, their decision to strike at the pinnacle of political power in Russia—the tsar himself—ultimately worked to the detriment of all oppositional groups. Rather than extending the government's crisis, the assassination of the tsar by the populists brought it swiftly to a head and permitted the forces of reaction to get a firm grip on the government. This failure was all the more tragic for the months of struggle, planning, and self-sacrifice that were poured into it.

The regrouping of the revolutionary forces was at first complicated by events that preceded the Turkish war. Some activists were temporarily diverted from the struggle in Russia by the revolt of Bosnia and Herzogovina in 1875, despite Lavrov's warning that they were wasting their energies in a cause that would only transfer the Slav peoples in the Balkans from one exploitative power to another. Others had to be enticed from studies abroad or from absorption in the day-to-day struggle against poverty, ignorance, and disease in the Russian villages. However, there were several extraordinarily talented organizers in the movement who were equal to the task.

---

17 P. A. Zaionchkovskii, *Krizis samoderzhaviia na rubezhe 1870–1880-kh godov* (Moscow, 1964).

The revolutionaries were aided in 1876 and 1877 by the government's false confidence that it had crushed the movement. Actually, there was some basis for this optimism. Of the more than 2,000 who had gone into the countryside, most had returned to their studies chastened by their bitter experiences. More than 200 were still incarcerated, awaiting trial. What seems remarkable in retrospect is that many of the young people who had been arrested between 1873 and 1875 were released—but not before experiencing the brutality of Russian prisons and seeing their comrades go mad or die from maltreatment, malnutrition, and disease. Some of those who were released emerged much more determined and hardened than they had been. Indeed, several of the defendants in the famous Trial of the 50 (March 1877) and Trial of the 193 (October 1877 to January 1878) later joined the revolutionary organizations. Such easy movement was possible because they had been confined to residence rather than imprisoned, or simply acquitted. A combination of judicial clemency, lax police surveillance, and escape artistry resulted in the liberation of numerous political prisoners who were recruited into the second "Land and Freedom."

From the moment of its inception in 1876, the new Land and Freedom displayed the contradiction that eventually split it into two separate groups in 1879. The *narodniki* still refused to abandon the idea of a fusion with the masses, and, as if to test the limits of the *narodnik* creed, deemphasized even further the programmatic contribution of the intelligentsia to the liberation movement. Indeed, this is the point in the revolutionary movement when the terms "*narodnik*" and "*narodnichestvo*" were first used to describe the putative subordination of the intelligentsia to the masses and their immediate needs. The traditional Bakuninist commitment to the idea of immediate social revolution was undiminished, but a new belief that the *obshchina*, the basis for native Russian socialism, was being eroded made active struggle seem all the more urgent. At first reluctantly, the *narodniki* began to assume new roles which had no real foundation in the ideologies of the earlier phases of the movement and which seemingly contradicted them.

The vague form of anarchism adopted by Land and Freedom in 1876 as its platform was in itself of little significance. It was a

Bakuninist program, reducing the autonomy and guiding role of the intelligentsia to a bare minimum. Deeds were considered to be more important than words. Unlike the earlier propagandists and agitators, those who went to the people in the spring of 1877 did not come with propaganda leaflets and brochures. They came to join the people, to live with them, and to help the *narod* achieve *their* immediate goals. The *narodniki* were also called *derevenshchiki,* which is best translated as "villagers," signifying the revolutionaries' total integration into the life of the villages. The *narodniki* no longer wanted to teach the peasants about socialism or to place before them long-term socialist goals. In some cases, they completely abandoned any attempt to arouse the peasants by the usual means and made a direct appeal to the peasants' faith in the tsar.

A logical outcome of the new attitude was the famous Chigirin episode of 1877, in which the old peasant belief that the tsar wanted to give them land but was prevented by the nobles from communicating with them, was cleverly exploited by Ia. V. Stefanovich, who was a member of an extremely resourceful and active intelligentsia group called the "Kiev Commune." Stefanovich learned about the discontent of a group of peasants in the area around Chigirin, not far from the city of Kiev. He and his comrades, L. G. Deich and A. N. Bokhanovskii, took advantage of the myth begun by a local peasant who had tried unsuccessfully in 1875 to petition the tsar and, upon his return home, had told the peasants that the tsar wanted them to take the land by force and divide it up among themselves. The large-scale resistance to authority that ensued led to numerous arrests, but the movement was still alive when Stefanovich intervened in 1876. He and Deich made up some fake documents, to which they affixed the tsar's "signature" and gold seals. The documents not only confirmed the myth about the tsar's being a captive of the gentry, but urged the peasants to organize themselves into secret armed bands of twenty-five. In less than a year hundreds of peasants had joined the organization, but it was discovered by the authorities in the autumn of 1877 and destroyed before any revolutionary action had taken place. The Chigirin "Fighting Brotherhood" *(Druzhina)* was the largest nonintelligentsia revolutionary organization of the 1870s, but its very nature attested to the populists' failure.

Although Stefanovich was not a member of Land and Freedom, and although his tactics were officially repudiated by the organization, they were not without appeal to some members. Continuing frustration in the countryside during 1877 and 1878 forced more and more *narodniki* to search for new modes of revolutionary expression.

The really significant aspects of Land and Freedom were its concern for its own internal organization on the one hand and for the "disorganization" of the forces of reaction on the other. Furthermore, organizers and "disorganizers" of Land and Freedom displayed a degree of resourcefulness without precedent in the history of the Russian revolutionary movement. For the first time, the revolutionaries attempted a systematic division of labor among several groups engaged in quite distinct tasks: one group worked at theoretical and programmatic questions, another edited the organization's publications, a third worked in Land and Freedom's clandestine printing operations, a fourth carried on in the villages and factories. Another group specialized in "disorganizing," which began as self-defense but later involved the execution of spies and traitors and the assassination of especially obnoxious officials. In addition, the organization developed its own security measures to a finer point by mastering techniques of secret communication, and by a modest venture in counterespionage. A. I. Zundelevich was an expert smuggler. One member, N. V. Kletochnikov, provided conspirators with an early warning system. He had the good fortune to gain the position of clerk in the Investigations Department of the Secret Police, a division of the Third Section. When the young revolutionaries began to concentrate on the disorganization of the state, specialists in explosives appeared, and they learned to manufacture their own dynamite. A talented young chemist, N. I. Kibalchich, was in charge of the laboratory.

Mark Natanson provided the initial organizational effort in creating Land and Freedom, and Alexander D. Mikhailov showed considerable genius in directing the operations of this group (he would also guide "The People's Will"). Creating a platform and rules of organization acceptable to the kind of people who were involved in the Going to the People was no mean accomplishment. There was, for example, a split between northerners and southerners, the former more cautious and concerned with rational planning, and the latter tending toward extremism and spontaneity in revolutionary action. There was the persistent and powerful bias against permanent ruling bodies, the subordination of individuals to an organization, and elaborate structures within the organization. However, outweighing these factors was the sense of urgency noted above, and a new militant spirit that included and transcended the moral passion that had inspired the *Chaikovtsy*. The bitter experiences of 1873–1878 developed in many the mentality of a suicide squad. They now saw themselves as an instrument of the masses. Strict subordination to party organization and the use of terror were ultimate acts of self-sacrifice for the *narod*. One should not lose sight of the deep personal loyalties that moved some of the young revolutionaries to act as avengers for their lost comrades. But this motive only reinforced the tendency toward depersonalization and the conversion of highly individualistic young men and women into instruments of the party. It is possible to mistake the new tendency for a fanatical kind of self-assertion. However, the exercise of power, especially the power of life and death over other human beings, was antithetical to the ideology and purposes of the young anarchists who formed the new organizations. The kinds of acts which they engaged in were acts of annihilation or extermination (*istreblenie*), and they were quite willing to use up their own lives in the process of destroying the obstacles to human liberation.

As was so often the case in the revolutionary movement, disorganizing activities appeared in practice before they were formally incorporated into the statutes of the new organizations. Escapes from prison and exile had a long history, and some of them, such as Peter Kropotkin's, were almost theatrical in planning and execution. The first instance of self-defense in the movement occurred in August 1875 when A. K. Tsitsianov, a Georgian prince and member of the Pan-Russian Social-Revolutionary Union, fired two pistol shots at the gendarme who came to arrest him. In June 1876 a group of Bakuninists, who had established a promising base of operations at Korsun in the Ukraine, unsuccessfully tried to assassinate a worker who had turned informer.

The era of assassinations was not launched properly until a young woman named Vera Zasulich shot at F. F. Trepov, the governor of St. Petersburg, in January 1878. Zasulich, an unhappy young woman from an impoverished gentry family, found the revolutionary calling a far more attractive option than the career of governess her family had planned for her. Her older sister had connections with the Ishutin circle, and during her teens she, too, became connected with the revolutionary underground. In St. Petersburg in 1868 she worked for a brief period in communes of the sort inspired by Chernyshevskii. In January 1869 Nechaev tried to recruit her into his organization. Arrested in April 1869 for her connection with the Nechaev conspiracy, Zasulich spent almost two years in prison, followed by internal exile, from which she was released in 1875. She promptly joined the revolutionary underground in Kiev. Although she moved back to St. Petersburg in 1877, Zasulich maintained her southern connections and through them became involved in the attempt on General Trepov. The southern branch of Land and Freedom decided to assassinate Trepov to avenge the flogging of a comrade, A. S. Emel'ianov.[18] The latter, who had used the pseudonym A. P. Bogoliubov, was a member of Land and Freedom. He had been arrested in December 1876 during a demonstration in St. Petersburg. Trepov had ordered the flogging in July 1877 for Emel'ianov's insubordinate behavior during a prison inspection. The disorganizing section of Land and Freedom was informed of Trepov's brutality, and V. I. Osinskii, the foremost advocate of disorganization, planned to assassinate Trepov after the Trial of the 193. Zasulich decided to take things into her own hands and on January 24, 1878, shot Trepov in his office in St. Petersburg. Her trial in March 1878 (Trepov did not die from the wound) ended in acquittal. Both the verdict and its popularity revealed more than moral outrage in St. Petersburg society against Trepov's behavior and the liberal qualities of Russia's reformed legal profession. They reflected the resurgence of the liberal opposition in the empire. There was disaffection within the sen-

18 Jay Bergman, *Vera Zasulich, a Biography* (Stanford, Calif., 1983), pp. 1–21.

ate itself. Zasulich's trial, following the moving mass trials of her comrades, galvanized the liberal opposition and gave the revolutionaries a new sense of righteousness. Both the revolutionaries and their liberal defenders turned the tables, putting the regime on trial by using the prisoner's dock as a rostrum to expose abuses of authority. I. S. Turgenev, the celebrated writer, wrote a prose poem in May 1878 entitled "The Threshold" portraying the virtuous woman terrorist. Whatever its value as a portrayal of the psychology and morality of those who made the commitment to terrorism, Turgenev's poem probably captured the sympathetic attitude of the liberal wing of the intelligentsia.

> I see a huge building. The front door is wide open: behind the door—deep gloom. A girl stands before a high threshold . . . a Russian girl. The impenetrable gloom chills the air; and together with an icy breath a solemn, hollow voice issues from the depths of the building.
>
> —"O you, who wish to cross this threshold, do you know what awaits you?"
>
> —"I know," the girl answers.
>
> —"Cold, hunger, hatred, ridicule, contempt, humiliation, imprisonment, disease, and death itself."
>
> —"I know."
>
> —"Total alienation, loneliness."
>
> —"I know, I'm ready. I'll endure all sufferings, all blows."
>
> —"Not only from enemies—but from kin, from friends?"
>
> —"Yes, from them, too."
>
> —"Very well. Are you ready to sacrifice yourself?"
>
> —"Yes."
>
> —"To be a nameless victim? You will perish and no one—no one will even know whose memory to honor!"
>
> —"I need neither thanks nor pity. I don't need to have a name."
>
> —"Are you prepared to commit crimes?"
>
> The girl bowed her head . . .
>
> —"I am even prepared to commit crimes."
>
> The voice did not immediately continue its questioning.
>
> —"Do you know—it said at last—that you might lose faith in your present beliefs, you might realize that you deceived yourself and sacrificed your young life in vain?"
>
> —"I know this, too. And yet I want to enter."
>
> —"Enter!"

> The girl strode across the threshold—and a heavy curtain closed behind her.
> —"Fool!"—hissed someone.
> —"Saint!"—came from somewhere, in reply.[19]

Henceforth both self-defense and assassination were carried out in a confident spirit of righteous retribution. During the course of 1878 and 1879 Land and Freedom attempted several assassinations, with some notable successes, including Sergei Kravchinskii's "execution" of General N. V. Mezentsev, chief of the Third Section, in August 1878.

Although the leaders of Land and Freedom had not intended to redirect the revolutionary movement from the countryside to the cities, there was a very visible shift in this direction after 1876. The publication of the party's organ, *Land and Freedom*, and occasional leaflets; the organization of demonstrations, such as the manifestation in December 1876 on Kazan Square in St. Petersburg; propaganda and agitation in the factories; assassinations carried out in Kiev, Odessa, and St. Petersburg—all of these kinds of activity encouraged a reverse migration from the villages into the cities. The "villagers," many of them already well-adapted to their role, left reluctantly, some only after the terrorist campaign gained momentum. Several who escaped arrest in the cities returned to the countryside.[20]

By 1878 Land and Freedom had become a recognized force in Russian society. The government no longer could ignore the existence of a group that had identified itself as "The Executive Committee of the Russian Social-Revolutionary Party." The latter title was the invention of Osinskii, who liked to do things with éclat. Actually, a large red banner carrying the slogan "Land and Freedom" had been unfurled during the demonstration on Kazan Square, but to the government the real focus of activity seemed to be the cities of the Ukraine, where Osinskii, G. A. Popko, M. F. Frolenko, and their fellow disorganizers carried out their executions. The government enacted several measures transferring powers ordinarily exercised by civil courts to the

19 I. S. Turgenev, *Sobranie sochinenii v desiati tomakh*, 10 vols. (Moscow, 1962), 10, pp. 24–25. The translation is mine.
20 D. Hardy, *Land and Freedom* (Westport, Conn., 1987), pp. 132ff.

police and military tribunals in order to deal with political criminals. In August 1878 the government appealed to the entire nation to join them in the struggle against the revolutionaries.

This sign of evident weakness encouraged left-leaning liberals to try to effect an alliance with the revolutionaries for the purpose of forcing a constitution upon Alexander. Nicholas Mikhailovskii was the liaison between the liberals and the revolutionaries because of his "political" orientation. The primary vehicle of Russian left liberals at this time was the *zemstvo,* which they hoped to transform into a popular, constitutional government at a national level. I. I. Petrunkevich, radical spokesman of the Chernigov *zemstvo,* entered into negotiations with Osinskii's group in December 1878 in the hope that a rational strategy of opposition could be worked out. However, his suggestion that terror be suspended was rejected, and the coalition between the *narodniki* and left liberals never materialized. This early venture was a foreshadowing of the strategy of coalition adopted by left liberals more successfully in 1904. In neither case, however, were terrorist groups willing to relinquish a weapon whose use seemed to them to be both morally and practically imperative. More and more members of Land and Freedom became convinced of the efficacy of political assassinations. In any case, the *zemstvo* movement was too weak to matter, and nothing concrete was lost by the rejection of the alliance. Petrunkevich was arrested in 1879 for his public opposition to the government.

Finally, in the period 1878–1879 the Russian government was faced by labor unrest of greater dimensions than that of previous years. There were twice as many labor disturbances in 1879 (fifty-four) as in 1876 (twenty-seven). More than 16,000 workers participated in eight strikes in 1879. The relationship of Land and Freedom to the labor movement was, in most respects, an extension of the contacts begun by the *Chaikovtsy* and continued by the Lavrovist circle in St. Petersburg. The party was still in embryonic form when several members who had been active among St. Petersburg factory workers decided to organize a joint intelligentsia-workers demonstration on Kazan Square. The demonstration was in most respects a failure. Less than 200 workers turned out on December 6, 1876, far fewer than the 2,000 that had been anticipated by the revolutionaries. The Kazan demonstration is more notable for the appearance of a new and talented leader within the intelligentsia, G. V. Plekhanov, than as a herald of an emerging alliance. When a spontaneous strike movement developed in the textile industry in St. Petersburg in 1878, Plekhanov and other members of Land and Freedom extended aid and advice to the strikers. However, a less spontaneous, more conscious and organized movement was simultaneously growing among the metal workers of the capital. The leaders of this movement had had their first contacts with student propagandists in the early 1870s and had absorbed Western socialist ideals. The ideas expressed in the program of the new workers' organization, "The Northern Union of Russian Workers" (1878–1879) revealed that traditional Russian attitudes and populist goals for the *obshchina* existed alongside those of the Western "social-democratic party." Several references were made in the Union's program to Christ, but none to any more recent socialist authority. Land and Freedom was not altogether pleased with the new organization's eclectic program, its political orientation, and its vagueness about "the active struggle." In replying to these and other objections, which appeared in the fourth issue of *Land and Freedom,* the workers displayed a rather mature spirit of rebellion against intelligentsia guardianship of their movement. The Northern Union of Russian Workers enrolled approximately 200 members and printed a leaflet of its own, *The Workers' Dawn,* before the police closed in. The need for political freedom asserted by the workers added one more stimulus to the increasingly political-minded element in Land and Freedom.

The final ingredient that went into the revolutionary ferment (there was an increase in peasant disturbances in 1878–1879, but they did not constitute as great a threat as those in the period after the Crimean War) was the student movement. This movement, no less than other expressions of a revived public opposition, was closely associated with the government's mishandling of the mass trials and of the Zasulich affair. The movement was suppressed with the use of troops, and hundreds of students were expelled and sent into exile.

Thus, the year 1878 was a psychological moment of profound significance for both the revolutionaries and the government.

The revolutionaries, though pessimistic about the chances for social revolution, began to believe in the vulnerability of the government. They perceived wide sympathy for themselves in the educated public, and despite crude tactics the government was unable to convince them that they were despised by the Russian people. Furthermore, it was widely believed in Europe that a Russian revolution was imminent. The Russian government, understandably alarmed, chose the course of repression in 1878 and 1879. The strengthening of the police yielded results, but by that time the revolutionary party was too extended and well organized to be destroyed quickly. The events of the years 1879–1881 in retrospect appear as a tragic series of vendettas, the consequence of the powerful commitment that many of the revolutionaries had made to terror and the government's equally powerful commitment to repression. One can safely say that the point of no return was reached by the spring of 1879.

On April 2, 1879, Alexander Solov'ev fired several pistol shots at Tsar Alexander in front of the Winter Palace. Alexander escaped unharmed. Solov'ev, in some ways repeating Karakozov's venture (he also shared his fate), acted without the full support of his party, but was encouraged by individuals and supplied with a pistol. The immediate effect of his attempt was, on the one hand, the division of Russia into six districts ruled by military viceroys, and on the other, a crisis in Land and Freedom. Arrests and the execution of several members of the party, including Osinskii, brought the crisis to a head. The growing split within the party over the use of terror had to be resolved.

The terrorist faction of the party organized a preliminary conference at Lipetsk in the province of Voronezh. Delegates to the conference began to arrive during the second week of June 1879. On June 18, an Executive Committee was formed, and the designation reflected the delegates' decision to carry on the work of Osinskii, who had invented the title for his southern terrorist organization. The delegates accepted the new emphasis upon centralization, discipline, and secrecy. Mikhailov and Frolenko were the leaders of the Lipetsk group, but Alexander Zheliabov, a man of peasant origins, began to show the qualities of leadership that would thrust him into the central role in the effort to assassinate the tsar. The Lipetsk meeting finally united in a single party the organizational meticulousness of the northerners and the somewhat picaresque daring of the southerners. At the time, it was not clear that the Lipetsk group were a distinct party. Indeed, they had called a preliminary meeting in order to prosecute their cause better against the other delegates to the conference in Voronezh that followed their own.

The Voronezh congress failed to define the relative importance of the political struggle and political goals (namely, the creation of a constitution) to the work in the villages and the preparation for a social revolution. A temporary compromise was worked out between "political terrorists" and "villagers." Thirteen of the nineteen delegates at Voronezh supported the terrorists. The first clear sign of the dissolution of Land and Freedom appeared when Plekhanov, an opponent of terror, left Voronezh and quit the party. In the weeks that followed, the Voronezh compromise collapsed. Two distinct parties emerged in the autumn of 1879. The minority party, led by Plekhanov, took the title "Black Repartition," signifying its continuing dedication to the peasants' immediate needs and aspirations. It became an émigré party and quickly lost its influence in Russia. Indeed, the leaders of Black Repartition were not even able to establish their influence abroad, once the exploits of the terrorists of the other party, The People's Will, began to excite the imagination of European and Russian émigré socialists. Lavrov, who was a free agent after resigning the editorship of *Forward!* in 1876, eventually allied himself with The People's Will. This peculiar situation illustrates the complexity and dynamism of the Russian revolutionary movement. The Black Repartition, a party based upon Bakuninism, had become a relatively conservative party, in that it did not stand for an *immediate* engagement with the old order. The People's Will, which had interposed an intermediate phase between the present and the socialist future—the phase of political struggle and constitutionalism—had assumed the character of a revolutionary vanguard by striking immediate blows against the Russian government. In short, not the consistent Bakuninism of The Black Repartition but the eclectic program of The People's Will became the latest word in revolutionary optimism. For this reason, however far its program deviated from orthodox *narodnichestvo,* The People's Will was able to attract hundreds of allies in the younger generation and to hasten the flow of revolutionary recruits, which had waned after 1875.

However, the central organization, the Executive Committee of The People's Will, consisted of revolutionary veterans, most of them over twenty-five years old, and some of them older than thirty in 1880–1881. They were professional revolutionaries supported by their own funds and by the contributions of sympathizers. From its inception until the assassination of Alexander II in March 1881, the Executive Committee was served by thirty-one members of the party, men and women of diverse ethnic backgrounds and from every stratum of Russian society. Most of them were "illegals," those with a record of arrests for revolutionary activity and a history of escapes from police supervision.

The story of The People's Will, with its numerous substructures, organs, affiliates, and connections could easily fill a separate volume. Land and Freedom, whose membership during the years 1876–1879 had probably exceeded 200, was a rather pale and unadvertised venture by comparison with the flamboyant and heroic People's Will. Not unnaturally, the history of The People's Will as usually recounted is little more than the saga of the assassins of Alexander II. However, The People's Will involved several hundred collaborators who desperately tried to sustain the party and resurrect the Executive Committee after the collapse of 1881–1882. They kept alive the revolutionary tradition and helped to raise the next revolutionary generation, even though they were not always able to inculcate *narodnik* ideals in them. The perpetuation of the revolutionary tradition and of the technique of secret organization was possibly a more substantial contribution than the Executive Committee's heroic activities. Yet it was precisely the exploits of the Executive Committee that made recruitment possible. The Executive Committee's heroic posture and the deceptions that were built into the organization created the impression that The People's Will was a vast and powerful organization capable of overthrowing the autocracy. Although such methods facilitated recruitment into the party, they could not change the fact that, no less than Land and Freedom, the new party was a vulnerable and tenuous web of conspirators, continually threatened by the secret police. Despite the large number of organizations (estimated at 300 by Soviet scholars), their wide distribution (seventy cities and towns in the Empire), and the sizable number of members (the lowest estimate is 500 on the eve of the assassination of Alexander II) and sympathizers (the upper estimate is 5,000), in many cases the "organization" must have been nominal, consisting of a contact or two. The activities of both The People's Will and Black Repartition among the several strategic groups that they believed would help them to bring about the revolution yielded some results, since the workers' and students' movements that had begun in 1878 were still in progress. But later events demontrated that there was not a revolutionary front sufficiently strong to support the revolutionaries in the critical period after the tsar's assassination.

The real struggle between the government and the revolutionary movement occurred during the period 1880–1882, and it was largely a contest between the Executive Committee and Count M. T. Loris-Melikov. There was at first almost a complete lack of faith in the government's ability to survive. In November 1880 the Executive Committee mined the rails of the Moscow-Kursk line but failed to blow up the tsar's carriage. Meanwhile, they had infiltrated the Winter Palace itself. Stepan Khalturin, an organizer of the defunct Northern Union of Russian Workers who had reluctantly accepted the idea of terror, obtained a job as carpenter in the Palace. Over the course of several months, he accumulated 100 pounds of dynamite in his trunk in the basement of the Palace. On February 5, 1880, he set off a huge blast, in the belief that it would destroy the Palace's dining room at the tsar's dinner hour. The tsar was not injured, but eleven persons were killed and more than fifty injured in the explosion.

After this episode, Count Loris-Melikov became a virtual dictator. He launched a two-pronged attack designed to crush the revolutionary organizations and at the same time to restore the popularity of the government by concessions. During the period of his "dictatorship of the heart" (February 1880 to March 1881), Loris-Melikov, who ruled Russia first as president of the Supreme Commission created by Alexander II in 1880 to cope with the revolutionary movement, and then as Alexander's last minister of the interior, tried to placate the liberal gentry and the educated public. He fired D. A. Tolstoy, the minister of education whose policies had kept the university students in a state of perpetual rebellion. He also dissolved the Third Section, which had become a symbol of tyranny (but his own police were no less effective). Relaxation of censorship, and finally, Loris-Melikov's proposal that the tsar convene a consultative assembly—another go-around with Count P. A. Valuev's scheme of 1863, which the former minister of the interior presented to the tsar again in 1880—have been correctly seen by historians as technical adjustments rather than the prelude to radical reforms. Loris-Melikov wanted to use the slogan "Constitution" but to restrict the new assembly's function to consultation with the State Council, a government body which itself had no genuine legislative power. Loris-Melikov was in many ways a forerunner of Peter Stolypin, one of the last effective servants of the old regime, who wrought havoc in the ranks of the revolutionaries while at the same time working to broaden the regime's base of support in society. The "dictator's" tactics were appreciated by the Executive Committee for what they were. Yet, as Alexander himself believed, any concession, however bogus, might open the way for a real constitution and a genuine parliament. Court conservatives feared Loris-Melikov's ambiguous program as much as the revolutionaries did. In any case, it was too late for such tactics. Police successes and the evident cessation of assassination attempts on the tsar merely inspired a false sense of confidence within the government. In fact, the revolutionaries' desire for revenge only increased as more and more prominent members of the party were arrested and tried. The death sentence that The People's Will had pronounced over Alexander II remained in force.

The dramatic story of the organization and execution of the assassination has been told by a number of historians with considerable narrative skill and will not be retold here. On March 1, 1881 in St. Petersburg, the Executive Committee, much reduced by arrests, sent its forces against the tsar. This time they were successful. One of the youngest members of the party, N. E. Rysakov, threw the first bomb, detaining Alexander's sleigh, and I. I. Grinevitskii threw the bomb that killed the tsar.

The confusion and wild rumors that followed the tsar's death had no issue. The really significant struggle of the succeeding weeks occurred in government circles between liberals, who tried to push through Loris-Melikov's "constitutional" project that had been provisionally approved by Alexander just before the assassination, and conservatives, led by Konstantin Pobedonostsev, the Procurator of the Holy Synod, and Michael Katkov, an extremely influential journalist. The Executive Committee tried to influence the successor to the throne, Alexander III, by publishing an open letter to him in which they demanded an amnesty for political criminals and a national assembly for the Empire. However, the new tsar committed himself to the conservative camp, and the Executive Committee was not able to make good its threat of revolution.

The trial of Zheliabov, Sofia Perovskaia (who had taken command when Zheliabov was arrested shortly before the assassination), Kibalchich, Rysakov, Gesia Helfman, and Timofei Mikhailov attracted worldwide attention, as had the struggle since 1878 between the tsarist government and the revolutionaries. The latter, as they had done before in previous trials, turned the court into a forum for their views of national liberation. Zheliabov and the Executive Committee seemed to be reasonable exponents of constitutionalism and civil liberties. However, despite pleas from some of the most prominent men of Russian letters, and the pressure of the foreign press, the revolutionaries were condemned to death by hanging. All except Gesia Helfman, whose execution was deferred because she was pregnant, were hanged on April 3, 1881.

The collapse of the Executive Committee was not apparent for more than a year after the assassination, but the price paid for Alexander's life was too great for the party to carry on at the same level of activity. Most of the prominent "specialists" had been executed or were in prison or exile. The final collapse of the party as a whole did not occur until 1882–1883. During the course of 1881 the party regularly issued proclamations calling for various social groups to carry on the struggle. In March 1882 the party assassinated General V. S. Strel'nikov, an especially harsh military judicial investigator, in Odessa. Indeed, to émigré groups the party's prestige was highest at a time when, unbeknownst to them, it was disintegrating. There is further proof that the Executive Committee's mystique was still intact during most of 1882. The government did not arrange any official negotiations with the Executive Committee, but the "Consecrated Guard," an unofficial group conceived by Sergei Witte and led by Count I. I. Vorontsov-Dashkov and Count P. O. Shuvalov, in the spring of 1881 actually contacted representatives of the revolutionary party. The story of the intrigues of the "Consecrated Guard" with Lavrov, who had become an associate of The People's Will, and the remaining members of the old Executive Committee, M. N. Oshanina, L. A. Tikhomirov, and Vera Figner (the former two having emigrated) is a curious footnote to the events of 1881. Nicholas Mikhailovskii was also drawn into the intrigue as an intermediary. In order to prevent an attempt on the life of Alexander III, the agents of the Consecrated Guard entered into various agreements with spokesmen of The People's Will, who hoped to arrange a political amnesty, the convening of a national assembly, and Chernyshevskii's release from Siberian exile. However, a more successful intrigue arranged by Lieutenant-Colonel G. D. Sudeikin, head of the St. Petersburg police, led to the infiltration of the party and the arrest of Vera Figner in February 1883. The central figure in this intrigue was Sergei Degaev, the first of a long series of double agents in Russian revolutionary history. Degaev helped to organize Sudeikin's assassination in December 1883, but not before his information had all but destroyed the remnants of the party. The total number of persons convicted for connections with the People's Will between 1881 and 1894 reached the impressive figure of 5,851, of which twenty-seven were executed and 342 either imprisoned or exiled to a labor camp.[21] The others received less severe sentences. However, the terrorists of the 1880s and 1890s rarely succeeded. They failed to create a unified, potent movement, and their prime targets escaped them.

For several years after 1883 Russian revolutionaries still refused to believe that the organization was destroyed. Lavrov and Tikhomirov published *The Messenger of The People's Will* in

---

21 Norman M. Naimark, *Terrorists and Social Democrats: The Russian Revolutionary Movement Under Alexander III* (Cambridge, Mass., 1983), p. 42.

1883–1886. After Tikhomirov's defection to the old regime, Lavrov and several other émigrés during the 1890s organized a group called "The Old *Narodovoltsy*" (the latter word is the plural of *narodovolets,* which means "member of The People's Will"). Individuals and groups in Russia never gave up the hope that the Executive Committee might be revived. Some simply took over the technique of terror and tried to carry on the unfinished work of The People's Will—namely the assassination of Alexander III. A young man named Alexander Ulianov became involved in an attempt on the life of the tsar in 1887 and was hanged for it. His younger brother, Vladimir, later known as Lenin, was drawn into the revolutionary movement largely as a consequence of Alexander's execution. Oddly enough, Lenin destroyed the party that was the real heir to The People's Will—the Socialist-Revolutionary Party.

The revolutionary actors of the 1870s did not disappear once and for all. Some returned to play major roles in the formation of new parties in the 1890s. Their dedication to the revolutionary cause had epic proportions. Twice or thrice arrested already, a few lived to see the revolution take the Jacobin direction that they had feared it would take. The heroic period of revolutionary *narodnichestvo* can be considered closed by 1883, but it is impossible to make a neat summary of the movement. An epitaph is easier. It was magnificent, but it was not revolution.

5 / THE REVOLUTIONARY ERA THROUGH 1905

THE DEVELOPMENT OF A REVOLUTIONARY FRONT

The years 1881–1896 in Russia can be described as a period of apparent remission of the malady of revolution. In much the same way that Nicholas I had succeeded in forcing the revolutionary movement into private hideaways where the revolutionary spirit was sustained and nourished, Alexander III's reactionary policies—his reign is often described as an era of counterreforms—forced the radical intelligentsia to resume modest tasks of enlightening the masses and helping them in their day-to-day lives. In the cities, *kruzhkovshchina* (an era of circles) prevailed. Little circles of populists, some of whom called themselves *narodovoltsy,* tried to rebuild what had been crushed, but their practical activity resembled that of the *Chaikovtsy* in the early 1870s and the Lavrovists in the mid-1870s. Indeed, the spirit of preparationism, of Lavrov's early revolutionary essays, closely corresponded to the mentality of a large segment of the intelligentsia and the growing workers' intelligentsia of this period, just as did Lavrov's eclecticism. Early Russian Marxism and left liberalism were both nourished by the predominantly populist radical intelligentsia. The populists reached out to both in order to carry on their struggle to liberate the working classes. The same was true for the countryside, where the populist theorist Abramov's doctrine of "small deeds" and Lev Tolstoy's Christian populism sustained the morale of the radical intelligentsia who worked in the villages.

However, just like the tsars before him, Alexander III was unable to reverse the cultural, social, and economic processes that continued to erode the autocracy's support in educated society, and at last, to destroy its popular support. His last two ministers of finance, I. A. Vyshnegradskii (1887–1892) and Sergei Witte (1892–1903), the latter serving Nicholas II as well, pursued a policy of forced industrialization that altered the complexion of both the cities and the countryside. The burdens imposed upon the peasants in the form of direct and indirect taxes, the policy of forced exports, Witte's tariff policies, and his successful bids for foreign loans and investment permitted Russia to enter an era of rapid industrial expansion. Large numbers of the rapidly increasing industrial proletariat (still a small percentage of the total population) were employed in large factories and herded into ghettos in the major cities of the empire. In spite of instances of relatively benevolent paternalism on the part of some factory owners, intervention in favor of the workers by the Russian government, and efforts by the government to gain control of the labor movement, Russian industrialization created social problems which far exceeded the government's resources to cope with them. Nonetheless, historians have speculated that the policy of forced industrialization might have succeeded but for external disasters: the unsuccessful Russo-Japanese War of 1904–1905 and especially the Russian failures in World War I. In view of the incredible ineptitude of Nicholas II and his governments, it is more reasonable to speculate that a different *kind* of revolution might have occurred at some other moment in his reign. Setting aside these speculations, in historical perspective what *did* happen looks very much like an unsuccessful gamble by the two ablest servants of the last reigns—Witte and Peter Stolypin—who believed that the autocracy could pursue a ruthless policy of modernization and simultaneously preserve its own position vis-à-vis the larger society. In fact, the empire did not modernize quickly enough to maintain its position in international politics, and the social and economic disequilibrium of the decades that preceded 1917 created an almost perpetually explosive internal situation.

The revival of the revolutionary intelligentsia during the 1890s and its complex development during the twentieth century were, for the first time, tied to social movements of considerable magnitude and genuine revolutionary potential. Indeed, elements within the revolutionary intelligentsia tended to lag behind the spontaneous movements in the urban and rural masses. Ideological and tactical adjustments were often made hastily to meet the needs of the moment. The debates of earlier revolutionary generations about the role to be played by the various participants in a nonexistent revolutionary front now became crucial calculations in rapidly unfolding revolutionary situations. That is not to say that the new intelligentsia factions were necessarily more correct, and that their ideologies were better guides to an understanding of the historical events in which they participated. Rather, all revolutionary factions had real constituencies and faced real opportunities for influencing mass behavior. In this new historical environment, the latest social and revolutionary theories of the intelligentsia were proven not so much correct as useful. They were useful because they inspired some members of the intelligentsia with the confidence and zeal that permitted them to adapt themselves to revolutionary situations and to act as astute manipulators rather than passive or fearful observers. Tactical flexibility, leadership skills, and the desire for real power and control over the revolutionary situation were far more important assets than the new and old theories that the intelligentsia ferociously debated. Although these qualities had been present in earlier generations of the revolutionary intelligentsia, they had been expended fruitlessly in an uncongenial historical environment.

When revolutionary factions subordinated tactics to elaborate and long-standing theoretical formulas, they tended to lose sight of the need of the moment and suffer defeats. One can spend long hours mulling over questions about the intrinsic superiority or inferiority of a given system of ideas for a revolutionary situation without coming to a definite conclusion. Complicated formulas could tell the revolutionaries what kind of revolution Russia should have, who should come to power, and what form the new government should take. These formulas were unquestionably important but often tended to restrain action. The great victories of revolutionary factions occurred when their leaders were able to find ways to adapt ideology to crisis conditions. After every major tactical adaptation such leaders made a correlative ideological adjustment. The populists had practiced this flexibility for years and continued to do so during the last phases of the revolutionary movement. Russian Marxists, who struggled for years before they were able to make converts in the intelligentsia, soon spread out over a wide spectrum of positions.

Recent scholarship dramatizes the extent to which Social Democrats and Socialist Revolutionaries collaborated once they got beyond the most intense period of ideological schism in the 1890s. The Socialist Revolutionaries, like many of the earlier populists, explicitly blended peasants and urban workers into a common "toiling" mass, and the Social Democrats came to appreciate the importance of the peasants in revolutionary struggle, particularly after 1902. Local groups collaborated in revolutionary projects despite the incessant clamor from abroad, where émigré theoretical leaders tried to maintain their factions' distinct boundaries. It is not too surprising that at any given moment a revolutionary subgroup belonging to a major "ism" could be temperamentally and strategically closer to a subgroup belonging to an alien "ism" than to fellow Marxists or populists. Thus, for the purpose of revolutionary *action,* Bolsheviks and left Socialist Revolutionaries might form an alliance against Mensheviks and right Socialist Revolutionaries.

Revolutionary theoreticians of all stripes had to define the historical moment and the roles of different social groups in the revolution to come. The problem of historical phases was a basic issue in an increasingly tortuous set of problems that the Russian revolutionary intelligentsia now shared with European socialist parties. During the 1870s, the revolutionary intelligentsia had operated under the assumption that the working classes were differentiated by location and employment but that all were imbued with revolutionary and socialist instincts. By the 1890s the intelligentsia was bitterly divided over the question of the role of the urban proletariat and the role of the peasants in the coming revolutions. It was not just a matter of who would be the vanguard at a given phase in the revolutionary process. The Marxists did not believe that the peasants were the true carriers of socialism. To them, the peasants had "petit-bourgeois" aspirations, and the populists were a petit-bourgeois party. Marxist factions created ever more complicated formulas describing the distribution of progressive and antiprogressive social forces, the roles envisioned for each of them in the revolutionary struggle at a given historical moment, the nature of the revolution to occur, and the political superstructure that would reflect new economic and social relationships. Several kinds of evidence were adduced to support the complicated revolutionary vision of the Marxists—economic theory, contemporary economic statistics, European revolutionary history, theories of class behavior, and class behavior as exhibited in contemporary situations—while their opponents defended themselves with quite similar modes of argument and demonstration. Marxism did not replace populism, but rather competed with it for recruits from the intelligentsia. Meanwhile, the radical liberal tradition gathered strength and competed with both of them. During the two final revolutionary crises in 1905 and 1917, several revolutionary parties, although bitterly divided internally, searched for alliances dictated by theoretical formulas and tactical considerations. Let us first examine briefly the theoretical bases of the competing ideologies.

Marxism, after all is said and done, bases itself upon the Hegelian theodicy. Marxists saw reason and order emerging from the seeming confusion of historical phenomena. Passions, struggle, violence, and suffering played a large part in the unfolding of human consciousness. For Marx, the theory of immiserization and of inevitable economic crises under capitalism led to an optimistic conclusion—to revolution and the victory of the proletariat. Thus, capitalism was neither an unqualified good nor an unqualified evil. It was good so long as it progressively transformed the technology of production, increased human mastery of the environment, and thus provided the basis for the next, higher stage in human development. Until that moment it had to be endured. But here was a major source of controversy. There was no certain way of knowing when the moment had arrived, and when one should refuse to suffer the bourgeoisie any longer. Nor was there any certainty about how the new phase would appear. Marx and Engels had made concessions to the variations of economic, social, and political development in several nations. They believed on the one hand that the proletariat might acquire power by legal means in some nations, and on the other, that a socialist seizure of power could occur in a nation like Russia, where bourgeois institutions had not yet developed, and where industrialism was still incipient. Marx accepted the populist assumption that Russia might pursue a more direct path to socialism, but only in the event of a general European revolution. He was certainly not dogmatic about Russia's need to endure a period of bourgeois institutions, and was therefore spiritually closer to the Bolshevik wing of Russian Marxism than to Menshevism.

The spiritual content of Marxism deserves comment. For all of its atheism, its emphasis on scientific analysis, and its elevation of prosaic economic data to a position of primacy and the centerpiece of a theory of historical change, Marxism attracted passionately moralistic types. The reasons are not difficult to discern. The system propounded by Marx and Engels promised that History, however devoid of divine inspiration, would reward the proletariat for its suffering by making it the carrier of progress. The proletariat, like the chosen people of the Old Testament, or like the saved in Christian doctrine, would enter the kingdom of socialism; the bourgeoisie would not. The last would be first. Perhaps shared moral and emotional impulses inspired both Judeo-Christian and Marxian teaching. Marxism might even be seen as a secular rationalization and extension of the Judeo-Christian tradition. On the other hand, the resemblance between the two doctrines may be adventitious, in that many intelligentsia doctrines have a "family resemblance." In either case, Marxism readily satisfied the hunger for social justice of people raised in the Judeo-Christian tradition.

History, of course, has shown that in its many permutations Marxism appealed to a great many people raised in other traditions, too. In the nineteenth and twentieth centuries it has inspired masses of people undergoing the painful early stages of industrialization. According to one view, it thrives in different cultures because it addresses the psychological needs of populations experiencing the stress of a transitional historical moment. Marxism ambivalently affirms the value of modernization and industrial production without abandoning nostalgia for a premodern world less controlled by the cash nexus and production.[1] Despite its defects in predicting historical change, Marx-

---

1 See Adam B. Ulam, *The Unfinished Revolution: Marxism and Communism in the Modern World* (Boulder, Colo. 1979).

ism still commands loyalty in the intelligentsias of developed as well as developing nations, given the failure of capitalism to solve problems of equality and social justice central to much intelligentsia thought. The rich array of neo-Marxist doctrines dramatically shows that Marxism still offers substantial intellectual, moral, and emotional benefits to its adherents. Nonetheless, as a global movement Marxism seems to have peaked in the 1970s, and the historical waning of Marxism appears to be linked to the continuing vitality of capitalism, to the tragedy of the Russian Revolution, and to the worldwide failures of Communist states. In the late twentieth century, it takes stubborn commitment, indeed, to insist that the factory proletariat is imbued with a special historical mission.

The first Russian Marxists, many of them former populists, sometimes savagely unmasked *narodnik* illusions about the peasants. Their new doctrine, however, simply substituted one sacred collectivity for another. The converts to Marxism (always theoretically and often in deed) committed themselves to the proletarian cause with the same selfless devotion that they had shown the peasants. And like members of religious communities, the Marxists split into warring sects, each claiming a new revelation and the last word in doctrine—in this case, a "scientific" word—and each clashing over the imminence of History's judgment of the bourgeoisie and elevation of the proletariat. To make things even more complicated, Marx and Engels, both still living when Russian revolutionaries first began to debate the relative merits of the populist and Marxian approaches to progress and social justice, interjected their own thoughts on Russia's development.

During Marx's lifetime, there had not been a Marxist party in Russia. Although he had found most of the Russian émigré revolutionaries insufferable for both theoretical and personal reasons, Marx had admired and encouraged the heroic young revolutionaries of The People's Will. The Russian populists for their part had admired Marx as a great socialist theoretician. *Das Kapital* had been translated into Russian by two populists—Herman Lopatin and N. F. Danielson—and had appeared in Russia in 1872, before it had been translated into any other European language. Some of the Lavrovists in St. Petersburg in the late

1870s had been called Marxists, although they had tended to see the urban proletariat as only one segment of the exploited masses and had not assigned it any special role. Leading populist theoreticians had found in Marx's writings not so much praise for the historically progressive role of bourgeois capitalism, as blame for its ruthless, exploitative character.

When several members of the Black Repartition, the *narodnik* faction that had split off from Land and Freedom in 1879, emigrated and converted to Marxism, they displayed all of the fervor of proselytes. During the 1870s it had been virtually impossible for Russian revolutionaries to abandon their faith in the peasants without abandoning their revolutionary optimism. Now, under the guidance of G. V. Plekhanov and the "Liberation of Labor Group" (1883), Russian Marxism began to take root in Geneva, Switzerland. Plekhanov repudiated the idea of Russia's unique path to socialism, even while recognizing the peculiarities of Russia's historical development in relation to the rest of Europe. Indeed, unlike former *narodnik* comrades who had drawn optimistic conclusions from their vision of Russian history, Plekhanov, Paul Akselrod, Lev Deich, and Vera Zasulich of the Liberation of Labor Group concluded that Russia would not lead but follow Europe to socialism. Plekhanov was not entirely free of the idea of the virtues of backwardness, but his emphasis was quite different. He declared that Russian backwardness had modified the character of the bourgeoisie and the development of bourgeois institutions, but that Russia could not skip the bourgeois phase of historical progress. This pitilessly "objective" vision embraced the inevitability of the destruction of the peasant commune, the transformation of the peasants into landless proletarians, and their exploitation by industrial capitalists.

Plekhanov's first major theoretical articles appeared in the course of a bitter debate with the Russian émigré group that published *The Messenger of the People's Will*. *Socialism and the Political Struggle* (1883) and *Our Differences* (1885) attempted to redirect the revolutionary movement and to demonstrate that the peasant socialism advocated by The People's Will was neither possible nor desirable according to Marx's scientific socialism. Plekhanov attacked the entire range of populist doctrine, from epistemology to revolutionary strategy. In some ways, his theoretical formulations pointed back to the 1860s. His hard-headed objectivism and materialism were far more complicated than Chernyshevskii's and Dobroliubov's, and his conclusions quite different from theirs, but like them he believed that he was liberating the intelligentsia from fantasies. However, in the 1880s and 1890s acceptance of a materialistic and objectivistic outlook signified a step back from the revolutionary aggressiveness of the *narodniki,* and a shift in emphasis toward conscious obedience to immutable historical laws. In Russia this meant acceptance of the priority of the bourgeois revolution. Plekhanov's belief that Russia's backwardness might permit its intelligentsia and proletarian class to avoid some of the defeats suffered by the European proletariat and thus hasten the downfall of capitalism was an important concession in the direction of voluntarism but was still retrograde relative to revolutionary populism. Plekhanov gave the intelligentsia an important role in the formation of proletarian consciousness in spite of his professed belief that the class struggle and class consciousness issued inevitably from objective conditions. This too was a concession to voluntarism. Indeed, such attempts to introduce factors that somehow acted from "above" upon the objective material conditions which, according to Marx's theory, produced proletarian class consciousness, were akin to the "idealist" heresies which Plekhanov condemned in the "utopian" socialism of his opponents.

On balance, it is correct to see Plekhanov as a fixed point of Marxist orthodoxy in the Russian Social Democratic movement. There is little question but that his theoretical acumen and literary talent provided Russian Marxism with a firm foundation. When inevitable right- and left-wing heresies (leanings toward trade unionism, evolutionary liberalism, or ultrarevolutionism) appeared among Russian Marxists, Plekhanov threw his weight to one side or the other, sometimes allying himself with groups that were far from orthodox. Nonetheless, he remained committed to the idea of two revolutions (a bourgeois revolution followed by a socialist revolution), a commitment which, not unexpectedly, made him an ally of the liberal Kadet Party during the revolutions of 1917 and an opponent of the ultrarevolutionary Bolsheviks. Plekhanovism and related strains of Menshevism, however, proved to be too inflexible and too artificial for a truly revolutionary situation. Plekhanov's orderly and optimistic historical vision led him into personal tragedy during his lifetime, the tragedy of his revolution going astray, and he himself being treated like a political criminal, but even his Bolshevik opponents posthumously conceded him a secure place in the apostolic succession of revolutionary theorists.

A sketch of Plekhanov's views is the merest introduction to the complex and extended history of Russian Marxism; the entry of Marx's ideas into Russia created a maze of philosophical, historical, economic, and sociological problems for the intelligentsia. Suffice it here to say that in the 1880s and 1890s Plekhanov and his major theoretical collaborator, Paul Akselrod, succeeded in adapting the views of Marx and Engels to Russian conditions. Early Russian Marxism had a pessimistic timetable in comparison with revolutionary populism, but it offered the Russian intelligentsia the certainties of science, the security of an international movement, and hope for at least an abbreviation of the bourgeois phase of historical development. On the other hand, the populists' urgent concern for the immediate suffering of the masses, their dedication to individualism, their emphasis upon the free exercise of human will, their attachment to smaller and (to them) more humane forms of association and economic organization continued to have great appeal. Marxist theories were assailable by populist critics, and the populists had a number of emotional advantages, among them a long martyrology and the recent memory of The People's Will, not to speak of the continuing appeal of terror. It took several historical shocks in the 1890s to permit Russian Marxists to proselytize successfully among the intelligentsia.

The first shock came in 1891–1892. The great famine and widespread typhus, typhoid, and cholera epidemics of this period confirmed what all oppositional elements in Russia knew—that a large segment of the peasant population lived on the verge of extinction, and that the Russian government's economic policies were indirectly responsible for hundreds of thousands of deaths. Both the spectacle of mass suffering and the government's appeal to Russian society in November 1891 for the organization of philanthropic work in the affected regions of European Russia revived the spirit of active opposition in "society." As in the preceding reigns, the crisis provoked a surge of public opinion and the revival of demands for reform. The new revival (1891–1894), although issuing from a crisis of lesser dimensions than those during the reigns of Nicholas I and Alexander II, created great expectations in educated society and the formation of a liberal-populist alliance. It was organized by none other than Mark Natanson, who had returned from Siberia with a number of other populist veterans. During its brief existence, "The Party of the People's Right" was less significant as a revolutionary party than as a symptom of the temporary weakening of the sectarian spirit within the intelligentsia during the early 1890s. This in turn was evidence of both the sheer numerical expansion of the educated and politically conscious elements in Russian society and the diversion of intelligentsia interest toward secondary but more immediately (or so it seemed to them) obtainable political goals. The Party of the People's Right began to form simultaneously with the regrouping of the literary forces of populism around Nicholas Mikhailovskii and his newly acquired journal, *Russian Wealth.* (After the creation of circles in several cities and the issuance of a number of pamphlets and proclamations in the period 1891–1894, Natanson's organization was destroyed by arrests in April 1894.) Mikhailovskii, who had allied himself with the Party of the People's Right, offered the younger generation, many of whom still hoped for the resurrection of the Executive Committee, a liberal-constitutionalist program. His journal and other populist organs such as *The Week* and *The New World* were divided over the strategies of populism and the proper path to socialism. Russian populism, having lost its sectarian spirit, also lost much of the theoretical appeal it had possessed for radical youths. Thus, during the period 1891–1894, the liberal-populist alliance stimulated the younger generation to look elsewhere for a consistent mode of radical thought.

Furthermore, the behavior of the peasants in 1891–1892 tended to confirm the Marxist view of the peasantry as a backward rather than progressive social group. The peasants proved to be either inert or hostile to the intelligentsia philanthropists who came to the villages to help them. Once again, this somewhat different kind of Going to the People disappointed populist-inclined radicals. To be sure, this was not a death blow either to liberal populism or to revolutionary populism. But it did help to prepare the way for competing systems of thought.

The real impetus for the development of Marxism came from the spontaneous development of the workers' movement, first in the western areas of the Russian Empire—Poland, Lithuania, and White Russia—and then in Great Russia. The turning point came in 1895–1896, when the liberal-populist campaign for constitutional reform bumped up against the inflexible conservatism of the new tsar, Nicholas II, and his government, and when the surge of industrialization begun in the reign of Alexander III yielded its first large-scale and extended strike movement. What had been a small and little known socialist sect trying to foster revolutionary class consciousness among the urban factory workers and to convince the intelligentsia that Marxism was the true socialist gospel was soon transformed into the nucleus of a revolutionary party. But acceptance of Marxism was only one of several responses within the intelligentsia to a rapidly changing historical environment.

Revolutionary populists, having conceded that during the 1890s the industrial proletariat was a more revolutionary force than the peasants, were forced into a defensive position. During the early 1890s the revolutionary intelligentsia had been so weak and disorganized that doctrinal disagreements had seemed less important than the pooling of resources and techniques in a common effort to further the struggle of the urban workers. In the nonsectarian atmosphere of this period the *narodovoltsy* in St. Petersburg had worked together with early Social Democratic circles, although their aims and methods were different. The *narodovoltsy* still felt that they were the true heirs of the strongest and most legitimate revolutionary party in Russia and did not yet see the Social Democrats as a real threat. The early populists and original *narodovoltsy,* after all, had never drawn a sharp line between the working class in the villages and the working class in the cities. Despite the fact that they tended to see the Social Democrats as nonrevolutionary, the *narodovoltsy* of the 1890s had sufficiently moderated their own position to accept the Marxists as colleagues. After 1894–1896, when Russian Marxist theoreticians began a major assault upon the populists, two hostile camps formed.

The revival of revolutionary populism did not occur in St. Petersburg, but in provincial capitals in the Volga region and the Ukraine. The leaders of the new movement were émigrés, veterans of revolutionary populism who returned to European Russia from Siberian exile during the 1890s, and young recruits who began their activities in the provinces. Like Russian Marxists during the mid- and late 1890s, revolutionary populists tried to form a party but did not possess either central leadership or a unified program. While Russian Marxists were experiencing their first bitter internal divisions over the heresies of economism and revisionism, revolutionary populists were still groping for a new theoretical foundation. The theoretical revamping of revolutionary populism was not possible until the period 1902–1906, when large-scale agrarian disturbances renewed the populists' faith in the peasants as a revolutionary force. Recent scholarship, however, stresses their ability to compete successfully with their Social Democratic colleagues in urban centers and factory settings.[2]

During the final phase of revolutionary populism, Victor Chernov was its dominant, indeed its only noteworthy theoretician. As if to symbolize the passing of the prophetic mantle, Chernov was present at Peter Lavrov's death in Paris in February 1900. Lavrov had given his final blessing to the "League of Agrarian Socialism," which was later amalgamated with the Socialist Revolutionary Party. Chernov's "constructive" (as opposed to utopian or scientific) socialism has never impressed students of social thought as a well constructed and coherent theory. Chernov labored very much within the subjectivistic tradition of Lavrov and Mikhailovskii, emphasizing ethics rather than pure knowledge, but strenuously attempting to assimilate his ethical vision of freedom and individuality to scientific thought. In order to establish the validity of ethical sociology, Chernov drew

---

2 See the following: Michael Melancon, " 'Stormy Petrels': The Socialist Revolutionaries in Russia's Legal Labor Organizations, 1905–1914," *The Carl Beck Papers* 703 (June 1988), University of Pittsburgh, and "The Socialist Revolutionaries from 1902–1907: Peasant *and* Workers' Party," *Russian History* 12 (Spring 1985); C. Rice, *Russian Workers and the Socialist-Revolutionary Party through the Revolution of 1905–1907* (New York, 1988).

upon new schools of epistemological and sociological thought in addition to earlier populist authorities. He was influenced by the neo-Kantian empiriocriticism of Richard Avenarius and Ernst Mach, and Lester Ward's dynamic sociology. The voluntarism deeply imbedded in the theoretical foundations of populism was reasserted in Chernov's revision.

Like Lavrov, Chernov was a catholic socialist, trying to avoid an exclusively peasant or proletarian orientation. Thus, he did not see any inconsistency in referring to Marx and Engels as his teachers, while at the same time perpetuating the populist vision of the peculiarly socialist character of the Russian peasantry. Chernov's ideas about Russia's special path also centered around the peasant commune and its fortunate ignorance of the conceptions of private property that Europeans had inherited from Roman law. However, unlike the earlier populists, Chernov had to take into account economic and social changes that had not only eroded the villages but had created an entirely new industrial sector in Russia. Chernov no longer saw Russia moving directly into the socialist phase. In this respect, he showed the influence of both Marxism and liberal populism. Yet he still clung to the populist faith that the village could be secured from the worst ravages of capitalism and thus ease Russia's entry into the phase of socialism. Regard for the small producer and small-scale agriculture, another deep populist bias, was incorporated into Chernov's projected postrevolutionary period.

The Socialist Revolutionary Party's program devised by Chernov was two-phased in that it envisioned a period in which the land would be socialized and cultivated by individual users or collectives. This phase would be followed by the socially and economically more advanced period of collective cultivation. The Socialist Revolutionaries' two-phase scheme was further complicated by the exclusion of industry from the process of socialization during the first phase. They proposed a dichotomous system in which agriculture would be socialized but industry privately owned (the urban land would be owned by municipalities). The socialization of industry would be deferred until the phase of full agricultural collectivization. Thus, the Socialist Revolutionaries' revolutionary goals reflected the fact that they were still, above all, agrarian socialists. While they were unwilling to see the peasants expropriated and proletarianized for the sake of large-scale production, the Socialist Revolutionaries were willing to accept the necessity of the continuance of industrial capitalism. It should be emphasized, however, that SR (the abbreviated form of Socialist Revolutionary) doctrine, modified though it was by Marxian theory and a notion of historical stages, still attracted impatient types prepared to attack the tsarist regime at any moment and with any possible means. The left wing of the party quickly asserted itself, and such "maximalist" personalities remained within the Socialist Revolutionary Party even after a Maximalist faction formally broke with the mainstream SRs in 1906.

The third major radical party that emerged during the last reign, the Constitutional Democrats, or Kadets, were associated less with the masses than with the expanding stratum of Russian professionals. The leaders of the left liberal movement during the late 1890s and after were often scholars from the urban intelligentsia, cosmopolitan men of culture. Some of them were defectors from the Marxist or populist camps. Unlike the Marxists and populists, the left liberals did not establish strong ties with an exploited social class which it felt to be its special constituency. Nonetheless, Russian left liberalism did have considerable popular appeal because of its advocacy of democratic constitutionalism and its commitment to social welfare. Many of the ideas of liberal populist and revisionist economists were incorporated into the program of the Kadet Party.

The theoretical leaders of Russian left liberalism during the period of the rise of the major oppositional parties (1898–1905) were Peter Struve and Paul Miliukov. Struve was a former "legal Marxist" who had played an important role in the debate between Marxists and populists in the mid-1890s. He had undergone an ideological evolution characteristic of a number of legal Marxists, from a scholarly variety of Marxism to Kantianism, and to Christianity. There is little question but that both philosophical and theological thought in Russia of the Silver Age, the extraordinarily diversified and creative cultural epoch that approximately coincided with the reign of Nicholas II, exceeded in sophistication and creativity the somewhat stale and sectarian varieties of ethical sociology and optimistic materialism of preceding intelligentsia generations. However, philosophical idealism often signified a lack of the combativeness and party spirit necessary for the ensuing struggle. Left liberalism, especially through the legal Marxists (Struve, Nicholas Berdiaev, S. N. Bulgakov, and S. L. Frank), became associated with a cosmopolitan variety of Westernism, which later tried to incorporate aspects of Russian national experience into a program of evolutionary change.

Paul Miliukov, a prominent historian, was the political leader of the left liberals. Miliukov belonged to a positivistic rather than Marxist or idealist school of thought, but this did not prevent him from joining Struve in an effort to organize the left liberal opposition into a party. Under the spur of Miliukov's radicalism, the left liberal organ *Liberation* (Stuttgart 1902–1904, Paris 1904–1905) and its organizational affiliate in Russia, "The Union of Liberation," attenuated their ties with the more moderate varieties of gentry liberalism based upon the *zemstvos.* Like the Social Democrats and Social Revolutionaries, the Union of Liberation had as its most immediate goals the destruction of the autocratic state and the establishment of a democratic constitution.

Operating as they did in a mass society and in an atmosphere of mass discontent, the three illegal parties very soon began to subordinate abstract theorizing to tactical and organizational matters. They were all faced with the problem of harnessing and guiding the numerous forces that had been unleashed by the government's economic, social, political, and cultural policies. Several distinct movements emerged, each of them interacting with the others during the most severe crises of the old regime, in the period 1904–1917. This resembled the previous interaction of several movements during the formation of revolutionary fronts in earlier periods of crisis such as 1856–1863 and 1878–1882. However, during the period 1904–1917 several new factors gave the revolutionary fronts a far more threatening character.

The first factor was the sheer size of the movements. The rate of population growth in the Russian Empire, especially in European Russia, exceeded that of any of the major European powers. The population of imperial Russia grew from 73,648,000 in 1861 to 169,759,000 in 1916. Although some of the growth can be accounted for by imperial expansion, population grew much faster than the capacity of Russia's urban and semiurban industrial centers to absorb it. At the turn of the century between 70 and 80 percent of the population was engaged in agriculture, and at the outbreak of World War I the agricultural population was still three to four times as large as the nonagricultural population. Despite the fact that Russia's urban population approximately tripled between 1861 and 1914, more than 85 percent of the Russian population still lived outside the jurisdiction of municipal governments and was officially rural in 1914.

However, there was a high degree of geographic industrial concentration in the empire and an unusally high degree of labor concentration in industrial enterprises. Almost half of Russia's industrial labor force in 1914 worked in enterprises that employed 1,000 or more workers. Even more significant is the fact that between 1910 and 1914 the government's economic and social policies (embodied in Stolypin's agrarian reforms of 1906–1911) led to a sudden increase in the industrial labor force. The average Russian industrial proletarian was quite young, even before we add the sudden influx of new hands mentioned above. St. Petersburg was the most developed Russian proletarian center in that the vast majority of its labor force was permanently employed in industry. In addition, St. Petersburg was strongly affected by the mass of new labor recruits, and on the eve of the revolutions of 1917 displayed in extreme form the social tensions that characterized European Russia as a whole.

By 1917 economic and social differentiation in the countryside had created a large mass of peasants who could no longer subsist on the land, yet could not be absorbed by industry. Moreover, the numerous peasants who did enter the industrial labor force just before World War I were newly experiencing proletarian life and were not at all reconciled to it.

The other significant social group (it is no longer historically appropriate to speak of estates, although estates continued to exist as legal entities after they had lost most of their social significance) was vaguely called "society." It consisted of the educated public who saw themselves as spokesmen for the nation, rather than for officialdom and the autocracy. By the turn of the century there were considerably more educated Russians outside the official apparatus than in it. The census of 1897 revealed that 1,384,143 persons in Russia had received either secondary or higher education. Only 10 percent of them had received higher education of any sort. More than 80 percent of the highly educated and about 70 percent of those who had received secondary educations lived in urban centers. A large number of educated persons who chose rural life did so out of a sense of dedication to the masses. They were employed by the *zemstvos* and became known as the "third element" to distinguish them from the state and local officials (the former appointed, the latter elected) who administered the *zemstvos*. The third element was responsible for much of the radical ferment at *zemstvo* conferences and at the meetings of professional societies and unions (*profsoiuzy*). Meetings, exhibits, and banquets sponsored by professional organizations and *zemstvo* conferences provided the basic framework for "society's" organized oppositional activity in 1904–1906. In spite of its relative numerical insignificance, "society" became an important revolutionary force in the first Russian revolution.

University students, although an even more insignificant group numerically than "society," also played a disproportionately large role. Despite the reactionary character of Count I. D. Delianov's tenure as minister of education (1882–1897), the process of democratization of the student body proceeded apace. In 1900 there were 16,357 students in eight Russian universities. By 1912 there were 34,538 in nine universities and almost 39,000 more enrolled in thirty other institutions of higher learning, fourteen of them in St. Petersburg and seven in Moscow. In addition, by 1912 28,274 women had enrolled in the program of higher courses designed for them. The pressures of modernization forced the regime to encourage enrollment in specialized institutes that prepared students for roles in a developing economy. The contrast in growth between these institutes and the more established universities can be seen in the shift in enrollment between 1912 and 1914; during this period the number of male university students remained stable, but the enrollment in specialized institutes increased dramatically to roughly 58,000. Approximately 34,000 women received higher education in special courses, and a smaller number in institutes.[3] By 1914 almost 39 percent of the students in Russia's nine universities were of working class or peasant origins, as well as 64 percent of the students in five higher state technical institutes. Furthermore, attempts to restrict student corporate activity played into the hands of the radicals in the student body, who converted illegal student organizations into affiliates of radical parties.

The student bodies of the expanded system of higher education in the major university cities were sufficiently large to cause serious disturbances and could occasionally provoke sympathy demonstrations by the proletariat. Finally, the brutal suppression of student demonstrations and mass expulsions in the period 1896–1901 (the movement was especially massive in 1899–1901) aggravated the situation. Expelled students who were not impressed into the army (an expedient employed by Nicholas II during this period) often became revolutionary agitators, propagandists, and terrorists. Thus, the universities and technical institutes, as in earlier periods, were important centers of recruitment for revolutionary parties. Still, compared to the mass worker and peasant movements and movements for national autonomy that developed in the first decades of the twentieth century, their importance was diminished.

The exacerbation of the nationalities problem within the Russian Empire was another important factor that spurred on the mass movements during the reign of Nicholas II. Between 55 and 60 percent of the inhabitants of the Russian Empire in 1897 were non-Russians. Of these, the Ukrainians, Turkic peoples, Poles, and Belorussians were the most numerous. The movements of greatest historical moment arose in Poland and the Ukraine, where the ruthless policies of cultural russification pursued by Alexander III and Nicholas II encountered the growing spirit of nationalism. Nationalism pervaded the borderlands. In the northwest, small ethnic groups aspiring to nationhood, such as the Estonians, Latvians, and Lithuanians, felt themselves to be culturally superior to their imperial oppressors. So too, in the south, Armenians and Georgians, though not numerous, looked

---

3 Patrick Alston, "The Dynamics of Educational Expansion in Russia," in Konrad H. Jarausch, ed., *The Transformation of Higher Learning* (Chicago, 1983), pp. 96–98.

back to a glorious past. The aspirations of the Moslem Turkic peoples in the south and east, and the mingling of different ethnic, racial, and religious communities in the southern and eastern borderlands created enormous complications. The Russian imperial government played an ambiguous role: at times it protected ethnic minorities against their more numerous and sometimes hostile neighbors, while at other times it suppressed national aspirations. The long-standing hostilities between, for example, Armenians and Azeri Turks points up the dilemma of the small nationalities and the ambiguous role of the Tsarist regime. Russian imperial governments played a protective role vis-à-vis Christian Armenians, whose superior socioeconomic status exacerbated the tensions between them and the more numerous Moslem, Turkic peoples in the area that became Azerbaijan.

The special position of the Jews in the Russian Empire created a very distinctive role for them. The discriminatory legislation against Jews and continuing persecution led to an unusually high level of Jewish participation in the revolutionary movement. This, of course, only added to the regime's hostility toward them. Faced with the alternatives of Zionism and emigration, introversion in their own communities, assimilation and a slow struggle for equal rights within the Empire, or a cosmopolitan revolutionary identity, many Jewish youths made the last choice. From this last category came important figures such as Trotsky and Martov, as well as some of the leading terrorists during the last three decades of the old regime.

More generally, all of the aggrieved minorities contributed leading figures to the revolutionary movement out of proportion to their numbers. These "marginal" groups played important roles at key moments during the revolutions of 1905 and 1917 and became special targets for the *Okhrana* (reorganized secret police), for chauvinist movements, for lynch-minded mobs such as the Black Hundreds, and for punitive expeditions by Cossacks. The benighted security forces of the regime expressed special contempt for and suspicion of Poles and Jews. It is not surprising that oppressed minorities had a greater stake in the success of revolution, and therefore were suspected by counterrevolutionaries of harboring motives of revenge. The ethnic composition of the first postrevolutionary government suggests the extent to which "marginals" had attained central positions in revolutionary parties. Oddly enough, the early Soviet regime's liberal employment of non-Russians resembled the practice of Russian imperial administrations. One found a disproportionate number of individuals of non-Russian ethnic background in elite positions during the old regime, too. The frequent amalgamation of nationalism with socialism, and the alliances formed by nationalist parties with the revolutionary parties after the turn of the century, created problems for both the old regime and the revolutionaries.

Given the extraordinary breadth and diversity of the oppositional groups, and the growth of underground organizations desiring to exploit and direct mass discontent, the major task before the Russian government was the prevention of the formation of a united revolutionary front. Even the repeated use of troops in the cities and countryside failed to quell mass discontent at the turn of the century. In retrospect, a wise counterrevolutionary policy would have entailed timely concessions to discontented groups and the creation of a broad and stable coalition of loyal forces. The old regime had several longstanding advantages—deep religious and national loyalties—that it could exploit. It commanded a widespread and reasonably effective network of security police, in addition to the regular army. As shall be seen, however, the old regime's attempts to manipulate the masses ultimately played into the hands of the revolutionaries.

On their side, the revolutionary parties, while fending off the police and trying to keep their own organizations from disintegrating into bitter factions, had to create tactics, programs, and slogans appropriate for mass movements. This task proved to be beyond the powers of all but the most astute manipulators, for at critical moments the masses always seemed to be demanding either too little or too much. The revolutionary intelligentsia's task was complicated by the extension of literacy to about one-third of the male population of the Empire at the turn of the century. On the one hand, this development led to the formation of an intermediate social stratum between the revolutionary intelligentsia and the illiterate masses that served as a medium of transmission for revolutionary ideas, and even as a source of leadership. On the other hand, the new, educated stratum of workers and peasants (often referred to as the worker or peasant intelligentsia) sometimes rebelled against the leadership of the revolutionary intelligentsia, still largely recruited from the upper strata of Russian society. Nonetheless, the higher cultural level of the masses utimately facilitated the work of the revolutionary parties and reduced the barriers that had separated the intelligentsia from them in earlier periods of the revolutionary movement.

We encounter several extremely difficult problems in studying the history of the relationship of revolutionary parties to mass movements. It is possible to discover real affinities between party programs and the aspirations of definite social groups. However, as historical scholarship advances, these affinities often prove to be limited to subgroups of a significant social entity, such as the urban proletariat, and are also discontinuous. Uneven development is the rule, rather than the exception, during the process of modernization. To paraphrase a prominent labor historian, modernization created "not an increasingly solid and uniform proletarian continent but a continually changing archipelago of working class categories."[4] Thus, it is not totally inaccurate to say that the Russian Social Democratic Workers' Party expressed the aspirations of the urban proletariat, but a statement of this sort glosses over the sometimes bitter struggle of revolutionary parties and factions, each of which appealed to different subgroups within the urban proletariat at different historical moments. Furthermore, the revolutionary parties and factions had aspirations that superseded those of any mass movement. While the parties had total programs, the mass movements had only partial, though radical goals. If the major revolutionary parties displayed a bias for a workers' revolution or a peasants' revolution, they did so because it suited their larger vision of social regeneration. It later became quite clear that leaders of revolutionary parties would not concede anything to the

4 William H. Sewell, Jr., "Uneven Development: The Autonomy of Politics, and the Dockworkers of Nineteenth-Century Marseilles," *American Historical Review* 93 (June 1988): 637.

masses that they felt would jeopardize their ultimate goals. Thus, the revolutionary intelligentsia parties and factions represented their own aspirations as well as those of the masses. The history of Bolshevik manipulations, concessions, and repressions is the clearest demonstration of this proposition.

The problem of leadership is possibly the most complex and interesting of all, for the character of the leaders of the revolutionary factions determined to a significant extent their success or failure in the upheavals of 1917. Neither Lenin's, Chernov's, Julius Martov's, nor Miliukov's behavior during the crucial months of 1917 and 1918, when policies, slogans, and actions had immediate consequences for the maintenance or creation of a power base, can be explained by their devotion to an ideology alone. Their decisiveness (or lack of decisiveness) and the decisions that they did make reflected very definite personality traits. Willingness to accept mass violence (concretely as well as abstractly), confidence that disorder can be brought under control once unleashed, and a strong desire to assert that control—a real desire for power—are deeply rooted in personality rather than ideology. The spectrum of positions in the minimalist or maximalist, Jacobin or anti-Jacobin programs of the revolutionary factions already reflected not only tactical adaptation, but the transformation of ideology by personality. The study of leading personalities becomes especially germane when examining the Social Democrats, whose leaders had a major impact on the shape of Russian history during and after 1917.

Both Marxist circles and labor organizations affiliated with them appeared in the non-Russian western areas of the empire before becoming a significant phenomenon in Russia proper. The first Russian Marxist circles were strongly influenced by the Jewish workers' movement in Poland, Lithuania, and White Russia. The "Bund," as the Jewish workers' union was later called, had itself been influenced by the Polish socialist movement. Veterans of these earlier movements could thus point the way to the first important Russian Marxist organization. For example, Martov, later the leader of the Menshevik movement, began his practical work in Vilno and applied what he had learned there in St. Petersburg. *On Agitation,* a pamphlet jointly prepared by Martov and Alexander Kremer early in 1894, was widely disseminated and accepted as a practical guide for Russian Social Democratic circles in the period 1894–1896. The new Social Democratic tactic was related to the old one of enlightenment and propaganda in much the same way that Lavrovist preparationism had been related to Bakuninist insurrectionism. The authors of *On Agitation* believed that the workers' consciousness of their class interests and goals would emerge out of their daily struggle with their oppressors. Resemblances to Bakuninism can be seen in the following passage:

> The ground is now prepared for political agitation. This agitation finds a class organized by life itself, with a well developed class egoism, with an awareness of the common interests of all who toil, and of the opposition of these interests to the interests of all other classes. A change in the political structure is only a matter of time. One spark—and the accumulated inflammable material will burst into life.[5]

On Agitation emphasized the "logic of things" and thus seemingly reduced the role of the critically endowed intelligentsia. However, the pamphlet displayed awareness of the danger that the workers could be manipulated by the bourgeoisie, and the fully conscious intelligentsia was still visualized as the vanguard of the working-class movement.

The very profound problems inherent in Marxist theory for any group trying to play the role of a revolutionary vanguard are already evident in *On Agitation*. Marx's theory did encourage faith in the inherent logic of things as opposed to abstract logic or consciousness. Yet the revolutionary spirit of Marxism, always in tension with the Marxist faith in an inexorable dialectic, spurred revolutionaries to take immediate action—to intervene in the historical process. *On Agitation* thus served the militant, voluntarist side of Marxism. When in 1895–1896 this realization fully dawned upon them, the more impatient types (including Lenin) within the Social Democratic movement adopted the

---

5 Quoted in Allan K. Wildman, *The Making of a Workers' Revolution* (Chicago, 1967), pp. 47–48.

strategy of the day-to-day struggle against the bougeoisie and the government.

The period 1894–1896 is of special interest to historians because it embraces the beginning of Lenin's career as a Social Democrat, his first contacts with Martov, and his first efforts at practical work. In Soviet historical writing Lenin is always credited with startling prescience, and early organizations and movements with which he was associated are accorded far greater historical impact than they actually had. In unmasking Soviet historiography Western historians have sometimes tended to go to the other extreme. Thus, there is some historical dispute about Lenin's position in the group of St. Petersburg Social Democrats (called the *stariki*—the elders) which merged with a group led by Martov in October 1895, and in December began to call itself "The St. Petersburg Union of Struggle for the Emancipation of the Working Class." The real impact of the activities of the Union of Struggle on the large-scale strike movement of 1896–1897 has also been debated.

In any case, Lenin missed the main action of the period 1896–1897, when the textile workers in St. Petersburg organized two massive, extended strikes. Lenin, Martov, and most of the other leaders of the St. Petersburg Social Democratic organization were arrested in December 1895 and January 1896. The agitation and strike support carried on by the Union of Struggle after the arrests were conducted by the remnants of the organization. Despite the arrests, the Social Democratic movement derived a sense of confidence and real achievement from its association with the strike movement. The Social Democratic agitators, whatever their real influence on the strikers, felt that their strategies were working and that the process of radicalization of the workers was proceeding according to their vision. This confidence proved to be premature. The divergence between the aspirations of the workers and those of the Social Democratic intelligentsia leaders became increasingly apparent towards the turn of the century. The journal *The Workers' Thought,* first published by K. M. Takhterev and later guided by August Kok, between 1897 and 1901 became the major organ of the workers' independence movement.

The Social Democratic movement was not only troubled by an intelligentsia-worker split, but by defections from the revolutionary orthodoxy established and sustained by Plekhanov and Akselrod. The development of a real movement and participation in it forced some Marxists to reexamine their theoretical assumptions. Some of them developed the idea of the spontaneous struggle for economic concessions into the heresy which became known as "economism." Expressed mainly in E. D. Kuskova's "Credo" (1899) it called for the separation of economic from political movements. While the workers were to pursue their economic goals, the Social Democratic intelligentsia was to reinforce the liberal opposition. "Credo" appeared almost simultaneously with Eduard Bernstein's more important revisionist heresy, which represented an abandonment of revolutionary Marxism for evolutionary, legal socialism. Revisionism was a symptom of the success of the German Social Democratic movement. To a militant socialist in a country without a constitution or legal parties, whose working class had only recently won an eleven-and-a-half-hour working day, Bernstein's doctrine could hardly seem appropriate. Yet some of the most important theoreticians in the Marxist movement, Peter Struve being the leading figure, defected from the Social Democratic camp altogether and became proponents of left liberalism.

Economism and revisionism forced the orthodox to marshal all of their literary forces for a counterthrust. The several essays and organs of the heretics, although representing several shades of opinion, were attacked with equally bitter invective. In 1900, the orthodox camp (Plekhanov, Akselrod, Zasulich, Martov, Lenin, and Alexander Potresov) began to publish their own journal, *The Spark* (*Iskra*). However, the exponents of the political struggle and intelligentsia leadership were by no means temperamentally or theoretically uniform. Although his colleagues on *The Spark* were not immediately or fully aware of it, Lenin was not simply expressing the orthodox belief in the political struggle and fear of the hegemony of bourgeois liberalism over the working class. He was developing a theory of the hegemony of the conscious Social Democratic intelligentsia over the "spontaneous" and blind working-class movement. Lenin's radical distinction between the conscious intelligentsia and the blind masses, and his ideas about the composition and role of a Social Democratic party, were unique in the orthodox camp. Although Lenin's position was fully exposed in *What Is to Be Done?* a pamphlet published in 1902, its full implications did not dawn upon his colleagues until July–August 1903, at the Brussels–London founding congress of the Russian Social Democratic Workers' Party.

The split that occurred at the congress had immense historical significance, for Lenin emerged as the exponent of a distinct revolutionary tendency—Bolshevism. The event, which had been planned as a reaffirmation of orthodoxy, proved to be a bid by Lenin to convert the Russian Social Democratic Workers' Party into a narrow, tightly disciplined, highly centralized party of professional revolutionaries. Although noteworthy for its programmatic debates and the various maneuverings of *The Spark's* supporters against a collection of opponents (the most powerful of which were associated with the economist publication *The Worker's Cause* and the Bund), the true significance of the congress lay in the mutual recognition of "hards" and "softs" that profound differences separated them. The "softs," led by Martov, though not always outvoted, at the congress became known as the Mensheviks (members of the minority), while Lenin's "hards" became the Bolsheviks (members of the majority). The titles were not true indications of the relative strength of the two factions. In the months that followed the congress, it became increasingly clear that Lenin had isolated himself from the leading figures in the Social Democratic movement—Martov, Plekhanov, and Akselrod. The Menshevik movement embodied on the one hand the fear of a premature mass uprising and the establishment of a new authoritarianism and on the other a desire to prepare the way for a proper revolution by the gradual transformation of the spontaneous workers' movement into a broad, conscious revolutionary party.

Trotsky, still a political novice, who had joined *The Spark* in 1902 and whom Lenin had cultivated as an ally, now turned his brilliant pen against Lenin. The Mensheviks complained that Lenin's methods would replace the proletariat by an organization of professional revolutionaries, but Trotsky, seeing in

Lenin's brand of Jacobinism a kind of "substitutionism," made the point most dramatically, succinctly—and prophetically:

> In the party's internal politics these methods lead, as we shall further see, to this: the party organization "substitutes" itself for the party, the C.C. [Central Committee] "substitutes" itself for the party organization, and, at last, a "dictator" substitutes himself for the C.C.[6]

While the Social Democrats were squabbling among themselves, events within Russia were creating an ever more complex revolutionary situation. Unlike earlier periods of revolutionary history, the new period does not permit narrow focus upon the activities of one major party and its problems. The mass movements of the period 1899–1904 precipitated the formation of the two other major parties—the Socialist Revolutionaries and the Kadets—and quickened the development of the anarchist movement, now led primarily by disciples of Peter Kropotkin.

In 1899 the student movement assumed mass dimensions. The labor strikes served the students as a model for their strike of February 1899, in which there participated an estimated 13,000 students enrolled in about thirty institutions of higher learning. The government's attempt to intimidate the students failed. While the student movement of 1899 had begun in St. Petersburg, that of 1900–1901 began in Kiev, after 183 students were inducted into the army in accordance with the government's new repressive rules. In February 1901 there were large-scale street demonstrations in Khar'kov, Moscow, and St. Petersburg. In the former two cities, factory workers joined the students, but in St. Petersburg the demonstrators were exclusively students and "society." The government's brutal handling of demonstrators in these and numerous other urban demonstrations that followed only aggravated the situation. By 1902 students, workers, and "society" comprised a kind of revolutionary front. Furthermore, it was a politicized front, in that students and workers had gone beyond

6 N. Trotsky, *Nashi politicheskie zadachi* (Geneva, 1904), p. 54. Trotsky used the initial "N." in his pseudonym at this time. His real name was Lev Bronstein.

demands for academic freedom and economic improvement to demands for political freedom. The latter was, of course, a long-standing demand of "society." Unified, disciplined, and coordinated leadership was impossible during this period. Programs were still being disputed, local groups tried to assert their autonomy, and firm loyalties to the nascent parties and their programs had not spread beyond the still relatively small cadres operating in the industrial centers and university cities.

The revolutionary situation that began to take shape in 1899 acquired a new complexion when the agrarian rebellions of 1902 in Poltava, Khar'kov, and Saratov provinces breathed life into revolutionary populism. In the late 1890s work in the villages was still carried on by isolated groups of revolutionary populists and *zemstvo* workers with few ties and little means to carry on their propaganda and agitation. However, by the turn of the century a combination of economic circumstances aided and abetted by administrative bungling created a favorable environment for revolutionary activity in the black earth region. Revolutionary populists gravitated toward the Volga and the black earth zones in the Ukraine.

After 1901 there was a larger supply of propagandists—many of them students expelled from the universities during the student uprisings of the period. The students sometimes had ties with veterans like Katherine Breshkovskaia, who had been arrested in the Going to the People but had returned to European Russia from Siberian exile in the 1890s. She and a group of students from the agricultural school near Saratov resurrected old populist brochures and distributed them to scattered groups working in the villages. In addition to Socialist Revolutionary propaganda and agitation, the peasants were exposed to the ideas of the Revolutionary Ukrainian Party, one of the several new nationalist and socialist groups that were forming at the turn of the century. Ukrainophile circles received propaganda brochures from Lvov and translated them into Ukrainian.

Although the peasants accepted some of the socialist ideas propagated by the students, traditional loyalty to the tsar was still strong. Just before the rebellion in 1902 started in Poltava, familiar rumors about golden deeds and manifestoes signed by the tsar began to circulate. The tsar's agents were rumored to be in the countryside preparing to lead the peasants against the landlords. Nonetheless, the Socialist Revolutionaries were encouraged to believe that the peasants had outgrown their hostility toward the revolutionary intelligentsia and were becoming a more conscious revolutionary force. This was especially true of the movement in Saratov province. *Revolutionary Russia,* the organ of the Socialist Revolutionary Party, expressed renewed optimism about a revolutionary peasantry.

In addition to their work among the peasants the Socialist Revolutionaries revived the tradition of political assassination. For this purpose they created the "Fighting Organization," a group devoted to terror. In the same way that terrorism had developed after Zasulich's exploit, the Fighting Organization was not really launched until an expelled student took revenge for the government's brutal handling of his comrades by assassinating N. P. Bogolepov, the minister of education. This was the first in an extended series of political assassinations, some of them conducted by SR organizations, others by free-lance assassins motivated by a desire for revenge. The most notable early exploits of the SRs were the assassinations of D. S. Sipiagin (1902) and V. K. von Plehve (1904), both ministers of the interior, the latter one of the most widely hated men in Russia.

The terrorism of the new generation was of a somewhat more complicated character than that of The People's Will. B. V. Savinkov, an SR terrorist who described the psychology of his colleagues in his memoirs, provides some understanding of the various types who were attracted to terror. A great many terrorists, both SR and anarchist, were young Jews, whose suicidal extremism can be traced to a large extent to the violent antisemitism during Nicholas's reign. The majority of acts of terror (70 percent) were now perpetrated mainly by nonintelligentsia members of the SR party. In the period 1905–1906 terror assumed a quite different character from the earlier crisis periods of 1878–1882 and 1902–1904. Not unexpectedly, with the influx of nonintelligentsia revolutionaries, it assumed a "plebian" character, with banditry, extortion, and revenge against local figures playing an ever-greater role during the revolutionary upsurge of 1905. Moreover, especially in the latter phases of the revolution of 1905, terrorism attracted Social Democrats and anarchists.[7]

Finally, the liberal movement quickened in response to the events of 1901–1902. One symptom of this was the first all-Russian *zemstvo* congress, held in Moscow in May 1902. The other important sign was *Liberation's* leftward movement in 1903, and the formation of the left liberal Union of Liberation in July 1903. The Union of Liberation was transformed into the Kadet (Constitutional Democratic) Party in 1905. The Kadet Party, too, moved with the radical tide and, in its zeal to find a striking force against the autocracy, encouraged the widespread terror that emerged in 1905. In their rhetorical support for terror, the Kadets had recourse to Turgenev's poem, "The Threshold," cited earlier.[8] The doctrine of "no enemies to the left," however, not only split the Kadets, but lost adherents when the Kadets emerged from their temporary intoxication with the struggle and reflected on the extent of anarchy and violence unleashed in 1905–1907.

Several conclusions can be drawn in considering the period 1899–1903. The movements of these years were a preview of the much more potent revolutionary front that would form in 1904–1905. They were large-scale, but lacked the truly mass character of the 1905 movements. The "return" of the peasants as a revolutionary force is possibly the most important single development of the period, not only because of the strengthened SR party, but because the Social Democrats were forced to fit the peasants into their revolutionary plans. Finally, the government, faced with large-scale disturbances, demonstrated that it no longer had the capacity to moderate popular movements by substituting its own paternalism for the leadership of radical groups. The failure of Colonel S. V. Zubatov's "police socialism" (1901–1903) was one clear example of this. Zubatov unions, which had been

---

7 For studies of SR terror see: Maureen Perrie, "The Social Composition and Structure of the Socialist-Revolutionary Party before 1917," *Soviet Studies* 24 (1972): 223–250; Anna Geifman, "Political Parties and Revolutionary Terrorism in Russia, 1900–1917," unpublished Ph.D. dissertation, Harvard University, 1991.

8 See Anna Geifman, "The Kadets and Terrorism, 1905–1907," *Jahrbücher für Geschichte Osteuropas* 36 (1988): 260.

formed with the blessing of the autocracy, joined the general strike in southern Russia in June 1903.[9] Another example was the government's convening of a conference in 1902 to deal with agrarian problems. Although Nicholas II was truly concerned about the peasantry, in keeping with his traditionalist philosophy (if one can call it that), he was of two minds about the course to be pursued in the countryside. His ambivalence was reflected in the conflict between Witte, his minister of finance, and von Plehve, minister of the interior (1902–1904). Nicholas was much closer to the archconservatives in his court and government, and eventually conceded more to them than to rational bureaucrats. Traditionalism, virulent antisemitism, and military adventurism more nearly reflected Nicholas's own sentiments than did the hard-headed manipulativeness of rational bureaucrats like Witte. The diversion of internal discontent into government-supported antisemitism (the great pogroms of 1903 in Bessarabia, the Ukraine, and White Russia) and the channeling of national energies into the Russo-Japanese War failed no less than Cossack whips and "police socialism" to arrest the developing mass movements.

On the other hand, the newly formed revolutionary organizations had wide influence but exercised only limited leadership and control over some elements in the mass movements. This was true in both peasant rebellions of 1902 and the general southern strike of 1903. The complexities of social change and the psychology of the mass movements were such that neither the government nor the revolutionary parties were fully prepared for the events of 1905.

THE REVOLUTIONARY INTELLIGENTSIA IN 1905

In the period 1899–1904, the Russian government could restore at least external order by the frequent use of troops. This was true

9 S. V. Zubatov (1864–1917), chief of the Moscow *Okhrana,* in 1901 created workers' organizations under police guidance that became quite popular in Moscow in 1902. Zubatov's efforts, however, only heightened worker militancy. He was dismissed in 1903.

because most of the demonstrations, insurrections, and strikes involved hundreds, thousands, or tens of thousands and either occurred separately in time or were limited geographically. The government was aware that eventually these separate movements might merge into a revolutionary front, but could do nothing to prevent it. The defeats suffered by Russia's armies and fleets in the Russo-Japanese War served as the catalyst for the formation of the revolutionary front of 1905.

The revolution of 1905, often regarded as a dress rehearsal for 1917, was actually something quite different. In fact, the behavior of the actors of 1917 was very much influenced by the way that they reacted to the experience of 1905. What seems extraordinary is that the leaders of the parties of 1905 were still present in 1917 to play their new roles—roles that some of them had been preparing for consciously, others unconsciously. The experience of mass violence, of revolutionary victories won and then snatched away, of leadership suddenly acquired and lost, of chances exploited or missed, could not but affect the plans of the revolutionary leaders. Above all, the revolution of 1905 confirmed Lenin's contempt for the "bourgeois" elements who were supposed to be the immediate beneficiaries of the revolution. He changed, however, his attitude toward spontaneity. Before the revolution of 1905, for Lenin spontaneity had connoted a soft, opportunistic, slothful, and "tailist" strategy, rendering the workers susceptible to trade-unionism instead of revolution. Quite the contrary, 1905 showed that spontaneity might spark aggressive revolutionary energy and self-mobilization.

The Russian Revolution of 1905 exhibited a number of "classical" features. There was a movement from right to left. The government's initial concessions to the right wing of the revolutionary front were insufficient appeasement for the left-wing elements. A period of relative anarchy followed, which frightened important groups and pushed them towards the right. The government's final concessions and its ability to use its instruments of force effectively against relatively uncoordinated mass resistance permitted it to stabilize the situation at a point much farther to the right than either left liberals or revolutionary socialists had expected. In this respect, all revolutionary parties were disappointed by the outcome of the revolution of 1905.

It is rather difficult to pick out the beginning point of the revolution of 1905, because the several social groups involved began their pressure upon the government at different moments. One must really begin the story in January 1904, with the outbreak of the Russo-Japanese War. The appeals to patriotism made by the government temporarily interrupted the growth of oppositional movements. The Japanese surprise attack on the Russian fleet at Port Arthur and the initial defeat suffered there had the effect of uniting Russian national sentiment around the figure of the tsar.

The first real pressure upon the government during this period of respite came from "society" in the form of the *zemstvo* movement. Von Plehve's refusal to confirm Dmitrii Shipov in office as chairman of the Moscow provincial *zemstvo* in April 1904 was the first sign of the struggle between "society" and the state in this period of crisis. The assassination of von Plehve by E. S. Sazonov, a member of the SR Fighting Organization, was an important turning point in that von Plehve's successor, Prince P. D. Sviatopolk-Mirsky, was seen as a conciliator and his appointment regarded as a concession to "society," just as at the end of Nicholas I's reign the articulate and politically conscious public sensed the beginning of a "thaw." Sviatopolk-Mirsky was indeed willing to take steps gradually to integrate the *zemstvo* movement with existing organs of central government, thus making a move in the direction of popular representation. However, opposition to the zemstvos in the central government was too strong, and Sviatopolk-Mirsky was powerless to yield real concessions. The government's vacillations in its dealings with the conservative, rather Slavophile gentry liberalism expressed by Shipov proved to be inconsequential, for Shipov spoke for a relatively weak faction within the liberal movement. While the government dickered with Shipov, militant left liberalism in the form of the Union of Liberation began to assert its leadership of "society."

Since the major revolutionary parties believed that the overthrow of autocracy and the establishment of a democratic constitution had to occur before they could accomplish their more distant goals, the program of the Union of Liberation served as a rallying point for the radical opposition. The first real cooperation between liberals and revolutionary socialists occurred at the Paris conference of September and October 1904. The conference was attended by the representatives of eight parties, the most important of which were the Union of Liberation and the Socialist Revolutionaries. The remaining parties represented nationalist and socialist movements—Polish, Finnish, Latvian, Georgian, and Armenian (two Polish parties attended). The program that they agreed upon called for the abolition of autocracy, the establishment of a democratic government, protection of national minorities in the empire, and the right to national self-determination. The Mensheviks and Bolsheviks had not yet worked out their tactical relationship to the liberal movement and did not participate in the conference. Operating under the assumption that the fall of the autocracy was imminent, they as well as the Liberationists had to find a way to make use of "society's" organizations within Russia. Since the *zemstvo* movement and the professional unions had at least the opportunity to hold congresses, exhibits, and banquets, they became the primary vehicles for all oppositional groups within "society." The second all-Russian *zemstvo* congress, which met in St. Petersburg early in November 1904, produced the "Eleven Theses" which, while carefully avoiding use of the word "constitution," in effect demanded one. Shipov represented the minority, which asked for a consultative rather than legislative assembly. Neither the majority nor the minority at the congress went along with the Union of Liberation's demand for the convening of a constituent assembly based upon universal, direct, equal, and secret suffrage. The Union of Liberation's program was set forth in the professional meetings and banquets held in a large number of cities toward the end of November 1904 precisely for the purpose of organizing political opposition. The banquet campaign was the zenith of liberal opposition in 1904.

During that same year, the Bolsheviks and Mensheviks were in a state of relative disorganization and had only tenuous ties with the labor movement. They engaged in hair-splitting debates about the relationship of Social Democracy and the labor movement to the coming revolution. But Social Democrats now had to move in the real world of political movements and had to choose some course of joint action with the class enemies of the proletariat. Both Mensheviks and Bolsheviks viewed the Russian "bourgeoisie" with a mixture of contempt and fear—contempt for their weakness and cowardice, but fear of the power that they might gain over the working-class movement. Social Democrats did not believe that the bourgeoisie could bring down the autocracy without the support of the working class, yet they did not want the working class to develop any real ties with the class enemy. Thus, they stood for both support of and opposition to the bourgeoisie. The Mensheviks chose to join the banquet campaign. Lenin, having acquired his own organ, *Forward!*, with which to criticize *The Spark*, now a Menshevik organ, evinced typical hostility toward any form of collaboration with a liberal movement. He proposed the tactic of a revolutionary uprising led by the proletariat.

The tactical debate over the banquet campaign seems rather academic in view of what followed. But Lenin's unwillingness to permit the proletariat to share the banquet halls with the bourgeoisie was a clear foreshadowing of his repudiation of "diarchy" in 1917, just as the Menshevik and SR tolerance for joint action, however restricted and infused with a spirit of antagonism, foreshadowed their support for the Provisional Government in 1917. In 1905 neither Bolsheviks nor Mensheviks had sufficient control over the labor movement to determine its larger course.

The real impetus for the labor movement came from an organization that had received government support, having been conceived in much the same spirit as Zubatov's earlier unions. The government still believed that it could exploit the religious and national sentiments of the working class by careful manipulation. George Gapon, a priest and former prison chaplain, became head of the St. Petersburg Assembly of Russian Factory Workers (February 1904). Toward the end of 1904, in keeping with the general tendency within Russia for mass discontent to seek legal channels, thousands of St. Petersburg factory workers enrolled in Gapon's organization. Gapon emancipated himself from Zubatov's conception of "police socialism" and pursued an independent course that eventually made him more an ally of the workers than of the government. The Social Democrats, primarily Mensheviks, and a few SRs tried to operate within the context of the Assembly meetings at the end of 1904. The simple, passionate, and direct appeal of Gapon and the workers who spoke at the organization's branch meetings (by January 1905 there were several thousand actual members and tens of thousands of sympathizers) mystified the agents of the revolutionary parties who tried to infiltrate and manipulate the Assembly. Although they spoke at the meetings and may have had some influence, it is certain that they were caught unawares by the movement and entered it only shortly before its demise. It is Gapon himself who gave his movement its peculiarly eclectic character. Gapon was evidently quite receptive to ideas, and had been exposed to the entire spectrum of liberal and radical thought. Like Zubatov, he passionately believed in his cause and his methods. Gapon's naiveté and eclecticism repelled the revolutionary intelligentsia, but his effectiveness made them all the more aware of their own remoteness from the masses.

Gapon proved his loyalty to his workers when he supported their strike against the management of the Putilov works. It began on January 3, 1905, and within five days grew into a general strike embracing more than 100,000 factory workers—the vast majority of St. Petersburg's factory labor force. Throughout this period, the Assembly maintained extraordinary discipline, given the mass character of the strike. Gapon felt fully confident that he could crown the strike movement by leading a solemn procession to the Winter Palace, where he would present the tsar with a petition from the Russian people. Gapon's naive faith and the government's incompetence led to the events of January 9, which became known as Bloody Sunday. Gapon's petition was written in the old style, addressed to a paternal tsar who was asked to mitigate the awful burdens imposed upon the Russian people by tyrannical bureaucrats and exploitative capitalists. However, substantively the petition was close to the program of left liberalism, demanding the election of a constituent assembly on the basis of universal, secret, direct, and equal suffrage. It also incorporated ideas propagated generally by the socialist parties that included "measures to eliminate" the poverty of the people and the exploitation of workers by capital, an eight-hour workday, and the legalization of trade unions. The long icon-bearing columns that converged from the working-class sections of the city toward the Winter Palace on the morning of January 9 were met at several points along the way by troops and were dispersed after being fired upon. Gapon never reached the tsar with his petition. Later in the day, troops fired upon a mob gathered on the square before the Winter Palace. Similar scenes occurred during the afternoon. After the workers had been dispersed, groups of students tried to keep the rebellion alive by building street barricades, but they were unsuccessful. Nonetheless, the events of January 9, occurring as they did against the background of an unsuccessful war and a vacillating government, signalled the entry of the masses into the revolution of 1905.

Gapon's historical role was over, although neither he nor the socialist parties who fought over him like a prize (he fled to Europe) knew it yet. At first he evidently thought that he could sustain leadership of the labor movement from abroad, now as an avowed revolutionary. After a time, however, Gapon gave up this design and returned to St. Petersburg. His moment had passed. Gapon found himself a leader without a mass following in the autumn of 1905. A complicated man who could not readily give up his projects and celebrity, he then tried to regain his standing with the tsarist authorities. His unscrupulous design to use both the police and the revolutionaries to reestablish his position ended when a group of SRs assassinated Gapon in March 1906.

The great service that Gapon rendered the revolutionary parties is not easily measured, but it is probably no exaggeration to say that no single event of the last two reigns so strongly affected the popular masses' attitude towards the tsar. The opposite of what both Gapon and the government had intended occurred, and the revolutionary parties became the ultimate beneficiaries of his movement. The masses became "political."

In the complex revolutionary situation that developed shortly after Bloody Sunday, all of the Empire's major urban centers were affected. By mid-January, hundreds of thousands of factory workers had struck and were supported by student bodies, faculties, professional organizations, industrial associations, and merchant guilds. Although the revolutionary front was not controlled or led by a single party, the left liberal program of the Union of Liberation was close to the general political tenor of "society" and was influential among the workers. The first real sign that the government was yielding under pressure came in

February, shortly after a member of the SR Fighting Organization assassinated the tsar's uncle, Grand Duke Sergei. Nicholas issued a rescript to the new minister of the interior, A. G. Bulygin, ordering him to establish a consultative assembly (duma). At this point, moderate concessions could not satisfy the major oppositional groups, who later boycotted elections to the "Bulygin Duma"; efforts to placate the factory workers failed; the war continued to go badly; and the peasants joined the revolutionary front on a significant scale in the summer of 1905.

As unrest continued, the government's ability to intercede diminished, and the rudimentary organizations among oppositional groups began to crystallize into wholly new kinds of sociopolitical entities. The first such entity appeared in May 1905, under the guidance of Paul Miliukov. It was the largest united segment of "society" ever to assemble under one banner. The Union of Unions, as the new organization was called, embraced fourteen "unions," mostly professional unions but also organizations representing railroad workers, clerks and bookkeepers, and civil rights causes. Next to appear was the Peasant Union, which had its first congress in Moscow in July 1905. The small number (125) of peasant and intelligentsia delegates could hardly claim to represent Russia's peasant masses, but the union can be regarded as an extension of the concept behind the Union of Unions into the countryside. Although the Union of Liberation played the largest role in creating the new sociopolitical form, the Mensheviks, Bolsheviks, and SRs continued to have influence over some of its elements.

However, the most significant development occurred in the factories. Once again, government attempts to channel the labor movement into safe organizations played into the hands of the opposition. The Shidlovskii Commission, named for its chairman, Senator N. V. Shidlovskii, in February 1905 arranged elections in the factories of St. Petersburg in order to select labor's representatives to a commission for the examination of labor problems. Unwittingly, the government was increasing the workers' experience in election procedures and accustoming them to the idea of workers' deputies. The Mensheviks and Bolsheviks were faced with their usual tactical problem: what could be gained by participation in or boycott of the Shidlovskii commission? The Menshevik vision of a broad Social Democratic labor organization, moving step by step toward revolution, at each step participating in the political process, once again contrasted with the Bolshevik preference for direct and swift revolutionary action against the government. Thus, while the Mensheviks prepared for the electoral campaign in hopes that the workers could use the Commission as a platform for political demands, the Bolsheviks were in favor of boycotting the elections. The Mensheviks assumed that, having elected their deputies to the Commission, the workers would show their solidarity with the deputies by conducting a general strike on the day the Commission's hearings opened. As it turned out, the workers' electors learned in advance that the Commission would not consider their demands, and so they did not proceed to elect deputies, and the general strike was called.

Even more serious tactical problems were raised by the appearance of a strong trade-union movement in 1905. Here the Mensheviks gained a distinct advantage because of their tendency to try to adjust their tactics to the spontaneous labor movement. The Bolsheviks, on the other hand, at first displayed considerable tactical rigidity when confronted with spontaneous forms of labor organization, but in the hurly-burly of 1905 began adapting themselves to them.

The most significant development in the labor movement did not occur until mid-October 1905, when under Menshevik leadership the Soviet of Workers' Deputies was formed in St. Petersburg. The soviet emerged (as did other similar organizations) from the massive strike movement that reached its peak in the Great October General Strike.[10] For about seven weeks, within the framework of the soviet, representatives of the major revolutionary parties debated and discussed questions of strategy with workers' deputies. Never before had the revolutionary intelligentsia had such a direct and open voice in the formation of the

10 The word "soviet" means "council" in Russian. The St. Petersburg Soviet, comprised of deputies from numerous industrial establishments and representatives of the radical parties, was the leading workers' assembly. It was widely imitated in provincial towns. Ultimately, hundreds of factories and tens of thousands of workers were represented.

strategies of mass action. The period of the first St. Petersburg Soviet is thus a crucial moment in the history of the relationships between the revolutionary intelligentsia and the revolutionary masses, and the hero of the moment was Lev Trotsky.

Unable to achieve parity with the leaders of the Social Democratic factions, and after a brief alliance with the Mensheviks, he began to play an independent role in the movement. Trotsky, though nominally a Menshevik, was already asserting his own interpretation of Marxism. In the milling crowds of St. Petersburg, Trotsky seemed to have found his element. He demonstrated an extraordinary grasp of the anatomy and psychology of mass movements and an equally unusual talent for engineering mass action. It was Trotsky who first fully realized the potential power of the soviets as a governing body.[11]

Trotsky's doctrine of permanent revolution is the most clearly focused and radical of several similar Marxist formulations, the most important of which had been expressed by A. L. Helphand (who wrote under the pseudonym, Parvus). Although one can find all of the essential features of the doctrine of permanent revolution in Trotsky's writings of 1905, he did not express them in systematic form until 1906, after he had been arrested and imprisoned for his activities in the St. Petersburg Soviet. Trotsky, in effect, discovered what the Russian populists and a number of Russian historians had always maintained: that Russia's historical development set it somewhat apart from Western Europe. Like the populists, Trotsky derived an optimistic conclusion from the weakness of the bourgeoisie, but he replaced the peasants with the proletariat as the vanguard of socialism. Russian backwardness and the weakness of the bourgeoisie were seen as conditions which would thrust the proletariat into power as a dictatorial class. Thus, a bourgeois revolution followed by a period of bourgeois rule was impossible in Russia. But in view of the distribution of social forces, the proletariat would not be able to consolidate its power without help from the proletariat of other countries. According to Trotsky's doctrine of permanent revolu-

---

11 Trotsky assumed leadership of the St. Petersburg Soviet after the arrest of G. S. Khrustalev-Nosar on November 27, 1905.

tion, the Russian revolution would have to be the prelude to a general European revolution.

Trotsky's vision of a dictatorship of the proletariat was far more radical than anything contemplated by either Mensheviks or Bolsheviks. By narrowing the base of revolutionary power and initiative to the proletariat, Trotsky had also theoretically narrowed the revolutionary government to the party of the proletariat. The relationship between proletariat and peasantry would be that of liberator to liberated, benefactor to beneficiary. As will be seen, this onesidedness was remedied by Trotsky's association with Lenin in 1917. While Trotsky at first tended to be wary of allying with the peasants and feared them as class enemies, Lenin prized them as allies and emphasized the process of stratification within the peasantry that would make the poor peasants class allies of the proletariat. The real weakness in Trotsky's theory lay in its failure to grasp fully the force of nationalism, the disunity of international socialism, and their consequences for permanent revolution.

Lenin, somewhat slower than Trotsky in 1905 to abandon the idea of two distinct revolutionary phases, believed that the soviets could become the nucleus for a provisional revolutionary government. However, this provisional government was seen as a force to be used to overthrow the autocracy rather than as a government for its own sake. Lenin believed that the soviets might serve as the means to create a democratic dictatorship of the proletariat and peasantry, itself a transitional type of revolutionary government containing both socialist and bourgeois elements. Lenin too was hopeful that this phase might be short, or that a European revolution might permit Russia to pass uninterruptedly into the socialist revolution. Like Trotsky, he had no patience with the liberal bourgeoisie. Lenin's initial reaction to the soviets was consistent with his long-standing wariness toward any mass movement or sociopolitical organization that had developed spontaneously rather than at his party's initiative. However, his flexibility distinguished him from many members of his own party, who were simply Bolsheviks and not Leninists. Lenin's sociology of the Russian peasantry was wrong, as was Trotsky's belief that successful European social revolutions would follow the Russian one, but their erroneous views became essential components of an optimistic outlook permitting Russian revolutionaries to justify their momentous gamble in 1917.

The painful experience of lagging behind the mass movement in the early phases of the revolution of 1905, of seeing charlatans like Gapon and (to him, at least) windbags like Trotsky assuming leadership of a mass labor movement taught Lenin a valuable lesson. The vanguard would have to be able to adapt itself to spontaneity before harnessing it. The Mensheviks were more successful in 1905 than the Bolsheviks because of their predisposition toward cooperative ventures and their faith in the potentialities of sociopolitical organizations that emerged spontaneously from mass movements. They continued to believe that power would have to pass to a bourgeois party, something that Trotsky no longer believed and that Lenin professed to believe but never really wanted to happen.

Meanwhile, the movement in "society" based upon the *zemstvos* and professional unions partially disintegrated under the impact of governmental concessions and the fear of mass violence. The left liberals maintained their attitude of "no enemies to the left," but several shades of liberal opinion feared a social revolution. In October 1905 Miliukov assumed leadership of the Kadet Party, which detached itself from the more moderate liberal elements in "society." The Kadets under Miliukov had a rather ambivalent attitude toward armed revolution. They believed that up to a point the revolutionary activities of the SDs and SRs would work to their own benefit, but they themselves did not want to encourage mass violence or an armed uprising against the government. It would be no exaggeration to say that the Kadets wanted an orderly revolution—one that went just far enough to topple the autocracy and establish true democracy in Russia. This was not too far from the Menshevik idea that the revolutionary proletariat, having pushed the bourgeoisie into power, would acquiesce in bourgeois rule. Thus, the community of interest that Miliukov believed existed between his party and the Social Democrats was not wholly a fantasy. By 1917, Miliukov's fear of revolution and anarchy had progressed to such an extent that he had become far more conservative about means to be used for the creation of a constituent assembly.

Finally, the SRs, who had played a significant role in both the Peasant Union and the soviets, continued to pursue an eclectic program with the socialization of the land as their most distinctive revolutionary goal. They did not believe in the necessity of a bourgeois revolution, but believed that their ultimate goal of socialism in both the countryside and the cities would be reached in two phases, as described earlier. In many respects, the vast jacquerie that broke out in the agricultural provinces of European Russia in the autumn of 1905 repeated the rebellions of 1902, though on a much grander scale. The SRs were quite successful in organizing the insurrections in areas where they had sunk deep roots, such as Saratov province, but had little real control over the uprisings as a whole. Agitation in the countryside issued from a variety of parties, and the peasants were easily inflamed. But they were also easily subdued by armed expeditions into the countryside. No less than for the Social Democrats and the liberals, the events of 1904–1905 created tactical problems for the SRs. In 1906 the party split into three groups—the left-wing Maximalists, who rejected the two-phase scheme proposed by Chernov and were temperamentally and doctrinally close to anarchism; the right-wing Popular Socialists who, in the spirit of "Legal Populism," tried to revive the more traditional populism that had existed before Chernov's revision, but without terror and with a longer time frame for social transformation; and the "orthodox" majority under Chernov's leaderhip, whose maximum program called for the achievement of socialism, and whose minimum program demanded a wide range of democratic reforms. Although quick to suspend terror in October 1905 when the government showed signs of yielding to the minimum program, orthodox SR leaders would not renounce terror as a method of revolutionary struggle and soon revived it.[12] Terror did not prove to be a liability, and the SRs' peculiarly eclectic approach, coupled with their efforts in both the factories and the villages, gave them broader appeal than the Social Democrats. Recent scholarship suggests that they expended a great deal of

12 See Maureen Perrie, *The Agrarian Policy of the Russian Socialist-Revolutionary Party* (Cambridge, U.K., 1976), pp. 160–167.

effort on the factory workers, with significant success.[13] Splits in the SR Party in some respects paralleled those in the Social Democratic Party. As it turned out, Chernov's commitment to two phases, and his belief that a constituent assembly was a necessary prelude to the first phase, eventually made him an ally of the Mensheviks and Kadets.

The newest formulas for revolution drawn up by the factions of the major parties, their peasant land programs, and their labor programs exhibited the influence of their historical and ethical sociologies, their bias for the proletariat or peasantry, their affinity for democratic or authoritarian political structures, and their patience or impatience with the course of the revolution. The Mensheviks, "orthodox" SRs, and Kadets already revealed the commitment to democratic procedures, cooperation, and orderly historical development that led them into disaster in 1917. Trotsky and Lenin displayed the ultrarevolutionary passion, tactical flexibility, and appreciation for the use of the masses as instruments that permitted them to harness mass action to their purposes in 1917. Adventurousness and authoritarianism—willingness to see things explode into temporary chaos, the confidence that order could be restored, and the fierce desire that their party should stand at the head of the new order—were the combination of traits that distinguished Trotsky and Lenin from the other major leaders in the final revolutionary crisis. It also distinguished them from the anarchists, who certainly possessed the first trait, but not the second.

In 1905 the old regime still had sufficient resources to cope with revolution. Witte, having played the major role in extricating Russia from the Russo-Japanese War in August 1905 and in yielding up the October Manifesto giving Russia the semblance of a parliament, waited for the rebellion to subside. Nothing of the sort happened. The revolution in the cities and countryside only gained in intensity, and the period between the granting of the Manifesto and the destruction of the Moscow Soviet in December 1905 became known as the Days of Freedom. This was a preview of the "diarchy" in 1917. Soviets and revolutionary com-

---

13 For example, see Michael Melancon, "The Socialist Revolutionaries from 1902–1907: Peasant and Workers' Party," *Russian History* 12 (Spring 1985): 2–47.

mittees in both the cities and countryside acted as local governments. Until the arrest of its leaders, the St. Petersburg Soviet was the organizational focal point of quasi-governmental activity during the Days of Freedom. However, insufficient solidarity and cooperation among the urban soviets, and the relative isolation of the agrarian revolts from the urban movement, permitted the government to reconquer both the cities and the countryside.

Numerous mutinies in the army and navy (the mutiny of June 1905 on the battleship *Potemkin* being the most celebrated) revealed the fragility of the regime's authority among those who were presumably trained to respond to its commands. They were sufficiently widespread to prompt a recent investigator to write that there was "a soldiers' rebellion akin to the workers' and peasants' rebellions."[14] However, when the loyal troops crushed the rebellions in the major centers in December 1905, the mutinous ones quickly came into line and proved to be reliable in the later stages of repression during 1906 and 1907. Neither the authority of the state nor its power collapsed in the period 1905–1907. The Russian heartland and the borderlands, where the nationalities problem had intensified the revolution and given it added political significance for the empire, were largely subdued by the beginning of 1906.

The undemocratic character of the Duma created by the new constitution was fully appreciated by the major parties, and they responded to it in much the same way that they had responded to the idea of the Bulygin duma. Nicholas had never intended to permit the Duma to become a genuine legislature. It was designed to be an instrument dominated by social groups loyal to the dynasty. However, the first two elections revealed that the autocracy rested upon a much narrower social base than had been assumed, and the government was unable to control the Duma until Prime Minister Stolypin dissolved the Second Duma in June 1907 and issued a new election law. Not only had the government failed to convene a constituent assembly elected by universal, direct, and equal suffrage; it had also, by

---

14 John Bushnell, "The Revolution of 1905–1906 in the Army: The Incidence and Impact of Mutiny," *Russian History* 12 (Spring 1985): 73.

Stolypin's coup d'état, changed the election law to favor moderate and right-wing social groups.

The Kadets, the strongest party in the first Duma, failed to force the government to transform the Duma into a genuine parliament. They compounded this failure by issuing the Vyborg Manifesto, which was supposed to revive mass opposition to the government, but in effect gave the government a pretext for destroying the left liberal opposition and thus ending the threat from "society."[15] Terror, however, persisted on a massive scale and lingered on well after Stolypin had succeeded in crushing most of it with thousands of military courts martial and summary executions—the familiar hangman's nooses were dubbed "Stolypin's neckties." The revolutionaries and the regime inflicted casualties whose magnitude suggests guerrilla war rather than the limited traditional style of Russian terrorism. During 1906–1907 the total of government officials killed and wounded reached approximately 4,500, with an additional 4,710 private citizens, for a grand total of more than 9,000 casualties.[16] Terrorism took on the character of banditry. The anarchists practiced indiscriminate terror. The SR command structure lost control over random violence perpetrated by raw recruits with weak party ties who often acted out of a desire for personal revenge or pecuniary gain. SR Maximalists and Bolsheviks collaborated, with the Bolshevik technical expert, Leonid Krasin, supplying bombs and Maximalists supplying the terrorists. Lenin was not above using the tactic of "expropriations" (robberies of state funds) to replenish the Party's coffers.

These tactics only served to increase the splintering of the Social Democrats. Lenin and the Bolsheviks embraced the new tactics enthusiastically, while the Mensheviks condemned them. Bolshevik association with the SR Maximalists in this period foreshadowed their alliance with the left SRs in 1917. In any case,

---

15 The Vyborg Manifesto was issued by mainly Kadet deputies to the Duma under the leadership of Miliukov. This appeal urged the people to refuse to pay taxes and to resist the draft as a way of protesting the dissolution of the Duma. The appeal failed.

16 A. Geifman, "The Kadets and Terrorism, 1905–1907": 250–51.

the new tactics were a sign of desperation, and Stolypin's extraordinary measures to cope with terror were quite successful. By 1907 he had curbed SRs, anarchists, and Bolsheviks and created at least external order in the empire.

6 | THE REVOLUTIONS OF 1917

THE PRELUDE

In the years 1907–1911 the old regime regained confidence; the revolutionary parties entered a period of defeat, schism, and scandal. Peter Stolypin's policy of reform combined with repression threatened at first to undercut all of the decades of struggle and sacrifice, all of the revolutionary successes of recent years. In 1913 the Romanovs celebrated the tercentenary of their dynasty in high spirits. Nicholas II and Alexandra could still dream of passing the throne to their only son. If the history of the Russian imperial regime could be written as Greek tragedy, then this would be the moment of blindness before the final *peripeteia*—the reversal of fortune—that led to the fall of Tsarism. But the personal weaknesses of Nicholas II make it difficult to cast him as a tragic hero. Perhaps Stolypin, the energetic social engineer who fell to an assassin's bullet in 1911, better qualifies for the role. Stolypin was probably doomed politically anyway by Nicholas's preference for archconservatives. It is difficult to assess his grandest project—the dissolution of the peasant commune in favor of individual ownership of farms—in view of the brevity of the experiment. Moreover, Stolypin's own high-handed methods and policies could satisfy neither the left-wing parties, the centrists, nor the right in the Duma and State Council, and finally earned him the enmity of a formidable coalition. His death probably spared him from an inglorious fall. It is not clear that any statesman, however skilled, could have managed the vast problems of the multinational empire while simultaneously catering to Nicholas and Alexandra. The ensuing tragedy was borne by the huge, impoverished population enclosed in the borders of the empire—and by the intelligentsia trying to liberate it. They were the ones who paid the costs of modernization, war, revolution, civil war, and famine with millions of lives.

Stolypin's assassination in 1911 left Nicholas free to indulge his preference for the unregenerate right. With Stolypin gone, Nicholas and Alexandra created further turmoil with their confused policies. Increasingly the leaders of the Fourth Duma (1912–1917) were pushed to the left. They formed the Progressive Bloc in 1915, which, in turn, became the incubator of the first Provisional Government of 1917.

Despite the numerous concessions yielded by the government during the revolutionary period, and in spite of Stolypin's major agrarian reforms, not one of the major problems facing the old regime was solved during the period 1907–1914. Stolypin's harsh treatment of the nationalities increased tensions among the minorities and in the borderlands. The standard of living of workers and peasants remained low, and their grievances against the bureaucracy, factory owners, and landowners were not significantly diminished by the social and economic changes that historians have often erroneously interpreted as a symptom of Russia's passage into an era of relatively stable economic and social progress. The pacification of "society" and the passivity of the intelligentsia have also been interpreted as signs of a growing spirit of moderation, but these were more often symptoms of despair, temporary withdrawal, or resignation to the apocalypse. The intelligentsia was still alienated; it had simply discovered that "decadence" was an alternative to activism. Finally, the revolutionary intelligentsia still clung to its faith in spite of arrests, desertions, party scandals, and new schisms.

The surge of modernization which had been promoted by Stolypin's agrarian reforms also led to the reradicalization of Russia's industrial centers, especially St. Petersburg. After 1912, there was a new period of massive strikes and labor violence. The revolutionary parties, especially the Bolsheviks and SRs, gained recruits from the newly urbanized masses who had been displaced from the countryside in the wake of Stolypin's agrarian reforms. One might conclude from this, as have some historians, that a revolution would have occurred even without World War I and Russia's military defeat. World War I did indeed interrupt an upsurge of labor militancy and the growth of Bolshevik strength. Until recently, all Soviet and some Western historians opined that only the Tsarist regime's brutal intervention and crushing of the Bolshevik organizations in 1914 arrested the development of the proletarian movement toward revolution under Bolshevik leadership. Moreover, according to this line of thought, the regime's actions permitted a revival of Menshevik and SR influence over urban labor.

The labor movement, never monolithic, responded to a variety of radical appeals, but also to patriotic ones. No socialist party could lay claim to the undivided and continuous loyalty of labor; nor did the process of social polarization mean that Bolsheviks were always the first choice of radicalized proletarians. The picture of the Bolsheviks as the natural vanguard of the urban proletariat and of History's dialectic has been fashioned by the historiography of the revolution's victors. Trotsky's *History of the Russian Revolution* still offers the most readable and dramatic rendering of the rise and triumph of Bolshevism; the writings of historians of similar ideological persuasion during the past half-century have mainly added detail to Trotsky's picture of the process.

To many historians, however, it seems that World War I gave those revolutionaries who had learned the lessons of 1905 a second chance in more favorable circumstances. The war destabilized and eventually toppled the sturdier Hapsburg and Hohenzollern dynasties, suggesting that the fall of the Romanovs was linked to a larger upheaval. But although Nicholas's downfall can be attributed to many factors, the *final* outcome of Russia's revolutionary experience—the October Revolution—may be attributed to the dynamic leadership of a handful of individuals—or even a single person, namely, Lenin. Even Trotsky, who firmly believed in the historical role of the proletariat, admitted that without Lenin the outcome of the revolution would have been quite different.

The conditions produced by World War I, and the scandalous behavior of the royal family and the government during a period of extreme crisis, set the stage for the kind of revolution that occurred. In 1917, a defeated and mutinous army, largely consisting of peasants with ancient grievances against the gentry class, and since 1905 against the tsar himself, now had weapons with which to express their fury. The deep social antagonisms of a society with fresh memories of serfdom, and the still acute unevenness of social development, set the stage for a major cultural disaster. All the harsh disciplines and stupidity of the last imperial regimes made the disaster all the more violent and anarchic when it finally happened. Indeed, only those revolutionary parties that accepted massive violence and chaos were psychologically prepared for 1917. These were the Bolsheviks, the left SRs, and the anarchists. But only Lenin and Trotsky had the astuteness to create or borrow from the SRs and anarcho-syndicalists the correct slogans for the masses, and to gather up and direct the scattered instruments of violence that the First World War had placed in the hands of the masses.

It has been noted often enough that a real desire for power distinguished the Bolsheviks from other revolutionary parties. All the bitter theoretical disputes of the two decades that preceded 1917, all the factional "isms," the reassessments of history, the changes in strategy and tactics, seem almost irrelevant in view of this fact. But they were not entirely irrelevant. Without Marxist "science" and its historical optimism, Lenin could hardly have survived the frustrations of imprisonment, exile, party splits, defections, and the near disintegration of the revolutionary movement in the period 1907–1912. It is difficult to believe that hate for the old order and vengeful thoughts alone could have sustained him. Lenin's treatises on the development of capitalism in Russia, on imperialism, philosophy, revolutionary strategy and tactics, although frequently elicited by direct threats to Marxism by outsiders and heretics (from his point of view) within the Marxist camp, are serious attempts to understand the historical moment on the basis of a "scientific" theory. But they are ultimately less significant than and subordinate to his desire for revolution—and for power.

LENIN AS LEADER

After some moments of unity forged during revolutionary struggle in 1905–1906, the leaders of the factions resumed their fissiparous course. The Social Democrats agonized over the prospect of entering a quasi-feudal, quasi-bourgeois parliament, but in the end decided to participate. The Bolsheviks, many still mobilized to continue the struggle in 1907, split over Lenin's decision to enter the Duma. His reversal of course alienated the left wing of his faction. Lenin's purge of the very men who had been his vanguard in 1905–1906 anticipated later fights with left oppositions during periods of retreat. Lenin's will to survive matched his passion for struggle: he retreated when the odds became overwhelming; he learned to exploit the legal opportunities afforded by the post–1905 reforms; he used expropriations, condemned by other Social Democrats, to finance his machinations; he schemed to dominate the Social Democratic deputies in the Duma and to use that assembly as a platform for socialist propaganda; he adjusted Bolshevik tactics in order to infiltrate the trade union movement and other newly created legal workers' institutions, and at the same time sustained an illegal party preparing for armed revolutionary action. In 1912, he organized a rump conference in Prague and declared his faction to be the true Party. In sum, he manipulated institutions that he fully intended to destroy and used all means, fair and foul, to establish the preeminence of his faction.

Lenin paid a price for all of this. His zigzag course and ruthless methods scandalized his fellow Social Democrats, disoriented even his loyal followers, and sometimes made him a favorite of the Tsarist *Okhrana*, which appreciated his divisive tactics. The secret police infiltrated the top ranks of Lenin's faction. For long periods of time between 1907 and 1917 the Bolsheviks seemed to be the most quixotic and suicidal faction of the Party. Yet Lenin's methods worked in the long run. The Mensheviks failed to keep pace with labor radicalism and lost significant ground to Bolsheviks and SRs in the labor movement. The desire of Menshevik "liquidators" to dissolve the underground and rely entirely on legal activities alienated many Social Democrats, including Trotsky, who spent much energy between 1907 and 1912 vainly trying to reconcile the warring factions. Martov, although a man of the left, refused to abandon the "liquidators," thereby losing any chance of maintaining an alliance with Trotsky. Lenin's flexibility, his expanding tactical repertoire, and his willingness to use to good advantage former opponents, permitted him to attract to his side extraordinary talents, like Trotsky, whom he had alienated earlier.

No one else combined so much energy, dedication, organizational skill, and tactical flexibility with a ruthless will to power, dogmatism, and sectarianism. Throughout his career Lenin stole the thunder of his opponents even while pinning derisive labels on them. When the SRs created combat squads in 1905, the Bolsheviks quickly followed suit, with Lenin strongly pressing the policy of organizing armed bands and expropriations. After 1906 Lenin forced his faction to follow the Mensheviks into legal activity in the Duma, the trade unions, and insurance councils. In 1912 Lenin appropriated *Pravda,* a newspaper Trotsky had made popular. Trotsky, not without justice, claimed that Lenin came around to his own idea of permanent revolution in 1917. In 1917 Lenin would also sound like an anarchist and appropriate the SR land program. Many more examples could be adduced showing Lenin's borrowing of the positions of the very people that he attacked and slandered.

Lenin's is the *modus operandi* of a politician for whom victory and power are central concerns. Like a certain species of politician, moreover, Lenin remained convinced that no one but he could be trusted with power, that he alone could interpret Marx and Engels correctly and lead the revolution. The implications of such convictions became clear after the October Revolution, when he toyed with coalition politics, but ultimately established a partocracy. A single-party regime had no warrant among Russian Social Democrats. Lenin changed the rules of the game when it suited him, but of course constructed "dialectical" rationalizations for his actions. Even before the revolution, Lenin's opponents correctly perceived the lineaments of a dictator.

Lenin's relationships with a series of mentors and subordinates, too, played a fateful role in his development. After the *Iskra* period he broke with the leading figures of Russian Social Democracy and after 1914 with Karl Kautsky, the premier theoretician of the Second International. Although he reestablished his alliance with Plekhanov from time to time, he never really trusted his former mentor. A tendency to break off relationships with all of his revered teachers and closest collaborators and to see them as betrayers, as Judas figures, marks Lenin's entire career. Time and again, he developed enthusiasms for individuals, quickly made them part of his inner circle, and later became contemptuous of them. Lenin's singular ability to develop ties with collaborators and then ruthlessly to jettison them permitted him to change course and maintain control over his organization, although the tactics of split and purge were costly ones. At times he had to recreate his general staff virtually *de novo.*

Lenin found it increasingly difficult to tolerate theoretical opponents and purged his faction of the ablest of them. A certain disgust for intelligentsia chatterboxes and innovators who fell prey to the latest European intellectual fads and tried to add frills to Marxism led Lenin to expel "heretics" like Alexander Bogdanov (A. A. Malinovskii), Anatole Lunacharsky, and other brilliant and inventive minds. He replaced them with less refractory types, like Gregory Zinoviev and Lev Kamenev, but even they later fought Lenin and provoked his wrath. More ominous still, Lenin placed more trust in people whom Trotsky called "primitives" than in typical members of the intelligentsia. These were "plebian" toughs, people who had done the dirty work of the Party but had no claim to theoretical eminence. Lenin admired the picaresque "expropriator" S. A. Ter-Petrosian (Kamo), and promoted provincial troubleshooters like Jacob Sverdlov, Sergo Ordzhonikidze, and Joseph Dzhugashvili (Stalin), who joined Zinoviev and Kamenev in Lenin's top echelon. Lenin made one of his costliest mistakes before 1917 when he sponsored Roman Malinovsky, a man with a criminal record, a tough proletarian organizer—and a police informer. Like Evno Azev in the SR Party, Malinovsky caused great damage to the Bolsheviks until they discovered his double-dealing. Resembling Bakunin in the 1860s and 1870s, Lenin after 1905 found solace and hope in fierce fighters, men of action, and like any self-ambivalent, Romantic *intelligent,* tended to lower his defenses when dealing with them. Only later—too late—did Lenin recognize the dangers of relying too much on "primitives."

Ability to reformulate the teachings of Marx and Engels remained central to the position of any leader in the revolutionary subculture. Lenin's commentaries on the fathers of "scientific socialism" suggests that to them, and them alone, he gave a full measure of devotion. No institution of Social Democracy remained sacred for Lenin, who abandoned the Second International and the label "Social Democrat" as readily as he had abandoned erstwhile comrades in the cause.

Like Plekhanov before him, Lenin believed he stood for orthodoxy. When Alexander Bogdanov and others combined Marxism with the ideas of Ernst Mach and Richard Avenarius, Lenin responded with *Materialism and Empiriocriticism* (1908). His major philosophical work, it seethes with intolerance and dogmatism of the sort that had only factional significance before 1917, but which after 1917 stultified Soviet culture. Lenin later used formerly refractory people like Lunacharsky, who headed the Commissariat of Enlightenment between 1917 and 1929, but kept them on a leash and responded wrathfully to any signs of a revival of the ideological ferment that characterized early Bolshevik heretics. He labeled anything that smacked of the collectivist, syndicalist ideas of the earlier era "an infantile disease" and revived this epithet to impeach the platform of Alexandra Kollontai and the Left Opposition in 1920–1921. Lenin later recognized the influence of Bogdanov on Bukharin, his rival for theoretical preeminence in the Party after 1917. Bukharin, like Bogdanov, translated dialectics into systems theory (an approach that eventually became popular in the Soviet Union and elsewhere), and Lenin consequently treated him like an errant schoolboy.

When he forced Bogdanov and other stellar thinkers out of his faction, Lenin deprived it of a high level of imagination, creativity, and vision. Bogdanov, recognized today as a prophet of the cybernetic revolution and of general systems theory, embodied his complex and sometimes tragic vision of the struggle for a collectivist society and culture in works of science fiction such as *Red Star* (1908) and *The Engineer Menni* (1913), and in treatises, *Empiriomonism* (1904–1907) and *Tectology* (1913–1929). Lunacharsky, on the other hand, had an excellent sense of deep religious needs, of the human hunger for, at the very least, symbolic immortality and for new myths to replace the old ones. Leading European socialists shared similar views about human spiritual needs and the resemblances between Christianity and Marxism.[1]

1 For good discussions of Bogdanov and Lunacharsky, see Robert C. Williams, *The Other Bolsheviks* (Bloomington, 1986); Zenovia A. Sochor, *Revolution and Culture* (Ithaca, 1988).

The authors of *Landmarks* (1909), Nicholas Berdiaev prominent among them, went even farther by rejecting not only Marxism, but the general orientation of the revolutionary intelligentsia. The essays in *Landmarks* surveyed all of the movement's cultural and spiritual failings. To Lenin, all of this (his former comrade, Peter Struve, contributed to the collection) seemed like so much rotten, reactionary debris churned up from the cultural depths in the wake of the failures of 1905.

In cultural matters, Lenin was conservative, even after the revolution of 1917. The brief period of experimentation in the 1920s in Soviet Russia occurred in spite of Lenin rather than with his sponsorship. Long before 1917 Bogdanov perceived the cultural conservatism coexisting with Lenin's revolutionism. In *Red Star,* he refers to a figure whom commentators recognize as Lenin: "But the Old Man of the Mountain is exclusively a man of struggle and revolution. Our order would not suit him at all. He is a man of iron, and men of iron are not flexible. They have a strong measure of inborn conservatism."[2]

Bogdanov, however, was only partially correct. Lenin did show considerable flexibility in political struggle—in which he displayed his greatest gifts—and his most inspired discussion of dialectics is infused with a political mentality. In his notes of 1914–1915 on Hegel's *Science of Logic,* Lenin dwelt on the law of the unity and interpenetration of opposites which signified for him perpetual tension and struggle. Above all, to him dialectics meant flexibility, and he wrote:

> All-sided, universal flexibility of concepts, a flexibility reaching to the identity of opposites—that is the essence of the matter. This flexibility, applied subjectively = eclecticism and sophistry. Flexibility applied *objectively,* i.e., reflecting the all-sidedness of the material process and its unity, is dialectics, is the correct reflection of the eternal development of the world.[3]

---

2 Alexander Bogdanov, *Red Star,* ed. by Loren R. Graham and Richard Stites, trans. by Charles Rougle (Bloomington, 1984), p. 134.

3 Edie, et al., *Russian Philosophy,* 3, p. 438.

Lenin's dialectical formula for adaptation to a continually changing reality suggests not so much conservatism as the potential for dogmatism, in that Lenin himself became the court of last resort (with appropriate references to Marx and Engels) for determining objectivity. His approach led to perpetual struggle and to the hegemony of politics over all activities. Even more important, Lenin's methods were not lost on his heirs.

Lenin's most important adaptation of the teachings of Marx and Engels sprung from the turmoil of World War I. In *Imperialism, the Highest Stage of Capitalism,* written in 1915–1916 but not published until 1917, Lenin produced the justification for abandoning the bourgeois phase of the Russian revolution and moving to a dictatorship of the proletariat. The struggle of the imperialist powers in the vast and bloody war signified the inability of capitalism to solve its inner contradictions. The advanced nations could no longer mitigate their internal problems by exploiting an external proletariat and buying off their own workers with higher wages; they had to fight for control over markets, raw materials, and cheap colonial labor. The workers, temporarily deceived, would soon rebel against those whom capitalism had bought off—the labor aristocrats and petit-bourgeois ideologues who objectively served the capitalists while calling themselves Social Democrats. The betrayal of the workers' cause by the German Social Democrats, who almost to a man voted for war credits in 1914, licensed Lenin to attack the most powerful and authoritative voices in the Second International.

With a handful of other Social Democrats, Lenin attended a conference at Zimmerwald, Switzerland, in 1915 designed to oppose the war and salvage the honor of the Second International. The majority of delegates, however, wanted merely to end the war without annexations and indemnities. Lenin and the Zimmerwald Left called for the workers of the belligerent nations to turn their bayonets against their officers and rulers—to work for defeat rather than victory, and to begin civil wars that would usher in the proletarian revolution. The Zimmerwald Left became the nucleus of a new Communist International. The chief splitter of Russian Social Democracy now worked his political art at an international level. Lenin would later complete the break with the Social Democrats of the defunct Second International and call his followers Communists. In Switzerland Lenin waited for the moment of revolution, sometimes despairing that it would happen in his lifetime. The collapse of the Tsarist regime in February (March, in the Gregorian calendar) 1917 spared him the fate of Marx and Engels, who died without ever having witnessed a successful socialist revolution, much less having led one.

THE FEBRUARY REVOLUTION

When women demanding bread in Petrograd (St. Petersburg) triggered the February Revolution on International Women's Day (February 23, 1917), they set into motion a process reminiscent of 1905, but in conditions far more favorable for a radical outcome. A vast number of troops, 15 million in all, had been mobilized during World War I. Many had been exposed to the propaganda of socialist agitators who, assisted by the agonies of trench warfare and the enormous casualties brought about by the bungling of the regime, at last wore down the patriotic feelings which had still been strong in the early stages of the war. The bitter feelings that had been accumulating for decades among the peasants and workers now serving in the ranks, the erosion of the authority of senior officers, and finally, of the very symbols of power, the Tsar and Tsarina, laid the groundwork for mutiny. The garrison in Petrograd decided the issue there, and on March 2, 1917, Nicholas II abdicated.

The scandalous and inept behavior of the last Tsar and his consort had hastened the outcome. Their indulgence of the notorious Rasputin, their mismanagement of the war, rumors of treason in high places, Alexandra's treacherous game of ministerial "leapfrog" during the crisis, and the rulers' open contempt for the Duma alienated even conservatives, who placed national survival above the preservation of the dynasty. Leaders of the prorogued Duma arranged Nicholas's abdication and formed a Provisional Government, which was supposed to rule for a few months until the election of a Constituent Assembly. The latter, in turn, would create a new, democratic constitution. The caretaker government, however, found itself in the odd position of having *de jure* power while remaining at the mercy of rebellious soldiers and sailors in the capital, who joined masses of workers in a revived soviet movement. Thus began in March 1917 the period of diarchy, or dual power.

As in 1905, the soviet movement spread rapidly across the vast empire. Not surprisingly, socialist parties dominated the revived soviets, which represented hundreds of thousands of workers who had been subjected to their propaganda and agitation for two decades, and whose militancy had only temporarily abated during the war. At first, mainly Mensheviks and SRs assumed leadership of the executive bodies that guided mass meetings of hundreds of deputies and wielded power for them between plenary sessions. When other leaders hurried back from internal and foreign exile (thanks to the amnesty issued by the Provisional Government), they found themselves treated like celebrities. Decades of sacrifice and struggle had not been spent in vain. A crowd of well-wishers with flowers, accompanied by a band, automobiles, an armored car, and a searchlight greeted Lenin on the night of April 3, 1917, when he arrived at the Finland Station in Petrograd. On the next day, to the shock of all but those who had read his "Letters from Afar," Lenin, sounding more like an anarchist than a Marxist, called for all power to the soviets and the formation of a new kind of socialist state in what became known as "The April Theses." Lenin quickly recognized that real power lay in the streets and, relying upon his own predictions in *Imperialism, the Highest Stage of Capitalism,* now called for something akin to Trotsky's permanent revolution.

The inspirational ideas propounded by Lenin in "The April Theses" and presented in finished form a few months later in *The State and Revolution* caught the antistate mood of the workers in the capital. The most optimistic and utopian of Lenin's major writings, *The State and Revolution* combined the ideal image of the Paris commune of 1871 created by Marx with other teachings of Marx and Engels on the state, and with Lenin's own vision of the dictatorship of the proletariat—also presumably derived from Marx. Lenin understood very well that the modern state apparatus in France, Russia, and elsewhere had crushed popular uprisings. Hence it was time to smash the apparatus of repression. The standing army and police should be disbanded in favor of a popular militia with broad police powers; the bureaucrats, technical experts, managers, and professional people should be replaced by employees receiving modest wages. On the other hand, material bourgeois achievements—the centralized banking system and the system of large-scale factory production—would fall like ripe fruit into the hands of the proletariat. The proletariat would create a new kind of commune state and run its finances and advanced productive system with minimal adaptation. Even the new commune state, a dictatorship of the proletariat, would be a transitional entity used to repress bourgeois resistance to the new order of things. With the end of class antagonism, the new state would wither away, just as Marx and Engels had prophesied.

This supremely confident vision seemed to fly in the face of common sense. To many socialists, the slogan, "All Power to the Soviets" and Lenin's teachings on the commune state and the dictatorship of the proletariat sounded like the ravings of the anarchists. Lenin, mindful of the similarities, made every effort to distinguish his vision of a centralized system, however democratized, from that of the anarchists. Everything still depended on the appropriation of an advanced system of production and the existence of skilled personnel to run it. Quite soon it became clear that Lenin would never place in peril the Marxian vision of efficient, large-scale production in favor of anything like an anarcho-syndicalist form of "workers' control." Indeed, Lenin's notions of management and his economic goals ultimately forced trade unions to act as instruments of the state rather than of a self-managing, liberated proletariat. In order to survive and modernize, the Communist regime reestablished a professional army, generated ever-larger bureaucratic structures, and, after temporary use of "bourgeois specialists," created a privileged stratum of "Red" experts and managers. The ideals of *The State and Revolution* were honored in the breach.

TROTSKY'S CONVERSION TO BOLSHEVISM

World War I catalyzed the process bringing together the most radical spirits in the socialist movement. In July 1914 it still would have been impossible to predict that Trotsky would become a Bolshevik and Lenin's second-in-command during the revolution. Trotsky did not become a Bolshevik until August 1917. Profound differences separated the two men, differences that surfaced again after the October Revolution. For most of his revolutionary career Trotsky, although differing sharply from the more moderate Mensheviks, could still work with them. Unable to join formally any of the factional Social Democratic groupings, Trotsky instead pursued his own path. He had strong connections with German and Austrian Social Democrats, wrote for their journals, and steeped himself in the rich cultural milieu of prewar Vienna. When his effort to unify the non-Bolshevik Russian Social Democrats collapsed after his short-lived "August Bloc" in 1912, he remained mainly a free-lance revolutionary journalist. As a war correspondent during the Balkan Wars of 1912–1913 he experienced the long, bloody prologue to the world war. In July 1914, just before the outbreak of World War I, Trotsky joined a broad array of Russian Social Democrats in Brussels who, under the sponsorship of the International Socialist Bureau, once again sought unity in the face of Lenin's splitting tactics. Among those in attendance were Plekhanov, Martov, Akselrod, and Rosa Luxemburg. The events of July 1914 were supposed to be a prelude to the Vienna Congress of the Second International, planned for August 1914, but the war intervened.

Trotsky, too, joined the Zimmerwald movement in 1915, but at first opposed Lenin's tactic of defeatism. Joining for a while with Martov in a fragile journalistic alliance to promote the Zimmerwald line, he broke with him in 1916. When he arrived in Petrograd in May 1917, Trotsky joined forces with other internationalists, some of them Bolshevik heretics like Lunacharsky, others left Mensheviks, in the so-called "Interdistrict Commission." Lenin quickly realized that the Bolshevik position and that of the Interdistrict Commission had converged and tried to convince this group to merge their organization of roughly four thousand with the larger Bolshevik organization in May 1917, but the merger did not occur until July. Trotsky's position remained the same as he had held in 1905—permanent revolution—but in the spring and early summer of 1917 he faced some painful decisions. He had to decide whether he could subordinate himself to a man whom he had consistently fought for more than a decade and whose political ideas smacked of dictatorship. That was what joining the Bolsheviks signified—subordination to Lenin. It took several months for Trotsky to decide that only the Bolsheviks could lead the soviets in the desired direction. By winning over Trotsky the Bolsheviks gained a leader with impressive intuitive capacities permitting him to adapt to fluid, battlefield situations.

TOWARDS OCTOBER

A ferocious process of selection for revolutionary leadership occurred between the arrival of the main actors between March and May and the October Revolution (since celebrated on November 7, in keeping with the Western-style calendar adopted by the Bolsheviks in 1918). The unstable chemistry of the mass movements put all leaders in peril. Radical soldiers, sailors, and workers in the cities increased their demands. The troops wanted an end to the war; workers agitated for a variety of benefits and increasingly demanded control of the factories; peasants began to seize private land and incorporate into their traditional communal structures both this property and land that had been taken from the communes as a consequence of the Stolypin reforms; aggrieved nationalities began the process of rebellion that would temporarily dissolve the Russian Empire.

The first Provisional Government proved inept in its handling of diplomacy and war. Alexander Kerensky, an SR, replaced Paul Miliukov as the leading figure in the Provisional Government, and Kerensky brought Mensheviks and other SRs into the ruling coalition. This tactic of coalition complicated matters for the left-wing socialists. They had found it easier to attack the Provisional Government as bourgeois and to hold up the Petrograd Soviet as its antithesis until Kerensky's action blurred the distinction between the two centers of power. Although circumstances seemed to favor the left, the main business of the revolution remained to be done. The demands of soldiers and sailors, peasants, workers, and minority nationalities remained unfulfilled.

The Provisional Government and its Menshevik and SR supporters in the Soviet started into motion the process that would bring them down when Kerensky called for a renewed military offensive against the Central Powers in June 1917. The unpopularity of the June offensive and the grassroots agitation of left-wing socialists (anarchists, left SRs, and Bolsheviks) led to the eruption in Petrograd called the "July Days." The leaders on the left, however, were unprepared and uncertain and the mood of the capital mercurial. When confronted by angry mobs, the Mensheviks and SRs in the Petrograd Soviet refused to take power. The Provisional Government, still able to command military support, survived the uprising, accused Lenin of treason, and forced him into hiding. Numerous Bolshevik leaders and Trotsky (still not officially a Bolshevik) were arrested. The Bolsheviks temporarily dropped their slogan, "All Power to the Soviets." However, the setback of July 3–5 only slowed the left's momentum temporarily. The failure of the Provisional Government's military offensive continued to cause unrest. Even more important, the Army's Supreme Commander-in-Chief, General Lavr Kornilov, attempted a right-wing putsch in August, ostensibly to "protect" the capital against insurrectionaries. Kornilov's failed coup during the last days of August revived the left, gave the Bolsheviks a second chance, and set the stage for the last act of the revolutionary drama. The Provisional Government now faced the left without the backing of the military establishment.

Lenin, realizing the vulnerability of the Provisional Government but fearing the instability of the situation, began calling in September for an immediate attack and seizure of power. Yet the Bolsheviks in the capital believed Lenin's pleas to be premature. Their power was growing markedly in the soviets. During September Trotsky, now a member of the Bolshevik Central Committee, became chairman of the Petrograd Soviet. It seemed to him, as well as to other Bolsheviks, that the Second Congress of Soviets scheduled for late October would be the appropriate occasion for the establishment of a Soviet government. Moreover, in October, not all of the Bolsheviks believed that the "correlation of forces" favored a try for power. Zinoviev and Kamenev opposed Lenin's design for a Bolshevik-led insurrection. Still in hiding, Lenin desperately and unsuccessfully searched for ways to precipitate it. Trotsky, as the Chairman of the Petrograd Soviet and head of its Military Revolutionary Committee in October, held the positions key to the success of the insurrection. Although prodded by Lenin to act earlier and with greater force, during October Trotsky maintained a course culminating in a virtually bloodless seizure of power in Petrograd.

VICTORY AND DEFEAT

Kerensky forced Trotsky's hand by launching an attack on the Bolsheviks once again on October 24 (November 6). Troops loyal to the Soviet and organized by the Bolsheviks quickly seized the strategic points in the capital. When Lenin arrived at Bolshevik headquarters late that night, the victory had been won. The "storming" of the Winter Palace, seat of the Provisional Government, had only symbolic value. Lenin felt that he had to overthrow those in power by military action, to show the delegates at the Second Congress of Soviets that the Bolsheviks had led them to victory. Bolshevik victory justified a Bolshevik government. Lenin rejected coalition with all but the left SRs, and their alliance lasted only a few months. When the elections to the long-anticipated Constituent Assembly returned a right SR majority, Lenin simply dissolved the Assembly in January 1918, after one session. After the alienation of the left SRs in March 1918, an exclusively Bolshevik (Communist) government emerged, one that would not yield power until 1991.

Hereafter, Lenin had to face the consequences of his actions: diplomatic isolation, civil war, economic ruin, famine, and a return of revolutionary militancy in the peasants and workers, this time against Communist power. In 1921 Lenin would retreat from his most revolutionary goals—the immediate transition to a fully socialist economy—but he would not retreat from political dictatorship. Between 1917 and 1922, the non-socialist opposition was crushed and expelled; then non-Communist socialists. Lenin, moreover, reined in the opposition within his own party and banned factions in 1921. In 1917, in seeming contradiction of his own style of politics, he had opened his party wide to mass participation. The concessions to spontaneity, to mass participation, like the ideas in *The State and Revolution*, proved to be fleeting ones. As the ruler of an encircled state, Lenin resorted to many of the same tactics that he had used as the leader of his prerevolutionary faction. Before his final incapacitation in March 1923 (he died in January 1924), Lenin gave no indication that he trusted even his closest comrades with political leadership. He passed on a dictatorial style and a confused set of instructions about the future. The cult that formed around Lenin's person and his "Testament" obscured his true legacy: a dictatorship that inflicted enormous damage upon its subjects.

Lenin's and Trotsky's erroneous predictions of world revolution lay behind the Communists' great gamble. Successful as revolutionaries, as rulers they had to face the consequences of their miscalculations. In keeping with the requirements of their ideology and the necessities of power politics, Lenin's heirs embarked upon a program of forced industrialization. After a period of concessions to the "petit-bourgeois" peasantry—still the overwhelming majority of the population—they carried through a ruthless program of collectivization of agriculture. A new breed of bureaucrat and administrator, the Communist Party *apparatchiki*, not the revolutionary intelligentsia, became the true heirs to the Tsarist state apparatus. One of the most repressive and conservative of all modern governments emerged from the experiments of the 1920s and the disasters of the 1930s and 1940s. The Communist Party of the Soviet Union was a far cry from the elite that the old revolutionary intelligentsia had envisioned—an elite embodying scientific truth, a vanguard of ethical sociologists.

When the Russian peasant masses and urban proletariat finally became revolutionary forces in 1905 and 1917, the several sects within the revolutionary intelligentsia were bitterly divided, and the historical fruits of the meeting of the masses with the revolutionary intelligentsia were equally bitter. But the impact of the intelligentsia was clear and undeniable, and the consequences of their doctrines for the shape, color, and texture of Soviet civilization, not to speak of its offshoots, were enormous. The deposition of traditional culture, the official enthronement of science and technology, the guardianship of truth by a self-perpetuating elite—these were neither conceived nor intended by the masses. Moreover, the Communist Party of the Soviet Union, with its neanderthalism, philistinism, and bureaucratic conservatism, perpetuated the very evils that the intelligentsia had struggled against so desperately in the nineteenth century. The meeting of the intelligentsia with the masses was undeniably responsible for what happened, although no one had intended such results. The history of the revolutionary intelligentsia of the nineteenth century therefore assumes the dimensions of a tragedy, profounder, perhaps, than that of any comparable historical movement in our era.

History, however, does not stand still; and the intelligentsia's voice was not stilled forever. The socialist dictatorships emerging from the ruins of two world wars presided over the channeling of scarce resources into heavy industry in societies groping toward modernity. The Stalinist system, a particularly brutal and durable variant, nonetheless created the conditions for its own destruction by forcing into existence a largely urban society with a sizable professional and managerial stratum. Like their Tsarist predecessors, the Soviet elite depended on censorship and a system of rewards and punishments to keep their people on a leash; like Tsarist modernizing bureaucrats, Communist reformers unleashed forces that they could not control. Urbanization and modernization brought new mentalities, contact with the West, and stimulated the desire for a freer and more open society. The Communists' calls for incessant struggle sounded increasingly hollow; their inability to implement and manage a productive and innovative economy gave the lie to their claims to be in the vanguard of material progress and threatened to undermine their power; and the existence of the Gulag shamed them in the eyes of the non-communist world. A new dissident intelligentsia emerged and spoke out bravely. The release of Andrei Sakharov from internal exile in December 1986 signalled the beginning of the end of the old regime. The contribution of the Soviet intelligentsia to the dissolution of one of the most brutal regimes in modern history cannot be doubted. Like their nineteenth-century ancestors, they showed vast courage, intelligence, and self-sacrifice in the cause of liberation. Now they must study their own tortuous history and find the vital elements that can be pressed into the service of human freedom and dignity. Then they will serve the only worthwhile permanent revolution: the ongoing, humane criticism of things as they are and the creation of new visions of things as they ought to be.

BIBLIOGRAPHICAL ESSAY

This bibliography is limited to books in English. It includes, in this order: general studies of Russian history, major collections of primary sources, broad studies of the Russian intelligentsia, and the more specialized literature on limited periods, individuals, or particular aspects of the revolutionary intelligentsia's history.

GENERAL TEXTBOOKS

General texts abound and many are quite good, but these are especially useful: M. T. Florinsky, *Russia: A History and Interpretation* (2 vols.; New York, 1953), II; Hugh Seton-Watson, *The Russian Empire, 1801–1917* (Oxford, 1967); Edward Thaden, *Russia Since 1801* (New York, 1971); James T. Billington, *The Icon and the Axe* (New York, 1966); David MacKenzie and Michael W. Curran, *A History of Russia and the Soviet Union*, 2d ed. (Belmont, Calif., 1991); and Hans Rogger, *Russia in the Age of Modernisation and Revolution, 1881–1917* (London, 1983). Florinsky's, Seton-Watson's, and Thaden's thoroughness and careful scholarship make them especially valuable resources. Billington approaches his subject from the point of view of cultural history and his book contains substantial material on the history of the intelligentsia. MacKenzie and Curran's text, though a more general survey, has the virtue of framing problems for students and, like Rogger's more specialized text, offers valuable and up-to-date information and interpretation.

PRIMARY SOURCES

The most comprehensive and valuable anthology of primary sources is *Russian Philosophy*, James M. Edie, James P. Scanlan, and Mary-Barbara Zeldin, eds. (3 vols.; Chicago, 1965). It contains concise introductions and bibliographies for individuals and schools of thought. The materials in *Russian Philosophy* are frequently cited in this book. Derek Offord has produced a relatively new anthology, notable for its broad coverage and its inclusion of documents hitherto unavailable in English: *A Documentary History of Russian Thought from the Enlightenment to Marxism,* W. J. Leatherbarrow and D. C. Offord, eds. and trans. (Ann Arbor, Mich., 1987). It begins in the late eighteenth century with A. N. Radishchev and ends in the 1880s with G. V. Plekhanov. Also notable for breadth are: Hans Kohn's *The Mind of Modern Russia* (New York, 1962) and Marc Raeff's *Russian Intellectual History: An Anthology* (New York, 1966). The second volume of Thomas Riha's *Readings in Russian Civilization* (3 vols.; Chicago, 1964) contains excellent material on the revolutionary intelligentsia, as does *Imperial Russia: A Source Book, 1700–1917,* Basil Dmytryshyn, ed. (New York, 1967). The first volume of Robert V. Daniels's *Documentary History of Communism,* rev. ed. (2 vols.; Hanover, N.H., 1984) contains brief but well-selected documents on Russian Marxism. A more comprehensive selection of documents especially valuable for tracing the history of Russian Marxism can be found in *Marxism in Russia, Key Documents 1879–1906,* Neil Harding, ed., Richard Taylor, trans. (Cambridge, U.K., 1983).

GENERAL SECONDARY WORKS

Of the general secondary works on the Russian intelligentsia, the most notable early study is one by Thomas G. Masaryk. It was first published in German in 1913 and then in a two-volume English edition that was reissued in 1955: T. G. Masaryk, *The Spirit of Russia,* Edan and Cedar Paul, trans., 2d ed. (2 vols.; London, 1955). Masaryk's insightful work, informed by a Kantian perspective, is the first broad and systematic non-Russian study of the Russian intelligentsia. Two compendious histories of Russian thought appeared at roughly the same time: Nikolai O. Lossky, *History of Russian Philosophy* (London, 1952); and Vasilii V. Zenkovsky, *A History of Russian Philosophy,* G. L. Kline, trans. (2 vols.; London, 1953). The able historian of philosophy F. C. Copleston has recently produced *Philosophy in Russia from Herzen to Lenin and Berdyaev* (Notre Dame, Ind., 1986). Nicholas Berdiaev's readable, essayistic *The Origin of Russian Communism* (London, 1937) and *The Russian Idea* (New York, 1948) continued the author's prerevolutionary thought about the spiritual background of Communism. The resurgence of Christianity in Russia today and the reevaluation of the revolutionary intelligentsia have given Berdiaev's ideas new currency.

During the 1950s, Franco Venturi produced the first major book in a Western language to focus upon the revolutionary intelligentsia as a social as well as a cultural or philosophical movement. It appeared in English translation as *Roots of Revolution: A History of the Populist and Socialist Movements in Nineteenth Century Russia* (New York, 1960). Venturi used to full advantage the previous scholarship on the revolutionary intelligentsia, and his work superseded anything previously written in scholarship and general excellence. It is written from a point of view sympathetic to the movement. Several of Venturi's more recent essays ranging widely over the history of the Russian intelligentsia appear in Franco Venturi, *Studies in Free Russia,* Fausta Segre Walsby and Margaret O'Dell, trans. (Chicago, 1982). Broad in coverage but less useful is Richard Hare, *Pioneers of Russian Social Thought* (London, 1951). Hare is interested mainly in the thinkers rather than the movement. Another excellent general study of the revolutionary movement which appeared at roughly the same time as Venturi's is Avrahm Yarmolinsky, *Road to Revolution: A Century of Russian Radicalism* (London, 1957). In a lively narrative style he covered a somewhat greater period of time than Venturi did, although in less depth and detail.

In the decade of the 1960s other notable books appeared. The most noteworthy is Fedor Dan, *The Origins of Bolshevism,* Joel Carmichael, ed. and trans. (New York, 1964). Although broad in treatment, it is devoted mainly to the Marxists and written from a Menshevik point of view. Dan was a major Menshevik leader. Sergei Utechin's useful *Russian Political Thought* (New York, 1964), more a handbook than a history, classifies the various intelligentsia movements and provides concise summaries of their basic ideas. Thornton Anderson produced a textbook on political thought covering the entire spectrum—Tsarist, intelligentsia, and Soviet—in *Russian Political Thought, an Introduction* (Ithaca, N.Y., 1967).

Moving now to the 1970s, another product of émigré scholarship, Tibor Szamuely's *The Russian Tradition,* Robert Conquest, ed. (New York, 1974) traces especially the role of the state in Russian history, the Jacobin-Blanquist tendency in the revolutionary movement, and the fateful impact of both. A detached and ironically witty view of Russian populism, particularly its terrorist current, can be found in Adam B. Ulam, *In the Name of the People* (New York, 1977). Ulam has also written essayistically about the entire range of Russian dissidence in the nineteenth and twentieth centuries in Adam B. Ulam, *Russia's Failed Revolutions, from the Decembrists to the Dissidents* (New York, 1981). One of the most comprehensive, scholarly treatments emphasizing ideas rather than actions is Andrzej Walicki, *A History of Russian Thought from the Enlightenment to Marxism,* Hilda Andrews-Rusiecka, trans. (Stanford, Calif., 1979). More specialized than Walicki's work, Alexander Vucinich's *Social Thought in Tsarist Russia: The Quest for a General Science of Society, 1861–1917* (Stanford, Calif., 1979) deals with both revolutionary and nonrevolutionary social thought in depth.

During roughly the last decade a number of general studies provided new perspectives. Vladimir Nahirny, a sociologist, produced a probing psychosocial study made up of several essays dealing with the pre-Marxist period: *The Russian Intelligentsia, from Torment to Silence* (New Brunswick, N.J., 1983). A number of Leonard Schapiro's illuminating essays written from the point of view of traditional liberalism and focussing mainly on Russian Marxism in the twentieth century were anthologized in Leonard Schapiro, *Russian Studies,* Ellen Dahrendorf, ed. (New York, 1986). The Soviet dissident movement is treated as an extension of the earlier intelligentsia's sense of individual worth and struggle for civil rights in Marshall S. Shatz, *Soviet Dissent in Historical Perspective* (Cambridge, U.K., 1980). One should also mention James Billington's stimulating overview of utopian and revolutionary traditions in *Fire in the Minds of Men, Origins of the Revolutionary Faith* (New York, 1980). Richard Pipes's recent *The Russian Revolution* (New York, 1990) presents a thoroughly disenchanted view of both the intelligentsia and the revolution.

For an opposing point of view, there is Boris Kagarlitsky, *The Thinking Reed,* Brian Pearce, trans. (London, 1988). Kagarlitsky still finds the possibility of building upon the revolutionary heritage that survived Stalinism and Brezhnevism. He provides insight into the system of beliefs that animated Gorbachev. Finally, in a recent study, Edward Acton, *Rethinking the Russian Revolution* (London, 1990), as part of his task classifies and gives brief accounts of the major schools of thought on the revolutionary intelligentsia, while taking a revisionist position and emphasizing history "from below."

LOST GENERATIONS: THE DECEMBRISTS

Turning now to the more specialized literature, it is appropriate to begin with the Decembrist movement. The relatively sparse literature in English does not do justice to the fascination the Decembrists hold for Russians. For documents, we have Marc Raeff's *The Decembrist Movement* (Englewood Cliffs, N.J., 1966) which not only contains primary sources but Raeff's valuable introductory essay; and the useful collection of translated documents, *Voices in Exile: The Decembrist Memoirs,* Glynn R. V. Barratt, ed. and trans. (Montreal, 1974). For secondary sources, there are two excellent general studies: Anatole G. Mazour, *The Decembrist Movement* (Berkeley, 1937) and Mikhail Zetlin, *The Decembrists,* George Pnin, trans. (New York, 1958). More recently, Glynn Barratt and Patrick O'Meara have enriched the biographical literature with O'Meara's *K. F. Ryleev: A Political Biography of the Decembrist Poet* (Princeton, N.J., 1984); and Barratt's two biographies: of Baron Andrei Rozen, *The Rebel on the Bridge* (Athens, Ohio, 1975), and *M. S. Lunin, Catholic Decembrist* (The Hague, 1976).

LOST GENERATIONS: THE INCUBATION OF SOCIALISM

The literature in English for the "lost generation" of the 1830s and 1840s is considerably richer. The influential writings of Peter Chaadaev are available in *The Major Works of Peter Chaadaev,* Raymond T. McNally, ed. and trans. (Notre Dame,

Ind., 1969) and Peter Yakovlevich Chaadayev, *Philosophical Letters & Apology of a Madman,* Mary-Barbara Zeldin, trans. (Knoxville, Tenn., 1969). A more inclusive collection with notes and fragments from Chaadaev's archives has been issued recently: *Philosophical Works of Peter Chaadaev,* Raymond McNally and Richard Tempest, eds. (Dordrecht, Netherlands, 1991). Raymond T. McNally has also written a scholarly work: *Chaadayev and His Friends* (Tallahassee, Fla., 1971).

There is a new abridged edition of Herzen's voluminous *My Past and Thoughts,* Constance Garnett, trans. (London, 1974). Herzen's memoirs shed light on generational change in the intelligentsia, as well as on the general ambience of the period of Herzen's main activities. His novel of 1845–1846, important for its insight into the alienated characteristics of his generation, is available in translation: A. I. Herzen, *Who Is to Blame?* Michael R. Katz, trans. (Ithaca, N.Y., 1984). Also available are the valuable observations of his contemporary, P. V. Annenkov, *The Extraordinary Decade,* Arthur P. Mendel, ed., Irwin R. Titunik, trans. (Ann Arbor, Mich., 1968). For useful excerpts from the writings of leading figures see *Russian Philosophy,* volume I.

The best single study of Herzen is Martin Malia's *Alexander Herzen and the Birth of Russian Socialism* (Cambridge, Mass., 1961). Edward Acton has written a useful, brief overview of the main part of Herzen's career, *Alexander Herzen and the Role of the Intellectual Revolutionary* (Cambridge, U.K., 1979). Edward H. Carr's story of the Herzen and Ogarev families in exile, *The Romantic Exiles* (New York, 1961), is a graceful collective biography. A more recent scholarly monograph about Herzen in the émigré community is Judith Zimmerman, *Midpassage: Alexander Herzen and European Revolution* (Pittsburgh, 1989). Martin Miller's *The Russian Revolutionary Émigrés, 1825–1870 (Baltimore,* 1986) provides a broader mapping of émigré life. Evgenii Lampert surveys the lives and thought of Herzen, Belinsky, and Bakunin in *Studies in Rebellion* (London, 1957). A collection of influential essays by Isaiah Berlin, *Russian Thinkers,* Henry Hardy and Aileen Kelly, eds. (New York, 1979) probes the ideas of Herzen, Bakunin, and Belinsky. The anthology also includes Berlin's classic, "The Hedgehog and the Fox." Two books on Belinsky's life and thought are: Herbert Bowman, *Vissarion Be-*

linski (Cambridge, Mass., 1954) and Victor Terras, *Belinskij and Russian Literary Criticism: The Heritage of Organic Aesthetics* (Madison, Wisc., 1974).

Bakunin, who outstripped his generation in radicalism and became a more influential revolutionary thinker and actor than his colleagues, Herzen and Ogarev, has attracted considerable attention. His writings have been collected into several easily accessible anthologies. There are also scholarly editions of *The Confession of Michael Bakunin,* Robert C. Howes, trans. (Ithaca, N.Y., 1977) and *The State and Anarchy,* Marshall S. Shatz, ed. and trans. (Cambridge, U.K., 1990). The earliest biography in English is E. H. Carr's *Michael Bakunin* (London, 1937) and it is still worth reading for its literary grace and lively depiction of Bakunin's career. Anthony Masters's *Bakunin, the Father of Anarchism* (New York, 1974) is a sympathetic biography, throughout which Bakunin is referred to as "Michael." More recent biographers probe Bakunin's psychology in greater depth: Aileen Kelly, *Mikhail Bakunin: A Study in the Psychology and Politics of Utopianism* (Oxford, U.K., 1982); and, considerably more thoroughly than Kelly and in a psychoanalytic vein, Arthur Mendel, *Michael Bakunin: Roots of Apocalypse* (New York, 1981). Richard B. Saltman's *The Social and Political Thought of Michael Bakunin* (Westport, Conn., 1983) is a recent monograph presenting Bakunin as a serious social and political theorist. A more specialized scholarly work on the rise and fall of Bakuninism in Italy is T. R. Ravindranathan, *Bakunin and the Italians* (Montreal, 1988).

The Slavophiles, too, have attracted a considerable amount of scholarly attention. Although I have deemphasized them in favor of the Westernizers for obvious reasons in this study, their historical importance should not be slighted in view of A. I. Solzhenitsyn's neo-Slavophilism and its impact in recent years. There are selections from the writings of the Slavophiles in the first volume of *Russian Philosophy* and in *Russian Thought* (cited in full above). Turning to scholarly studies, one should mention first of all Nicholas V. Riasanovsky's useful early study, *Russia and the West in the Teachings of the Slavophiles* (Cambridge, Mass., 1952). More recently, Peter K. Christoff studied the foremost Slavophile thinkers in depth in his four-volume series, *An Introduction to Nineteenth-Century Russian Slavophilism:*

Vol. 1: *A. S. Xomjakov* (The Hague, 1961); Vol. 2: *I. V. Kireevskij* (The Hague, 1972); Vol. 3: *K. S. Aksakov* (Princeton, N.J., 1982); and Vol. 4: *I. F. Samarin* (Boulder, Colo., 1991). Abbott Gleason added to the scholarly literature *European and Muscovite: Ivan Kireevsky and the Origins of Slavophilism* (Cambridge, Mass., 1972) and A. Walicki contributed his probing study, *The Slavophile Controversy: History of a Conservative Utopia in Nineteenth-Century Russian Thought,* Hilda Andrews-Rusiecka, trans. (Oxford, U.K., 1975).

Two recent studies of several important Russian liberals (T. N. Granovsky, V. P. Botkin, P. V. Annenkov, A. V. Druzhinin and K. D. Kavelin) in Derek Offord, *Portraits of Early Russian Liberals* (Cambridge, U.K., 1985) and P. R. Roosevelt, *Apostle of Russian Liberalism: Timofei Granovsky* (Newtonville, Mass., 1986) help fill out our picture of the 1830s and 1840s. Leonard Schapiro, a deservedly influential émigré scholar, produced several essays on the 1830s and 1840s published in *Rationalism and Nationalism in Russian Nineteenth-Century Political Thought* (New Haven, Conn., 1967). Finally, to complete this survey of works on the thinkers of the 1830s and 1840s, there are two studies of the Petrashevskii circle. The first is slight but useful: John L. Evans, *The Petraševskij Circle, 1845–1849* (The Hague, 1974). The second, based on archival work, significantly enriches our picture of the circle: J. H. Seddon, *The Petrashevtsy: A Study of the Russian Revolutionaries of 1848* (Manchester, U.K., 1985).

NIHILISM

Materials in English for the study of nihilism, though not abundant, are adequate for undergraduate study. English translations of selected works of Chernyshevskii, Dobroliubov, and Pisarev were issued by the Soviet Foreign Languages Publishing House, but their value is limited by tendentious selecting and editing. There are, however, non-Soviet English translations of Chernyshevskii's most influential work. Of the new translations, the most useful for historical study is Chernyshevskii's *What Is to Be Done?* Michael Katz, trans. (Ithaca, N.Y., 1989). There is good material on the nihilists in the second volume of *Russian Philosophy* and in *Russian Thought.* Individual biographies of nihilist thinkers in English are somewhat scarce. However, Chernyshevskii, the single most important figure, has a thoughtful and thorough biography devoted to him: William F. Woehrlin, *Chernyshevskii: The Man and the Journalist* (Cambridge, Mass., 1971). Two other useful works are: Francis Randall's *N. G. Chernyshevskii* (New York, 1967) and N. G. Pereira's *The Thought and Teachings of N. G. Černyševskii* (The Hague, 1975). F. Venturi's *Roots of Revolution: A History of the Populist and Socialist Movements in Nineteenth Century Russia*, cited above, contains excellent biographical material on the major figures of nihilism. One can turn also to E. Lampert's *Sons against Fathers* (Oxford, U.K., 1965) for good biographical work on Chernyshevskii, Dobroliubov, and Pisarev. Abbott Gleason's *Young Russia, the Genesis of Russian Radicalism in the 1860s* (New York, 1980) mixes biography with sociocultural analysis of the student movement and radical underground. Daniel Brower's *Training the Nihilists: Education and Radicalism in Tsarist Russia* (Ithaca, N.Y., 1975) explores the institutional framework in which nihilism developed. Rufus Mathewson's *The Positive Hero in Russian Literature*, 2d ed. (Stanford, Calif., 1975) is an excellent monograph examining the values and images conveyed by nihilist literature.

The more unruly figures in the movement have attracted considerable attention. For Tkachev, whose activities spanned the 1860s and 1870s, there are two biographies: Albert Weeks, *The First Bolshevik: A Political Biography of Peter Tkachev* (New York, 1968) and Deborah Hardy, *Petr Tkachev, the Critic as Jacobin* (Seattle, 1977). Hardy's work significantly surpasses Weeks's. Three studies have been devoted to Nechaev: Michael Prawdin, *The Unmentionable Nechaev* (New York, 1961); Stephen Cochrane, *The Collaboration of Nečaev, Ogarev and Bakunin in 1869: Nečaev's Early Years* (Giessen, 1977); and Philip Pomper, *Sergei Nechaev* (New Brunswick, N.J., 1979). Prawdin's is quite readable, though not as scholarly as the other two. Cochrane's is a specialized work (his dissertation), and my own is a psychological study of Nechaev and his companions. There is another study of émigrés, although with a somewhat different focus and a revisionist perspective: Woodford McClellan, *Revolutionary Exiles: The Russians in the First International and the Paris Commune* (London, 1979). Michael Confino has contributed to Nechaev studies with documents about Natalie Herzen and Nechaev in *Daughter of a Revolutionary* (La Salle, Ill., 1973). Paul Avrich's thoughtful essay, *Bakunin and Nechaev* (London, 1974) has been issued in softcover. Finally, one should note Dostoevsky's *The Possessed* and *Crime and Punishment* and Turgenev's *Fathers and Sons,* three literary classics that provide insight into the period of nihilism and Nechaev.

POPULISM

Like nihilism, revolutionary populism has been thoroughly investigated. The memoir literature is particularly good in this area. One should note first of all Peter Kropotkin's *Memoirs of a Revolutionist* (Montreal, 1989), the latest reprint of the memoirs originally appearing in 1899. Kropotkin cannot easily be confined to a single decade and his own impact as a major anarchist thinker occurred considerably later than the 1870s and 1880s, the high tide of revolutionary populism. Three other important books by participants are: Sergei M. Kravchinskii, *Underground Russia* (New York, 1892); Katherine Breshkovskaia, *Hidden Springs of the Russian Revolution* (Stanford, 1931); and Vera Figner, *Memoirs of a Revolutionist* (DeKalb, Ill., 1991). The latter is a recent reprint with an introduction by Richard Stites. Stites has also authored a sweeping study of women in the movement, *The Women's Liberation Movement in Russia: Feminism, Nihilism, and Bolshevism, 1860–1930* (Princeton, N.J., 1978). All of these studies provide insight into the motivations of the young revolutionaries who devoted their lives to the *narod* and give vivid portrayals of their self-sacrifice. Several of the major women participants aside from Breshkovskaia and Figner have had their memoirs excerpted in *Five Sisters: Women against the Tsar,* Barbara Engels and Clifford Rosenthal, eds. and trans. (New York, 1975). One of the most important influences on the young revolutionaries, Peter Lavrov's *Historical Letters,* James P. Scanlan, ed. and trans. (Berkeley, Calif., 1967), is available in a complete edition with Scanlan's valuable introduction. There are useful excerpts from the writings of Lavrov and Nicholas Mikhailovskii in *Russian Philosophy,* volume II (cited in full above).

Among secondary sources in English one should mention again F. Venturi's *Roots of Revolution,* A. Yarmolinsky's *Road to Revolution,* and A. Ulam's *In the Name of the People* (all cited in full above). Ronald Hingley's *Nihilists* (New York, 1969) covers in a brief survey the entire reign of Alexander II. David Footman's *Red Prelude* (New Haven, Conn., *1945*) is a readable account of the rise and fall of The People's Will. Still another survey of terrorism, although not a scholarly one, is Robert Payne, *The Terrorists: The Story of the Forerunners of Stalin* (New York, 1957). Of the recent books on terrorism, one should mention first of all Deborah Hardy, *Land and Freedom: The Origins of Russian Terrorism, 1876–1879* (Westport, Conn., 1987). Two studies of the later period (the 1880s) of populist terrorism appeared in rapid succession: Norman Naimark, *Terrorists and Social Democrats: The Russian Revolutionary Movement under Alexander III* (Cambridge, Mass., 1983); and Derek Offord, *The Russian Revolutionary Movement in the 1880s* (Cambridge, U.K., 1986). Hardy and Naimark have written penetrating, scholarly accounts; Offord's is a useful study, but not as thorough as Naimark's.

There are several studies of the major theoreticians of populism: James H. Billington, *Mikhailovskii and Russian Populism* (Oxford, U.K., 1958); Philip Pomper, *Peter Lavrov and the Russian Revolutionary Movement* (Chicago, 1972); A. Mendel, *Dilemmas of Progress in Tsarist Russia* (Cambridge, Mass., 1961); and A. Walicki, *The Controversy over Capitalism* (Oxford, U.K., 1969). The first two focus on the thinkers who launched the movement in the late 1860s and 1870s, the last two on the dilemmas created for populist theoreticians when industrialization quickened in Russia in the 1880s and 1890s. Kropotkin, who succeeded Bakunin as the theoretical inspiration of Russian anarchism, has had two scholarly biographies devoted to him: Martin Miller's psychobiography, *Kropotkin* (Chicago, 1976) and Caroline Cahm's more focused *Kropotkin and the Rise of Revolutionary Anarchism, 1872–1886* (Cambridge, U.K., 1989). A good, readable biography has been reprinted: George Woodcock and Ivan Avakumovic, *Peter Kropotkin, from Prince to Rebel* (Montreal, 1990). Finally, the Russian populist writers trying to create an image of the *narod* have been studied with an eye to their psychological needs in

Richard Wortman, *The Crisis of Russian Populism* (Cambridge, U.K., 1967).

THE REVOLUTIONARY ERA THROUGH 1905

The literature in English on the Russian revolutionary movement expands enormously for the period of the emergence of Marxism and the revival of revolutionary populism and militant liberalism. For primary sources concerning Marxist theory and programs I refer the reader to *Russian Philosophy,* volume III, and *Marxism in Russia, Key Documents 1879–1906* (cited in full above). There is also a volume devoted to the Mensheviks, *The Mensheviks in the Russian Revolution,* Abraham Ascher, ed. (Ithaca, N.Y., 1976), and a recent and valuable collection of the memoirs of three Mensheviks, *The Making of Three Russian Revolutionaries: Voices from the Menshevik Past,* Leopold Haimson, ed. (Cambridge, U.K., 1987). For the years of the split in Russian Marxism featuring the writings of an Economist and a useful introduction on the struggle of generations, see *Vladimir Akimov on the Dilemmas of Russian Marxism, 1895–1903,* Jonathan Frankel, ed. (Cambridge, U.K., 1969). The literature on individual thinkers is voluminous. The most influential theoretical works of the theoretical father of Russian Marxism are available in Georgi Plekhanov, *Selected Philosophical Works* (3 vols.; Moscow, 1974–1976). The Soviet editors saw fit to include only the early works and other philosophical works not conflicting obviously with Leninist doctrine. Plekhanov has had a good scholarly biography devoted to him, Samuel Baron's *Plekhanov* (Stanford, Calif., 1963). Lenin's collected works have been translated and the most important of them anthologized. Perhaps the most useful collection is *The Lenin Anthology,* Robert C. Tucker, ed. (New York, 1975). Trotsky's most important writings have been issued in many editions and are readily available.

Biographies of Lenin abound and not all deserve to be included. Two that appeared in the mid-1960s still have value: Louis Fischer's *The Life of Lenin* (New York, 1964) and Adam Ulam's *The Bolsheviks* (New York, 1965). The latter is really a biography of Lenin introduced by a nice summary of the revolutionary movement preceding Lenin. The most recent scholarly biography of Lenin, still in process, is Robert Service, *Lenin, a Political Life* (2 vols.; Bloomington, Ind., 1985, 1991). The two volumes already published are relevant to the period studied here, in that they embrace Lenin's career through the consolidation of Bolshevik state power. One of the best sources for Lenin's early career is Nicholas Valentinov (N. V. Volsky), *Encounters with Lenin,* Paul Rosta and Brian Pearce, trans. (London, 1968). Isaac Deutscher never finished his projected biography of Lenin but left for posthumous publication *Lenin's Childhood* (New York, 1970), an effort to understand the origins of Lenin's revolutionism. For a powerful critique of the tradition leading to Lenin and of Leninism see Alain Besançon, *The Rise of the Gulag: Intellectual Origins of Leninism* (New York, 1981) and for a standard work on Leninism see Alfred G. Meyer, *Leninism* (Cambridge, Mass., 1957). For a scholarly reading of Lenin's corpus, see Neil Harding, *Lenin's Political Thought* (2 vols.; London, 1977, 1981).

Like Lenin, Trotsky has had several biographers. The most useful short biography is Robert Wistrich's *Trotsky, Fate of a Revolutionary* (London, 1979). Joel Carmichael's *Trotsky, an Appreciation of His Life* (London, 1975) is insightful and well-written. Isaac Deutscher's three-volume biography, written from a Marxian perspective, remains the most thorough account of Trotsky's career in English. The first volume, *The Prophet Armed* (New York, 1954), deals with Trotsky's career before 1921 and is therefore relevant to the period of history covered here. Trotsky's autobiography, *My Life* (New York, 1970) is an invaluable source. Baruch Knei-Paz's *The Social and Political Thought of Leon Trotsky* (Oxford, U.K., 1978) is a thorough, scholarly study of Trotsky's ideas.

Rosa Luxemburg, akin to Trotsky in her radicalism, has also inspired biographers. The first major biography was J. P. Nettl's *Rosa Luxemburg* (2 vols.; London, 1966). Raya Dunayevskaya, a Trotskyist, wrote *Rosa Luxemburg, Women's Liberation and Marx's Philosophy of Revolution* (Atlantic Heights, N.J., 1982), and Elzbieta Ettinger contributed a more psychoanalytically oriented study, *Rosa Luxemburg: A Life* (London, 1987). There are also scholarly biographies of Vera Zasulich, Julius Martov, and Paul Akselrod: Jay Bergman, *Vera Zasulich, a Biography* (Stanford, Calif., 1989); Israel Getzler, *Martov* (Melbourne, 1967); and

Abraham Ascher, *Pavel Axelrod and the Development of Marxism* (Cambridge, Mass., 1972). A biography has been devoted to Nadezhda Krupskaia, Lenin's lifelong companion and an important revolutionary functionary: Robert McNeal, *Bride of the Revolution: Krupskaya and Lenin* (Ann Arbor, Mich., 1972). Recently, some of the lesser-known but for a time extremely influential Bolshevik "heretics" have received attention in perceptive studies: Robert C. Williams, *The Other Bolsheviks: Lenin and His Critics, 1900–1914* (Bloomington, Ind., 1986) and Zenovia Sochor, *Revolution and Culture, the Bogdanov-Lenin Controversy* (Ithaca, N.Y., 1988). Alexandra Kollontai has received much attention. The best scholarly biography is Barbara E. Clements, *Bolshevik Feminist: The Life of Alexandra Kollontai* (Bloomington, Ind., 1979).

Several works examine the interactions among leading Russian Marxists and trace connections among individual and group psychology, theory, and political practice. For a Freudian approach to the psychology of bolshevism see Nathan Leites's *A Study of Bolshevism* (Glencoe, Ill., 1953), which deals with bolshevism in its broader intelligentsia context. Leopold Haimson's *The Russian Marxists and the Origins of Bolshevism* (Cambridge, Mass., 1955) studies the impact of individual psychology on Marxian theory by examining the early careers of Plekhanov, Akselrod, Lenin, and Martov. Bertram Wolfe's justly celebrated *Three Who Made a Revolution* (New York, 1948) remains one of the best combinations of biography (Lenin, Trotsky, and Stalin) and history for the period before the revolutions of 1917. E. Victor Wolfenstein psychoanalyzes Lenin and Trotsky in *The Revolutionary Personality: Lenin, Trotsky, Gandhi* (Princeton, N.J., 1967). Philip Pomper, *Lenin, Trotsky, and Stalin: The Intelligentsia and Power* (New York, 1990) is a more recent psychological approach to the interactions of the three men against the background of the intelligentsia subculture.

There is an abundant literature on the Social Democrats as a movement, all of it worthwhile: J. L. H. Keep, *The Rise of Social Democracy in Russia* (Oxford, U.K., 1963); Richard Pipes, *Social Democracy and the St. Petersburg Labor Movement, 1885–1897* (Cambridge, Mass., 1963); Allan K. Wildman, *The Making of a Workers' Revolution: Russian Social Democracy, 1891–1903* (Chicago, 1967); R. C. Elwood, *Russian Social Democracy in the Underground* (Assen, Netherlands, 1974). This literature tends to broaden the context and shift the focus from the leading figures in the intelligentsia to the labor movement itself. Even more focused on the labor constituency of the Social Democratic Party is David Lane's sociological study, *The Roots of Russian Communism* (Assen, Netherlands, 1969) and Oskar Anweiler's study of the Soviet movement, *The Soviets: the Russian Workers, 'Peasants,' and Soldiers' Councils, 1905–1921* (New York, 1975).

The literature on the non-Marxist parties has expanded significantly. For quite a time Oliver Radkey's *The Agrarian Foes of Bolshevism* (New York, 1958) remained the only study in English of the prerevolutionary SRs and his book is more concerned with their failure in 1917 than with the rise of the party. More recently Maureen Perrie in *The Agrarian Policy of the Russian Socialist-Revolutionary Party from its Origins through the Revolution of 1905–1907* (Cambridge, U.K., 1976) has provided a scholarly study of the SRs, their social background, and the evolution of their tactics and programs. Christopher Rice contributes to a revision of the image of the SRs as a mainly agrarian-based party in *Russian Workers and the Socialist-Revolutionary Party through the Revolution of 1905–1907* (New York, 1988). For a collection of studies of social and political evolution in a province where the SRs played a major role see *Politics and Society in Rural Russia: Saratov, 1590–1917,* Rex Wade and Scott Seregny, eds. (Columbus, Ohio, 1989). Donald Treadgold wrote of the contest among the Bolsheviks, Mensheviks, SRs, and Constitutional Democrats in *Lenin and His Rivals: The Struggle for Russia's Future, 1898–1906 (New York,* 1955).

The liberals first received broad treatment in George Fischer, *Russian Liberalism, from Gentry to Intelligentsia* (Cambridge, Mass., 1958). The role of Russian liberals (mainly focused on the Constitutional Democrats, also known as Kadets) in the revolution of 1905 has been examined in two recent scholarly works, of which Emmons's is the more distinguished: Shmuel Galai, *The Liberation Movement in Russia 1900–1905* (Cambridge, U.K., 1973) and Terence Emmons, *The Formation of Political Parties and the First National Elections in Russia* (Cambridge, Mass., 1983). Paul Miliukov, the leader of the Kadets in 1905 and again in 1917, receives biographical treatment in Thomas Riha, *A Russian European: Paul Miliukov in Russian Politics* (Notre Dame, Ind., 1969). Richard Pipes's voluminous study of Peter Struve illustrates the evolution of one important thinker from a scholarly variety of Marxism to conservative liberalism: Richard Pipes, *Struve, Liberal on the Left, 1870–1905* (Cambridge, Mass., 1970) and *Struve, Liberal on the Right, 1905–1944* (Cambridge, Mass., 1980). Richard Kindersley's earlier study of thinkers undergoing an evolution similar to Struve's, *The First Russian Revisionists: A Study of "Legal Marxism" in Russia* (Oxford, U.K., 1962) remains useful. A recent translation of important essays by Struve, Berdiaev, and others is an invaluable source for the period after 1905: *Landmarks: A Collection of Essays on the Russian Intelligentsia, 1909*, Boris Shragin and Albert Todd, eds., Marian Schwartz, trans. (New York, 1977). For a study devoted to this period and to the debate around *Landmarks* see Christopher Read, *Religion, Revolution and the Russian Intelligentsia, 1900–1912* (New York, 1980).

The revolution of 1905 itself has begun to receive greater attention. For quite a while the only general treatment in English was Sidney Harcave's *First Blood: The Russian Revolution of 1905* (New York, 1964). Solomon Schwarz's *The Russian Revolution of 1905* (Chicago, 1967) is actually a collection of essays written from a Menshevik point of view. More recently, Theodore Shanin produced a voluminous but not altogether successful study of Russian modernization, *The Roots of Otherness: Russia's Turn of the Century* in two volumes, of which volume II deals with the revolution: *Russia, 1905–1907: Revolution as a Moment of Truth* (New Haven, Conn., 1986). The best single work available is Abraham Ascher, *The Revolutions of 1905: Russia in Disarray* (Stanford, Calif., 1989). For a study of the social and cultural background of the mutinous troops in 1905, see John Bushnell, *Mutiny and Repression, Russian Soldiers in the Revolution of 1905–1906* (Bloomington, Ind., 1985). Andrew Verner analyzes the politics of the regime in *The Crisis of Russian Autocracy: Nicholas II and the 1905 Revolution* (Princeton, N.J., 1990). Two other studies show how the autocratic regime tried, but failed to curb the labor movement before 1905: Jeremiah Schneiderman, *Sergei Zubatov and Revolutionary Marxism: The Struggle for the Working Class in Tsarist Russia* (Ithaca, N.Y., 1976) and Walter Sablinsky,

The Road to Bloody Sunday: Father Gapon and the St. Petersburg Massacre of 1905 (Princeton, N.J., 1976).

The lives of the more picaresque figures in the movement—the double agents and terrorists—make for lively biographies: Boris Nicolaevsky, *Azeff, the Spy* (New York, 1934); Ralph C. Elwood, *Roman Malinovsky: A Life without a Cause* (Newtonville, Mass., 1977); and, most recently, Richard B. Spence, *Boris Savinkov, Renegade on the Left* (Boulder, Colo., 1991). Evno Azev became infamous as the police agent who headed the SR Combat Organization. Malinovsky spied for the *Okhrana* while serving Lenin as a high-ranking Bolshevik. Savinkov's adventures as SR terrorist and then plotter against the Soviet regime extended into the 1920s. For a more general study, see Nurit Schleifman, *Undercover Agents in the Russian Revolutionary Movements: The SR Party 1902–1914* (London, 1988).

THE REVOLUTIONS OF 1917

No attempt will be made to include in this bibliography even the major works on the revolutions of 1917. For the interested student, two recent books that contain useful bibliographies are Edward Acton, *Rethinking the Russian Revolution* (cited in full above), and *The Russian Revolution and Bolshevik Victory: Visions and Revisions,* 3d ed., Ronald Suny and Arthur Adams, eds. (Lexington, Mass., 1990). Many of the books listed above apply to 1917 as well as to the period under which they appear. I add here two biographies dealing with figures playing a major role in 1917: Richard Abraham, *Alexander Kerensky: The First Love of the Revolution* (New York, 1987); and W. H. Roobol, *Tsereteli, a Democrat in the Russian Revolution: A Political Biography,* Philip Hyams and Lynne Richards, trans. (The Hague, 1976). The first is particularly valuable—a sympathetic and scholarly account of a sometimes misunderstood figure. Roobol's equally sympathetic study of Tsereteli sheds light on the failure of the Mensheviks, as does Ziva Galili y Garcia, *The Menshevik Leaders in the Russian Revolution: Social Realities and Political Strategies* (Princeton, N.J., 1989). Vladimir Brovkin has gathered Menshevik documents concerned with 1917 and the Civil War in *Dear Comrades: Menshevik Reports on the Bolshevik Revolution and the Civil War,*

Vladimir N. Brovkin, ed. and trans. (Stanford, Calif., 1991). One should note, too, a new translation particularly valuable for undergraduate courses, Vasilii V. Shulgin, *Days of the Russian Revolution: Memoirs from the Right, 1905–1917,* Bruce F. Adams, ed. and trans. (Gulf Breeze, Fla., 1990). Shulgin presents a point of view often neglected in studies of the revolution. At the other extreme, the too often neglected role of the anarchists in 1905 and 1917 has been well studied by Paul Avrich in *The Russian Anarchists* (Princeton, N.J., 1967) and in a collection of related documents: *The Anarchists in the Russian Revolution,* Paul Avrich, ed. (Ithaca, N.Y., 1973). Finally, there is a new monograph in a revisionist mode rectifying, to some extent, the distortions issuing from the historiography of the victors, Michael Melancon, *The Socialist Revolutionaries and the Russian Anti-War Movement, 1914–1917* (Columbus, Ohio, 1990).

GLOSSARY

apparat Communist party bureaucracy

apparatchiki members of the Communist party bureaucracy

arteli workers' cooperative associations in both villages and towns

barshchina labor rent owed by Russian serfs to their landlords

Bolsheviks the "hard" Social Democratic faction led by Lenin that evolved into the Communist party. Literally, "the majority."

buntarstvo the Bakuninist tactic of igniting revolutionary instincts in peasants

burlak barge hauler

Carbonari early nineteenth-century Italian movement for cultural and political autonomy

derevenshchiki populist propagandists who settled in the countryside. Literally, "villagers."

Druzhina an old Russian term denoting a prince's retinue adopted by the Chigirin Fighting Brotherhood, the largest non-intelligentsia revolutionary organization of the 1870s

Duma a Prussian-style parliament created after the revolution of 1905 which, contrary to the government's intentions, became an oppositional force and the source of the Provisional Government in 1917

dvorianin member of Russian gentry estate

dvorianstvo gentry estate

garde perdue suicide squad

kruzhok study circle

Mensheviks the "soft" Social Democratic faction led by Martov. Literally, "the minority."

narod the people, usually signifying the peasantry

narodnichevstvo populism

narodniki populists

narodovoltsy members of the terrorist organization, *Narodnaia Volia* (The People's Will)

noblesse d'épée the nobles who achieved their status through military service. Literally, "nobility of the sword."

obshchina peasant commune

Okhrana political "secret" police

raznochintsy term popularized by Nicholas Mikhailovskii, who used it to describe educated commoners who became prominent writers and ideologists in the late 1850s and 1860s

Tugendbund early nineteenth-century German movement for cultural and political autonomy

zemliachestvo mutual aid society with a regional basis that existed in Russian institutions of higher education

zemstvo created in 1864, the system of provincial and district assemblies elected by landowners, peasant communes, and propertied urban groups

INDEX

The Russian Revolutionary Intelligentsia, Second Edition
Copy editor, J. Michael Kendrick
Proofreader, Claudia Siler
Sponsoring editor, Maureen Hewitt
Production editor, Lucy Herz
Typesetter, Point West, Inc.
Printer, McNaughton & Gunn, Inc.
Book designer, Roger Eggers

About the author: Philip Pomper is William F. Armstrong Professor of History at Wesleyan University. Other books he has published include *Lenin, Trotsky, and Stalin; Trotsky's Notebooks, 1933–1935* (ed.); *The Structure of Mind in History; Sergei Nechaev;* and *Peter Lavrov and the Russian Revolutionary Movement.*